PHILOSOPHY
OF
RELIGION

PHILOSOPHY

OF

RELIGION

AN INTRODUCTION

SECOND EDITION

WILLIAM L. ROWE
Purdue University

WADSWORTH PUBLISHING COMPANY
Belmont, California
A Division of Wadsworth, Inc.

Philosophy Editor: Kenneth King
Editorial Assistant: Gay Meixel
Editing and Production: Proof Positive/Farrowlyne Associates, Inc.
Print Buyer: Randy Hurst
Designer: John Odam
Cover: Al Burkhardt
Compositor: TCSystems, Inc.
Printer: Maple Press

This book is printed on acid-free paper that meets Environmental Protection Agency standards for recycled paper.

2 3 4 5 6 7 8 9 10—97 96 95 94 93

Library of Congress Cataloging in Publication Data

Rowe, William L., 1931–
    Philosophy of religion : an introduction / William L. Rowe.—2nd
ed.
        p.   cm.
    Includes bibliographical references and index.
    ISBN 0-534-18816-8
    1. Religion—Philosophy.   I. Title.
BL51.R5988   1992
200'.1—dc20   92-4823
                                                                  CIP

To Peggy

CONTENTS

ACKNOWLEDGMENTS

I would like to thank the reviewers of the first edition: George L. Abernathy, Monroe C. Beardsley, Donald Burrill, John Fisher, Robert O. Long, Geddes MacGregor, and Walter Stromseth. I am also grateful to the reviewers of the present edition: Pieranna Garavaso, University of Minnesota-Morris; S. S. Rama Rao Pappu, Miami University; Louis Pojman, University of Mississippi; William L. Power, University of Georgia; Paul Tidman, Illinois State University; and Donald J. Zeyl, University of Rhode Island.

W.L.R.

PREFACE TO THE
SECOND EDITION

This book, first published in 1978, is designed to introduce students to a range of topics in philosophy of religion. The aim has been to cover these topics in some depth without sacrificing clarity or presupposing any previous study of philosophy. Since 1978 the field of philosophy of religion has been very active, producing new and important ideas. This second edition endeavors both to take account of important new work and to make some improvements on the first edition. In addition to minor changes, this edition includes a discussion of God's moral goodness and its relation to human morality, a section on ordinary (as opposed to mystical) experiences of the divine, an examination of soul-making theodicy, a section on religious beliefs without evidence, and a chapter on some important differences among the world's major religions.

INTRODUCTION

Religion, along with art and science, must surely count as one of the most fundamental and pervasive aspects of human civilization. As such it is worthy of the most careful scrutiny and study. But religion is such a complex, far-reaching aspect of human life that no single discipline can hope to achieve a comprehensive study of it. For this reason religion is studied through a number of distinct disciplines: philosophy, history, anthropology, sociology, and psychology.

Philosophy of religion is one of the branches of philosophy, as are philosophy of science, philosophy of law, and philosophy of art. We may best understand what philosophy of religion is by beginning with what it is not. First, philosophy of religion must not be confused with the study of the history of the major religions by which human beings have lived. In studying the history of a particular religion, Christianity, for example, one would read something about its origin in Judaism, the life of Jesus, the emergence of the Christian church within the Roman Empire, and the development of the doctrines distinctive of the Christian faith. Similar studies might be carried out with respect to other major religions: Judaism, Islam, Buddhism, and Hinduism. While such studies are important to the philosophy of religion, and at times may overlap with it, they should not be confused with it.

Second, philosophy of religion is not to be confused with theology. Theology is a discipline largely *within* religion. As such, it develops the doctrines of some particular religious faith and seeks to ground them either within the reason common to humankind (natural theology) or within the revealed word of God (revealed theology). Although philosophy of religion is fundamentally concerned with the study of the ways in which religious beliefs are justified by those who hold them, its primary concern is not to justify or refute some particular set of religious beliefs but to assess the sorts of reasons that thoughtful people have advanced for and against religious beliefs. Philosophy of religion, unlike theology, is not primarily a discipline *within* religion, but a discipline which studies religion from a vantage point beyond. Like philosophy of science and philosophy of art, philosophy of religion is not a part of the subject matter it studies. It is important to recognize, however, that there is considerable overlap between theology, particularly *natural* theology, and philosophy of religion. When Aquinas discusses the various arguments for God's existence, or tries to analyze what is meant by the idea that God is omnipotent, or when Anselm examines certain important notions like eternity and self-existence, it is difficult to classify their work as belonging solely to theology. It clearly can also be viewed as philosophizing about certain issues in religion. Despite these overlaps, however, the philosophy of religion, as a discipline, should not be identified with theology.

We may best characterize philosophy of religion as *the critical examination of basic religious beliefs and concepts*. Philosophy of religion critically examines basic religious concepts like the concept of God, the concept of faith, the notion of a miracle, the idea of omnipotence. To critically examine a complex concept like the concept of God is to do two things: to distinguish the basic conceptions of God that have emerged in religion, and to analyze each conception into its basic components. The notion of God, as we shall see, stands for several distinct conceptions of the divine. There is, for example, the *pantheistic* idea of God, as well as the *theistic* idea of God. What the philosophy of religion seeks to do is to distinguish these different ideas of God and to elaborate each of them. A comprehensive philosophy of religion would analyze each of these distinct ideas of God. In this introductory text, however, we shall need to limit our detailed analysis to the major conception of God that has emerged in western civilization, the *theistic* idea of God.

Philosophy of religion critically examines basic religious beliefs: the belief that God exists, that there is life after death, that God knows before we are born whatever we will do, that the existence of evil is somehow consistent with God's love for his creatures. To critically examine a religious belief involves explicating the belief, and examining the reasons that have been given for and against the belief, with a view to determining whether there is any rational justification for holding that belief to be true or holding it to be false. Our purpose in carrying out this examination is not to persuade or convince but to *acquaint* the reader with the sorts of reasons that have been advanced for and against certain basic religious beliefs. In the course of examining religious beliefs, it would be dishonest to say that my own views concerning these beliefs, and the reasons offered for and against them, do not appear in the text. They surely do. But I have tried to present the views with which I disagree in as forceful and cogent a manner as their strongest proponents might do. And my hope is that the reader will treat my own judgments in the way I have sought to treat the judgments of others, not as points to be accepted as true, but as points worthy of serious reflection and careful examination. To read the text in this spirit is to engage in the very discipline to which the text is designed as an introduction; it is to philosophize about the fundamental issues in religion.

I have tried in the text to cover a good number of the topics that are generally considered by philosophers of religion. No beginning text, however, can hope to be comprehensive. Topics such as the nature of religion, the concept of prayer, religious ethics, are important topics. But the limitations imposed on an introductory text have precluded their inclusion. Nevertheless, a goodly number of topics central to the discipline have been covered in what I hope is as thorough a manner as can be reasonably accomplished in a first course in the philosophy of religion.

The book falls into five segments. In the first (Chapter One), the particular conception of deity that has been predominant in western civilization—the *theistic* idea of God—is explicated in some detail and distinguished from several other notions of the divine. The second segment considers the major reasons that have been advanced in support of the belief that the theistic God exists. In Chapters Two through Four the three major arguments for the existence of God are discussed, arguments which appeal to facts supposedly available to any rational person, whether religious or not. Chapter Five considers religious and mystical experience as a source and justification for theistic belief.

The third segment undertakes an examination of some of the major reasons which have been thought to provide rational grounds for atheism, the belief that the theistic God does not exist. The most formidable of these is the problem of evil (Chapter Six), but we also shall consider the attack on the meaningfulness of religious language (Chapter Seven) and Freud's attempt to account for religious beliefs on psychological grounds, thereby discrediting the claim that they are true (Chapter Eight).

A number of topics quite central to theistic religion are considered in the fourth segment of the book, Chapters Nine through Thirteen. These topics include miracles, the question of life after death, problems in relating the idea of divine foreknowledge to the belief in human freedom, the questions of what is faith and how is it related to human reason, and problems arising from the existence of diverse religions. The final segment (Chapter Fourteen) gives some account of the views of two modern theologians, Paul Tillich and Henry Nelson Wieman, views which represent recent attempts to provide alternatives to traditional theism.

At the end of each chapter the reader will find a study guide. The first five topics in the guide seek to focus the student's attention on the major points developed in the chapter. The last two topics seek to direct the student's thinking to new ideas about, and new ways of responding to, the issues raised in the chapter. They also may serve as suggestions for student papers.

At the end of the book the reader will find a bibliography of some of the major writings that might be usefully consulted in connection with a number of topics discussed in the text.

Chapter

1

THE IDEA OF GOD

In 1963 a small book was published by an Anglican bishop, a book that caused a religious storm both in England and America.[1] In *Honest to God* Bishop John Robinson dared to suggest that the idea of God that has been dominant in western civilization for centuries is irrelevant to the needs of modern men and women. The survival of religion in the West, Robinson argued, requires that this traditional picture of God be discarded in favor of a profoundly different conception of God, a conception Robinson professed to perceive emerging in the work of twentieth-century religious thinkers such as Paul Tillich and Rudolf Bultmann.

Robinson correctly predicted the reaction to his thesis, pointing out that it was bound to be resisted as a betrayal of what the Bible says. Not only would the vast majority of Church people oppose his view, but those who rejected belief in God would resent the suggestion that the idea of God was already dead or at least dying. In letters to the editor of the London *Times*, in articles in scholarly journals, and in pulpits on two continents, Robinson was attacked as an atheist in bishop's garments, and only infrequently defended as a prophet of a new revolution taking place within the Judeo-Christian religious tradition. A look at some of Robinson's ideas will help us in our effort to sort out different ideas of God and to focus on that idea of God which will be the center of our attention throughout most of this book.

Before the emergence of the belief that the whole world is under the sovereign control of a single being, people often believed in a plurality of divine beings or gods, a religious position called *polytheism*. In ancient Greece and Rome, for example, the various gods had control over different aspects of life, so that one naturally worshipped several gods, a god of war, a goddess of love, and so forth. Sometimes, however, one might believe that there are a number of gods but worship only one of them, the god of one's own tribe, a religious position called *henotheism*. In the Old Testament, for example, there are frequent references to the gods of other tribes, although the allegiance of the Hebrews is to their own god, Jahweh. Slowly, however, there emerged the belief that one's own god was the creator of heaven and earth, the god not only of one's own tribe, but of all people, a religious view called *monotheism*.

According to Robinson, monotheism, the belief in only one divine being, has passed through a profound change, a change he describes with the help of the expressions "up there" and "out there." The god "up there" is a being located in space above us, presumably at some definite distance from the earth, in a region known as the heavens. Associated with this idea of God is a certain primitive picture in which the universe consists of three regions, the heavens above, the earth beneath, and the region of darkness under the earth. According to this picture, the earth is frequently invaded by beings from the other two realms— God and his angels from the heavens, Satan and his demons from the region beneath the earth—who war with one another for control over the souls and destiny of those who inhabit the earthly realm. This idea of God as a powerful being located "up there" at some definite place in space was slowly abandoned, Robinson claims. We now explain to our children that heaven is not in fact over their heads, that God is not literally somewhere up in the sky. In place of God as "the old man in the sky," there has emerged a much more sophisticated idea of God, an idea Robinson refers to as the God "out there."

The fundamental change from the God "up there" to the God "out there" is the change from thinking of God as located at some spatial distance from the earth to thinking of God as separate from and independent of the world. According to this idea, God has no location in some spot or region of physical space. He is a purely spiritual being, a supremely good, all-powerful, all-knowing, personal being who has created the world, but is not a part of it. He is separate from the world, not subject to its laws, judges it, and guides it to its final purpose. This rather majestic idea of God was slowly developed over the centuries by great western theologians such as Augustine, Boethius, Bonaventure, Avicenna, Anselm, Maimonides, and Aquinas. It has been the dominant idea of God in western civilization. If we label the God "up there" as "the old man in the sky," we can label the God "out there" as "the God of the traditional theologians." And it is the God of the traditional theologians that Robinson believes has become irrelevant to the needs of modern people. Whether Robinson is right or wrong— and it is rather doubtful that he is right—it is undeniably true that when most of us who are the cultural heirs of western civilization think of God, the being we think of is in many important respects like the God of the traditional theologians. It will be helpful, therefore, in clarifying our own thoughts about God to explore more thoroughly the conception of God that emerged in the thinking of the great theologians.

THE ATTRIBUTES OF GOD

We have already noted that according to many major theologians, God is conceived of as a supremely good being, separate from and independent of the world, all-powerful, all-knowing, and the creator of the universe. Two other features that were ascribed to God by the great theologians are *self-existence* and *eternity.* The dominant idea of God in western civilization, then, is the idea of a supremely good being, creator of but separate from and independent of the world, all-powerful (omnipotent), all-knowing (omniscient), eternal and self-existent. Of course, this list of the major elements in this idea of God will be illuminating to us only insofar as the elements themselves are understood. What is it for a being to be omnipotent? How are we to understand the idea of self-existence? In what way is God thought to be separate from and independent of the world? What is meant when it is said that God, and God alone, is eternal? Only to the extent that we can answer these and similar questions do we comprehend the central idea of God to emerge within western civilization. Before turning to a study of the question of the existence of God, therefore, it is important to enrich our grasp of this idea of God by trying to answer some of these basic questions.

Omnipotence and Perfect Goodness

In his great work, the *Summa Theologica,* St. Thomas Aquinas, who lived in the thirteenth century, undertakes to explain what it is for God to be omnipotent. After pointing out that for God to be omnipotent is for God to be able to do all things that are possible, Aquinas carefully explains that there are two different kinds of possibility, *relative possibility* and *absolute possibility,* and inquires as to which kind of possibility is meant when it is said that God's omnipotence is the ability to do all things that are possible. Something is a relative possibility when it lies within the power of some being or beings to do. Flying by natural means, for example, is possible relative to birds but not relative to humans. Something is an absolute possibility, however, if it is not a contradiction in terms. Defeating a chess master in a game of chess is something that is very hard to do, but it is not a contradiction in terms; indeed, it occasionally has been done. But defeating a chess master in a game of chess *after* he has checkmated your king is not just something that is very hard to do, it cannot be done at all, for it is a contradiction in terms. Becoming a married bachelor, making one and the same thing both round and square at the same time, defeating someone at chess after he has checkmated your king, are not possible in the absolute sense, for they are activities which, implicitly or explicitly, involve a contradiction in terms.

Having explained the two different kinds of possibility, Aquinas points out that it must be absolute possibility which is meant when God's omnipotence is explained as the ability to do all things that are possible. For if we meant relative possibility, our explanation would say no more than that "God is omnipotent" means that he can do all things that are in his power to do. And while it is certainly true that God can do all things that are in his power to do, it explains nothing. "God is omnipotent," then, means that God can do whatever does not involve a contradiction in terms. Does this mean that there are some things God cannot do? In one sense it clearly does mean this. God cannot make one and the same thing both round and square at the same time and he cannot defeat me at a game of chess after I have checkmated his king. Of course, God could always checkmate my king before I am in a position to checkmate his. But if he should—for whatever reason—engage me in a game of chess and allow it to happen that I checkmate his king then he *cannot* win that game of chess. He could annihilate me and the chessboard, but he could not win that game of chess. So there are many things that God, despite being omnipotent, cannot do. It would be a mistake, however, to conclude from this that God's power is somehow limited, that there are things he cannot do which, if only his power were greater, he could do. For power, as Aquinas points out, extends only to whatever is possible. And there is nothing that is possible to be done that God's power is inadequate to accomplish. Thus Aquinas concludes, "Whatever implies contradiction does not come within the scope of divine omnipotence, because it cannot have the aspect of possibility. Hence it is more appropriate to say that such things cannot be done, than that God cannot do them."[2]

But aren't there some things which, unlike making a round square, are not contradictory and yet such that God cannot do them? Committing suicide or some evil deed are not contradictory. Many theologians, however, have denied that God can destroy himself or do what is evil. For the doing of such things is inconsistent with God's nature—his eternity and perfect goodness. It might be objected that God's perfections imply only that he will not destroy himself or do evil, not that he cannot—he has the power to do evil, but because he is supremely good it is a power he will never exercise. What this objection overlooks, however, is that to attribute to God the power to do evil is to attribute to him the power to cease to have an attribute (perfect goodness) which is part of his very essence or nature. Being perfectly good is as much a part of God's nature as having three angles is part of the nature of a triangle. God could no more cease to be perfectly good than a triangle could cease to have three angles. In view of this difficulty, it is perhaps necessary to amend Aquinas' explanation of what it means for God to be omnipotent. Instead of saying simply that what it means is for him to have the power to do anything that is an absolute possibility, we shall say that it means that God can do anything that is an absolute possibility *and not inconsistent with any of his basic attributes*. Since doing evil is inconsistent with being perfectly good, and since being perfectly good is a basic attribute to God, the fact that God cannot do evil will not conflict with the fact that he is omnipotent.

The idea that God's omnipotence does not include the power to do something inconsistent with any of his basic attributes can help us solve what has been called the paradox of the stone. According to this paradox, either God has the power to create a stone so heavy that he cannot lift it, or God does not have that power. If he does have the power to create such a stone, then there is something God cannot do: lift the stone he can create. On the other hand, if God cannot create such a stone, then there is also something he cannot do: create a stone so heavy he cannot lift it. In either case there is something God cannot do. Therefore, God is not omnipotent.

The solution to this puzzle is to see that *creating a stone so heavy that God cannot lift it* is doing something inconsistent with one of God's essential attributes— the attribute of omnipotence. For if there exists a stone so heavy that God lacks the power to lift it, then God is not omnipotent. Therefore, if God has the power to create such a stone, he has the power to bring it about that he lacks an attribute (omnipotence) that is essential to him. So, the proper solution to the puzzle is to say that God cannot create such a stone, any more than he can do an evil deed. This does not mean, of course, that there is some stone in the infinite series of stones weighing 1000 lb., 2000 lb., 3000 lb., 4000 lb., and so on, that God cannot create. In the case of an evil deed, God cannot perform that deed because his perfect goodness is essential to him. In the case of a stone so heavy that God cannot lift it, God cannot create such a stone because his omnipotence is essential to him.

We've seen that God's omnipotence is not to be understood as including the "power" to bring about logically impossible states of affairs or to perform actions inconsistent with his essential attributes. What about changing the past? Clearly, God could have prevented Nixon from being a President of the United States. But can God *now* do so? Nixon's never having been President is not a logically impossible state of affairs; nor does bringing it about appear to be inconsistent with God's goodness, or any of his other essential attributes. But it does seem that it is not *now* in the power of any being, including an omnipotent being, to bring about Nixon's never having been President. So, although we have refined our understanding of the notion of omnipotence and come to see that God's omnipotence isn't the power to bring about absolutely anything whatever, we cannot claim to have provided a full explication of the idea that God is omnipotent. For, as we've just seen, certain past happenings cannot now be changed even by an omnipotent being. And there may be other states of affairs that an omnipotent, divine being cannot bring about.

The idea that God must be perfectly good is connected to the view that God is a being who deserves unconditional gratitude, praise, and worship. For if a being were to fall short of perfect goodness, it would not be worthy of unreserved praise and worship. So, God is not just a good being, his goodness is unsurpassable. Moreover, God doesn't simply happen to be perfectly good; it is his nature to be that way. God logically could not fail to be perfectly good. It was for this reason that we observed above that God does not have the power to do evil. For to attribute such a power to God is to attribute to him the power to cease to be the being that he necessarily is.

Are we saying that God is perfectly good by definition? Yes. But we are also noting that the definition of God as perfectly good is connected to, if not grounded in, the religious requirement that God be an object of unconditional praise and worship. And we are making an additional point. For we also have said that *the being who is God* cannot cease to be perfectly good. A bachelor is unmarried by definition. But someone who is a bachelor can cease to be unmarried. Of course, when this happens (our bachelor marries), he no longer is a bachelor. Unlike our bachelor, however, the being who is God cannot give up being God. So, we are not simply saying that God is by definition perfectly good. We are also saying that a being who is God cannot ever be anything other than God. The bachelor next door can cease to be a bachelor. But the being who is God cannot cease to be God. We can put it this way. Being a bachelor is not part of the nature or essence of a being who is a bachelor. So, although by definition someone cannot be a bachelor without being unmarried, that person can cease to be unmarried because he can cease to be a bachelor. But being God is part of the nature or essence of the being who is God. So, since the being who is God cannot cease to be God, that being cannot cease to be perfectly good.

But what is it to be perfectly good? Since God is unsurpassably good, he has all the features that unsurpassable goodness implies. Among these is absolute *moral goodness*. Moral goodness is a vital part, but not the whole of goodness. For there is nonmoral goodness as well. Thus we distinguish two statements that might be made on the occasion of someone's death: "He led a good life." "He had a good life." The first statement concerns his moral goodness, the latter centers chiefly on nonmoral goodness such as happiness, good fortune, etc. God's perfect goodness involves both moral goodness and nonmoral goodness. Of chief interest here is his absolute moral goodness (perfect justice, benevolence, etc.). For God's moral goodness has long been thought to be in some way the source or standard of what it is for human life to be moral. Furthermore, by virtue of his essential moral perfection, some judgments can be made about the world he has created. We may be certain, for example, that God would not create a morally bad world. It might even be true that by virtue of his moral perfection God would be led to create the morally best world he can. These are important topics. We will pursue the second of these topics (what sort of world God would create) when we later consider the problem of evil. It will be helpful here to consider briefly the connection between God's moral perfection and morality in human life.

God has been held to be the source or standard of our moral duties, both negative duties (for example, the duty not to take innocent, human life) and positive duties (for example, the duty to help others in need). Commonly, religious people believe that these duties are somehow grounded in divine commandments. A believer in Judaism may view the ten commandments as fundamental moral rules that determine at least a good part of what one is morally obligated to do (positive duties) or refrain from doing (negative duties). Clearly, given his absolute moral perfection, what God commands us to do must be what is morally right for us to do. But are these things morally right because God commands them? That is, does the moral rightness of these things simply consist in the fact that God has commanded them? Or does God command these things to be done because they are right? If we say the second, that God commands them to be done because he sees that they are morally right, we seem to imply that morality has an existence apart from God's will or commands. But if we say the first, that what makes things right is God's willing or commanding them, we seem to imply that there would be no right or wrong if there were no divine being to issue such commands. While neither answer is without its problems, the dominant answer in religious thinking concerning God and morality is that what God commands is morally right independent of his commands. God's commanding us to perform certain actions does not make those actions morally right; they are morally right independent of his commands and he commands them because he sees that they are morally right. How then does our moral life depend on God? Well, even though morality itself need not depend on God, perhaps our *knowledge* of morality is dependent (or at least aided) by God's commands. Perhaps it is the teachings of religion that lead human beings to view certain actions as morally right and others as morally wrong. Also, the practice of morality may be aided by belief in God. For although an important part of the moral life is to do one's duty out of respect for duty itself, it would be too much to expect of ordinary humans that they would relentlessly pursue the life of duty even though there were no grounds for associating morality with well-being and happiness. Belief in God may aid the moral life by providing a reason for thinking that the connection between leading a good life and having a good life is not simply accidental. Still, what of the difficulty that certain things are morally right apart from the fact that God commands us to do them? Consider God's belief that $2 + 2 = 4$. Is it true that $2 + 2 = 4$ because God believes it? Or does God believe that $2 + 2 = 4$ because it is true that $2 + 2 = 4$? If we say the latter, as it seems we should, we imply that certain mathematical statements are true independent of God's believing them. So, we already seem committed to the view that the way some things are is not ultimately a matter of God's will or commands. Perhaps the basic truths of morality have the same sort of status as the basic truths of mathematics.

Self-Existence

The idea that God is a *self-existent* being was developed and explained by St. Anselm in the eleventh century. By various arguments Anselm had satisfied himself that among those beings that exist there is one that is supremely great and good—nothing that exists or ever did exist is its equal. Of anything that exists, however, Anselm was equally persuaded that we can ask of it, what accounts for or explains the fact that it exists? If we come upon a table, for example, we can ask what accounts for the fact that it exists. And we might answer our question, at least partially, by learning that a carpenter took some wood and made it. So too, for a tree, a mountain, or a lake, we can ask the question, what explains the fact that it exists? In an effort to learn more about the supremely great and good being, Anselm asks it of this being. What is it that accounts for the fact that this being exists?

Before trying to answer the question, Anselm observes that there are only three cases to consider: either something's existence is explained *by another*, explained *by nothing*, or its existence is explained *by itself*. Clearly, the existence of the table is accounted for by something else (the carpenter). So too for the existence of a tree, a mountain, or a lake. Each of them exists because of the activities of other things. Indeed, the familiar things in our lives all seem to be explained by other things. But even when we don't know what, if anything, explains the fact that a certain thing exists, it's clear that the answer must be one of the three Anselm proposes. The fact that a certain thing exists is explained either by reference to something else, by nothing, or by itself. There simply are no other causes to consider. What then of the existence of the supremely great and good being? Is its existence due to another, to nothing, or to itself? Unlike the table, the tree, the mountain, or the lake, the supremely great and good being cannot have its existence due to another, Anselm reasons, for then it would be dependent for its existence on that other thing and, consequently, would not be the supreme being. Whatever is supreme over all other things cannot be (or have been) dependent for its existence on any of them. The existence of the supreme being, therefore, must be explained either by nothing or by itself.

For something to have its existence explained by nothing is for it to exist and yet for there to be no explanation whatever of the fact that it exists rather than not. Could there by something of this sort—something whose existence is simply an unintelligible, brute fact, having no explanation whatever? Anselm's answer, whether correct or not, is perfectly clear: "It is utterly inconceivable that what is something should exist through nothing."[3] Unfortunately, Anselm gives us no explanation as to why we cannot conceive of something whose existence is an unintelligible brute fact. Presumably, he thought the point so obvious as not to require explanation. In any case, we must carefully note the principle Anselm is here expressing, for it will figure later in one of the major arguments for God's existence. Anselm's basic conviction is that *whatever exists must have an explanation of its existence*—there must be something that accounts for the fact that it exists rather than not, and that something must be either something else or the thing itself. To deny this is to view the existence of something as irrational, absurd, utterly unintelligible. And this, thinks Anselm, can no more be true of the supreme being than it can be true of a tree or mountain. The existence of the supreme being, therefore, cannot be explained by nothing. There remains, then, only the third case. Anselm draws the conclusion that the supreme being's existence is due *to itself*.

Of course, it is one thing to conclude that the explanation of the supreme being's existence is to be found within the nature of that very being, and quite another thing to understand what it is within the supreme being's nature that accounts for the existence of that being. Anselm does not profess to understand *what* it is within the divine nature that accounts for God's existence. Nor does he understand just *how* a being's nature might provide the explanation of that being's existence. All that he professes to be sure of is that the existence of the supreme being is due to the supreme being itself. He does not mean, of course, that the supreme being brought itself into existence. For it would then have to exist before it existed in order to bring itself into existence, and clearly that is impossible. Moreover, as we noted earlier, eternity is one of God's characteristics, so he clearly did not come into existence at a certain time.

Anselm does, however, offer an analogy in an effort to help our understanding of this very difficult idea. Using our own example, his point can be expressed as follows: Suppose on a cold night we come upon a blazing campfire. We note that a rock a few feet from the campfire is warm. If we ask what explains this fact about the rock (that it is warm), it would be absurd to suggest that the explanation is to be found within the rock itself, that there is something about the nature of the rock that makes it warm. The fire and the nearness of the rock to the fire explain the rock's warmth. Suppose we then note that the fire is also warm. What accounts for the fact that the fire is warm? Here it does not seem absurd to suggest that the explanation lies within the fire itself. It is the nature of a fire to be warm just as it is the nature of a triangle to have three angles. To avoid confusion here we must keep clearly in mind that it is the fact of the fire's warmth we are trying to explain, and not the fact of the fire's existence. The fact of the fire's existence is not due to the fire but to the camper who built the fire. The fact that the existing fire is warm, however, is a fact about the fire that is accounted for by the nature of the fire, by what it is to be a fire. We have here, then, an example of a fact about a thing (the fire's warmth) that is accounted for not by something else but by the nature of the thing itself (the fire). Anselm's hope is that if we once see that a certain fact about a thing may be explained not by something else but by that thing's nature, the idea of self-existence will seem less strange to us. Whether this is so or not, it should be clear both what is meant by *self-existence* and why the traditional theologians felt it to be a basic feature of the divine being. For something to be a self-existent being is for it to have the explanation of its existence within its own nature. Since no thing can exist whose existence is unintelligible, lacking any explanation (Anselm's basic principle), and since the supreme being would not be supreme if its existence were due to something else, the conclusion is inevitable that God (the supreme being) has the explanation of his existence within his own nature.

Separation, Independence, and Eternity

We have been exploring the notions of *omnipotence, perfect goodness,* and *self-existence* in an effort to enlarge our grasp of the dominant idea of God to emerge in western civilization. Some of the other elements in this idea of God will be explored in later chapters. To complete this beginning exploration, however, it will be instructive to consider the notion that God is *separate from and independent of the world* and the conception of God as an *eternal being*.

We have noted the emergence of monotheism out of henotheism and polytheism. Monotheism is the dominant tradition in Judaism, Christianity, and Islam. Another view of God has persisted since ancient times, and still flourishes, particularly in the major religions of the East, Buddhism and Hinduism, a view called *pantheism.* According to pantheism, everything that exists has an inner nature that is one and the same in all things, and that inner nature is God. Later, when we examine the experiences of some of the great mystics, we shall consider pantheism more fully. The fundamental idea in monotheism that God is *separate from* the world constitutes a rejection of pantheism. According to the Judeo-Christian and Islamic conception of God, the world is entirely distinct from God; everything in it could be entirely annihilated without the slightest change in the reality of the divine being. There are, of course, things in the world more like God than other things. Since human beings are living and rational they are more like God than are stones and trees. But being *like God* and *being God* are enormously different. The world is not the divine, and the notion that God is separate from the world is meant to emphasize the fundamental difference between the reality of God and the reality of the world.

That God is independent of the world means that he is not governed by any of the physical laws according to which the universe operates. But it means much more than this. It also means that God is not subject to the laws of space and time. According to the law of space, no object can exist at two different places at one and the same time. Of course, a part of an object can exist at one place in space while another part of it (if it is a large object) can exist at a different place. The law doesn't deny this. What it denies is that the whole of an object can exist at two different places in space at the same time. Now if this law applied to God either God would be at some place in space at a certain time and not at other places at that time or he would be everywhere in space at once, but only a part of him in each part of space. Neither of these alternatives was acceptable to the great theologians of the past. On the first alternative, while God might be present in

Boston at a certain moment, he couldn't, at that moment, be present in New York. And, on the second alternative, although God could be both in Boston and in New York at the same time, it would be one part of God in New York and a different part in Boston. On the traditional idea of God, not only must God be at every place at the same time, the *whole of God* must be at each distinct place at the same time. The whole of God is in Boston and in New York at one and the same time, indeed, at every time. But such a view conflicts with the law of space. And so the idea of God that emerged in western civilization is the idea of a supreme being who is independent of the laws of nature and transcends even the basic law of space.

The idea that God is not subject to the law of time is, as we shall see, closely related to one meaning of *eternity*. According to the law of space, nothing can exist as a whole in two different places at the same time. According to the law of time, nothing can exist as a whole in two different times at the same time. To understand the law of time, we need only consider the example of a man who existed yesterday, exists today, and will exist tomorrow. The whole man exists at each of these different times. That is, it is not that only his arm, say, existed yesterday, his head today, and his legs will exist tomorrow. But even though the whole man exists at each of these three times, the whole *temporal life* of the man does not exist at each of these times. The temporal part of his life that was yesterday does not exist today; at best he can share in it only by remembering it. And the temporal part of his life that will be tomorrow does not exist today; at best he can share in it only by anticipating it. Although the *whole man* exists at each of these three times, his *whole life* exists at none of them. His life, then, is divided up into many temporal parts and at any particular time only one of these temporal parts is present to him. Thus a person's life exemplifies the law of time. For according to that law the individual temporal parts of a person's life cannot all be present to him at once. For reasons we need not pursue here, the great medieval theologians were reluctant to view God's life as split up into temporal parts, and so took the view that God transcends the law of time, as well as the law of space. Even though it is scarcely intelligible, they took the view, as Anselm expresses it, that "the supreme Nature exists in place and time in some such way, that it is not prevented from so existing simultaneously, as a whole, in different places or times. . . ."[4] According to this idea the whole beginningless and endless life of God is present to him at each moment of time, and the whole of God is simultaneously present at every place in space.

Eternal has two distinct meanings. To be eternal in one sense is to have endless temporal existence, without beginning and without end; it is to have infinite duration in both temporal directions. Now there is nothing in this meaning of *eternity* that conflicts with the law of time. The law of time would imply only that anything that is temporally infinite has an infinity of temporal parts making up its life such that at no time does it have more than one of these temporal parts present to it, the other temporal parts would be either in its past or in its future. According to the second meaning of *eternal*, however, an eternal being does not have its life broken up into temporal parts, for it is not subject to the law of time. So, according to this meaning of *eternal*, a being having infinite duration in each temporal direction and subject to the law of time would not be eternal. As the Roman scholar Boethius (A.D. 480–524) noted:

> Whatever is subject to the condition of time, even that which—as Aristotle conceived the world to be—has no beginning and will have no end in a life coextensive with the infinity of time, is such that it cannot rightly be thought eternal. For it does not comprehend and include the whole of infinite life all at once, since it does not embrace the future which is yet to come. Therefore, only that which comprehends and possesses the whole plenitude of endless life together, from which no future thing nor any past thing is absent, can justly be called eternal.[5]

Boethius, Anselm, Aquinas, and other traditional theologians interpreted the *eternity* of God in the second of the two senses just distinguished. They held that God is outside of time, not subject to its fundamental law. Other theologians, however, took the view that God is eternal in the first sense distinguished, that he has infinite duration in both temporal directions. The eighteenth-century English theologian, Samuel Clarke, for example, rejected the idea that a being might transcend time as a senseless idea, and took the view that to be eternal is simply to be *everlasting*, existing in time but having neither beginning nor end. When we later study the problem of divine foreknowledge and human freedom we shall reconsider these two senses of *eternity* and note their implications for the doctrine of divine foreknowledge. For the moment, however, it is sufficient to recognize that eternity is a central element in the traditional idea of God and that it has been interpreted in two distinct ways.

We have been exploring some of the basic features making up the idea of God that have been central in the western religious tradition. According to this idea, God is a supremely good being, creator of but separate from and independent of the world, omnipotent, omniscient, eternal, and self-existent. In the course of exploring this idea of God, we have also noted various other conceptions of the divine associated with polytheism, henotheism, monotheism, and pantheism. The idea of God that will be of central importance in this book, however, is the idea elaborated by the traditional western theologians. It is the major idea of God in the three great religions of western civilization: Judaism, Christianity, and Islam. Up to this point we have used Robinson's expression "the God out there" and the expression "the God of the traditional theologians" to refer to this idea of God. From this point on, however, we shall call this view of God the *theistic* idea of God. To be a theist, then, is to believe in the existence of a supremely good being, creator of but separate from and independent of the world, omnipotent, omniscient, eternal (in either of our two senses) and self-existent. An *atheist* is anyone who believes that the theistic God does not exist, whereas an *agnostic* is someone who has considered the theistic idea of God but believes neither in the existence nor in the nonexistence of the theistic God.

We have just used the terms *theist, atheist,* and *agnostic* in a restricted or narrow sense. In the broader sense, a theist is someone who believes in the existence of a divine being or beings, even if his idea of the divine is quite different from the idea of God we have been describing. Similarly, in the broader sense of the term, an atheist is someone who rejects belief in every form of deity, not just the God of the traditional theologians. To avoid confusion, it is important to keep in mind both the narrow and the broader senses of these terms. In the narrow sense, the Protestant theologian Paul Tillich is an atheist, for he rejected belief in what we have called the theistic God. But in the broader sense he is a theist since he believed in a divine reality, albeit different from the theistic God. For the most part I shall use the terms *theism, atheism,* and *agnosticism* in the narrow sense. Thus when we consider the question of what grounds there are for theism, we shall be concerned with whether there are rational grounds for the existence of the theistic God (the God of the traditional theologians). And when we ask, for example, whether the facts about evil in the world prove the truth of atheism, we shall be asking whether the existence of evil provides rational grounds for the conclusion that the theistic God does not exist.

Having clarified the idea of the theistic God, we can now consider some of these larger questions. And we shall begin with the question of whether belief in his existence can be rationally justified.

Notes

1. John A. T. Robinson, *Honest to God* (London: SCM Press Ltd., 1963).
2. St. Thomas Aquinas, *Summa Theologica,* I, Q 25, Art. 3. in *The Basic Writings of Saint Thomas Aquinas,* ed. Anton C. Pegis (New York: Random House, 1945).
3. St. Anselm, *Monologium,* VI in *Saint Anselm: Basic Writings,* tr. Sidney N. Deane (La Salle, Illinois: Open Court Publishing Co., 1962).
4. St. Anselm, *Monologium,* XXII in *Saint Anselm: Basic Writings.*
5. Boethius, *The Consolation of Philosophy,* Prose VI, tr. Richard Green (New York: The Bobbs-Merrill Company, Inc., 1962).

Topics for Review

1. Briefly define the concepts *polytheism, henotheism,* and *monotheism.*
2. Explain how God can be omnipotent and yet not have it in his power to do evil.
3. What is meant by a self-existent being, and for what reasons does Anselm think that God is a self-existent being?
4. State the law of space and the law of time, and indicate the connection between the law of time and what is meant by the eternity of God.
5. Describe the theistic idea of God and what is meant by *theism, atheism,* and *agnosticism.*

Topics for Further Study

6. How would you define the term *God*? If your definition of *God* is different from the theistic idea of God, explain the differences and give reasons why your idea of God might be a better one.
7. What reasons would you give to show that God exists, as you've defined *God*? What reasons might someone give for rejecting either your definition of *God* or your claim that God (as defined by you) actually exists? How would you respond?

Chapter

2

THE COSMOLOGICAL ARGUMENT

Since ancient times thoughtful people have sought to justify their religious beliefs. Perhaps the most basic belief for which justification has been sought is the belief that there is a God. The effort to justify belief in the existence of God has generally started either from facts available to believers and nonbelievers alike or from facts, such as the experience of God, normally available only to believers. In this and the next two chapters, we shall consider some major attempts to justify belief in God by appealing to facts supposedly available to any rational person, whether religious or not. By starting from such facts, theologians and philosophers have developed arguments for the existence of God, arguments which, they have claimed, prove beyond reasonable doubt that there is a God.

STATING THE ARGUMENT

Arguments for the existence of God are commonly divided into *a posteriori* arguments and *a priori* arguments. An *a posteriori* argument depends on a principle or premise that can be known only by means of our experience of the world. An *a priori* argument, on the other hand, purports to rest on principles all of which can be known independently of our experience of the world, by just reflecting on and understanding them. Of the three major arguments for the existence of God—the Cosmological, the Teleological, and the Ontological—only the last of these is entirely *a priori*. In the Cosmological Argument one starts from some simple fact about the world, such as that it contains things which are caused to exist by other things. In the Teleological Argument a somewhat more complicated fact about the world serves as a starting point, the fact that the world exhibits order and design. In the Ontological Argument, however, one begins simply with a concept of God. In this chapter we shall consider the Cosmological Argument; in the next two chapters we shall examine the Ontological Argument and the Teleological Argument.

Before we state the Cosmological Argument itself, we shall consider some rather general points about the argument. Historically, it can be traced to the writings of the Greek philosophers, Plato and Aristotle, but the major developments in the argument took place in the thirteenth and in the eighteenth centuries. In the thirteenth century Aquinas put forth five distinct arguments for the existence of God, and of these, the first three are versions of the Cosmological Argument.[1] In the first of these he started from the fact that there are things in the world undergoing change and reasoned to the conclusion that there must be some ultimate cause of change that is itself unchanging. In the second he started from the fact that there are things in the world that clearly are caused to exist by other things and reasoned to the conclusion that there must be some ultimate cause of existence whose own existence is itself uncaused. And in the third argument he started from the fact that there are things in the world which need not have existed at all, things which do exist but which we can easily imagine might not, and reasoned to the conclusion that there must be some being that had to be, that exists and could not have failed to exist. Now it might be objected that even if Aquinas' arguments do prove beyond doubt the existence of an unchanging changer, an uncaused cause, and a being that could not have failed to exist, the arguments fail to prove the existence of the theistic God. For the theistic God, as we saw, is supremely good, omnipotent, omniscient, and creator of but separate from and independent of the world. How do we know, for example, that the unchanging changer isn't evil or slightly ignorant? The answer to this objection is that the Cosmological Argument has two parts. In the first part the effort is to prove the existence of a special sort of being, for example, a being that could not have failed to exist, or a being that causes change in other things but is itself unchanging. In the second part of the argument the effort is to prove that the special sort of being whose existence has been established in the first part has, and must have, the features—perfect goodness, omnipotence, omniscience, and so on—which go together to make up the theistic idea of God. What this means, then, is that Aquinas' three arguments are different versions of only the first part of the Cosmological Argument. Indeed, in later sections of his *Summa Theologica* Aquinas undertakes to show that the unchanging changer, the uncaused cause of existence, and the being which had to exist are one and the same being and that this single being has all of the attributes of the theistic God.

We noted above that a second major development in the Cosmological Argument took place in the eighteenth century, a development reflected in the writings of the German philosopher, Gottfried Leibniz (1646–1716), and especially in the writings of the English theologian and philosopher, Samuel Clarke (1675–1729). In 1704 Clarke gave a series of lectures, later published under the title *A Demonstration of the Being and Attributes of God*. These lectures constitute, perhaps, the most complete, forceful, and cogent presentation of the Cosmological Argument we possess. The lectures were read by the major skeptical philosopher of the century, David Hume (1711–1776), and in his brilliant attack on the attempt to justify religion in the court of reason, his *Dialogues Concerning Natural Religion*, Hume advanced several penetrating criticisms of Clarke's arguments, criticisms which have persuaded many philosophers in the modern period to reject the

Cosmological Argument. In our study of the argument we shall concentrate our attention largely on its eighteenth century form and try to assess its strengths and weaknesses in the light of the criticisms which Hume and others have advanced against it.

The first part of the eighteenth-century form of the Cosmological Argument seeks to establish the existence of a self-existent being. The second part of the argument attempts to prove that the self-existent being is the theistic God, that is, has the features which we have noted to be basic elements in the theistic idea of God. We shall consider mainly the first part of the argument, for it is against the first part that philosophers from Hume to Russell have advanced very important objections.

In stating the first part of the Cosmological Argument we shall make use of two important concepts, the concept of a *dependent being* and the concept of a *self-existent being*. By *a dependent being* we mean *a being whose existence is accounted for by the causal activity of other things*. Recalling Anselm's division into the three cases: "explained by another," "explained by nothing," and "explained by it-self," it's clear that a dependent being is a being whose existence is explained by another. By *a self-existent being* we mean *a being whose existence is accounted for by its own nature*. This idea, as we saw in the preceding chapter, is an essential element in the theistic concept of God. Again, in terms of Anselm's three cases, a self-existent being is a being whose existence is explained by itself. Armed with these two concepts, the concept of a dependent being and the concept of a self-existent being, we can now state the first part of the Cosmological Argument.

1. Every being (that exists or ever did exist) is either a dependent being or a self-existent being.
2. Not every being can be a dependent being.

Therefore,

3. There exists a self-existent being.

Deductive Validity

Before we look critically at each of the premises of this argument, we should note that this argument is, to use an expression from the logician's vocabulary, *deductively valid*. To find out whether an argument is deductively valid, we need only ask the question: If its premises were true, would its conclusion have to be true? If the answer is yes, the argument is deductively valid. If the answer is no, the argument is deductively invalid. Notice that the question of the validity of an argument is entirely different from the question of whether its premises are in fact true. The following argument is made up entirely of false statements, but it is deductively valid.

1. Babe Ruth is the President of the United States.
2. The President of the United States is from Indiana.

Therefore,

3. Babe Ruth is from Indiana.

The argument is deductively valid because even though its premises are false, if they were true its conclusion would have to be true. Even God, Aquinas would say, cannot bring it about that the premises of this argument are true and yet its conclusion is false, for God's power extends only to what is possible, and it is an absolute impossibility that Babe Ruth be the President, the President be from Indiana, and yet Babe Ruth not be from Indiana.

The Cosmological Argument (that is, its first part) is a deductively valid argument. If its premises are or were true, its conclusion would have to be true. It's clear from our example about Babe Ruth, however, that the fact that an argument is deductively valid is insufficient to establish the truth of its conclusion. What else is required? Clearly that we know or have rational grounds for believing that the premises are true. If we know that the Cosmological Argument is deductively valid, and can establish that its premises are true, we shall thereby have proved that its conclusion is true. Are, then, the premises of the Cosmological Argument true? To this more difficult question we must now turn.

PSR and the First Premise

At first glance the first premise might appear to be an obvious or even trivial truth. But it is neither obvious nor trivial. And if it appears to be obvious or trivial, we must be confusing the idea of a self-existent being with the idea of a being that is not a dependent being. Clearly, it is true that any being is either a dependent being (explained by other things) or it is not a dependent being (not explained by other things). But what our premise says is that any being is either a dependent being (explained by other things) or it is a self-existent being (explained by itself). Consider again Anselm's three cases.

a. explained by another
b. explained by nothing
c. explained by itself

What our first premise asserts is that each being that exists (or ever did exist) is either of sort a or of sort c. It denies that any being is of sort b. And it is this denial that makes the first premise both significant and controversial. The obvious truth we must not confuse it with is the truth that any being is either of sort a or not of sort a. While this is true it is neither very significant nor controversial.

Earlier we saw that Anselm accepted as a basic principle that whatever exists has an explanation of its existence. Since this basic principle denies that any thing of sort b exists or ever did exist, it's clear that Anselm would believe the first premise of our Cosmological Argument. The eighteenth-century proponents of the argument also were convinced of the truth of the basic principle we attributed to Anselm. And because they were convinced of its truth, they readily accepted the first premise of the Cosmological Argument. But by the eighteenth century,

Anselm's basic principle had been more fully elaborated and had received a name, the *Principle of Sufficient Reason*. Since this principle (PSR, as we shall call it) plays such an important role in justifying the premises of the Cosmological Argument, it will help us to consider it for a moment before we continue our enquiry into the truth or falsity of the premises of the Cosmological Argument.

The Principle of Sufficient Reason, as it was expressed by both Leibniz and Samuel Clarke, is a very general principle and is best understood as having two parts. In its first part it is simply a restatement of Anselm's principle that there must be an explanation of the *existence* of any being whatever. Thus if we come upon a man in a room, PSR implies that there must be an explanation of the fact that that particular man exists. A moment's reflection, however, reveals that there are many facts about the man other than the mere fact that he exists. There is the fact that the man in question is in the room he's in, rather than somewhere else, the fact that he is in good health, and the fact that he is at the moment thinking of Paris, rather than, say, London. Now, the purpose of the second part of PSR is to require an explanation of these facts, as well. We may state PSR, therefore, as the principle that *there must be an explanation (a) of the existence of any being, and (b) of any positive fact whatever*. We are now in a position to study the role this very important principle plays in the Cosmological Argument.

Since the proponent of the Cosmological Argument accepts PSR in both its parts, it is clear that he will appeal to its first part, PSRa, as justification for the first premise of the Cosmological Argument. Of course, we can and should enquire into the deeper question of whether the proponent of the argument is rationally justified in accepting PSR itself. But we shall put this question aside for the moment. What we need to see first is whether he is correct in thinking that *if* PSR is true then both of the premises of the Cosmological Argument are true. And what we have just seen is that if only the first part of PSR, that is, PSRa, is true, the first premise of the Cosmological Argument will be true. But what of the second premise of the argument? For what reasons does the proponent think that it must be true?

The Second Premise

According to the second premise, not every being that exists can be a dependent being, that is, can have the explanation of its existence in some other being or beings. Presumably, the proponent of the argument thinks there is something fundamentally wrong with the idea that every being that exists is dependent, that each existing being was caused by some other being which in turn was caused by some other being, and so on. But just what does he think is wrong with it? To help us in understanding his thinking, let's simplify things by supposing that there exists only one thing now, A_1, a living thing perhaps, that was brought into existence by something else, A_2, which perished shortly after it brought A_1, into existence. Suppose further that A_2 was brought into existence in similar fashion some time ago by A_3, and A_3 by A_4, and so forth back into the past. Each of these beings is a *dependent* being, it owes its existence to the preceding thing in the series. Now if nothing else ever existed but these beings, then what the second premise says would not be true. For if every being that exists or ever did exist is an

A and was produced by a preceding A, then every being that exists or ever did exist would be dependent and, accordingly, premise two of the Cosmological Argument would be false. If the proponent of the Cosmological Argument is correct there must, then, be something wrong with the idea that every being that exists or did exist is an A and that they form a causal series. A_1 caused by A_2, A_2 caused by A_3, A_3 caused by A_4, . . . A_n caused by A_{n+1}. How does the proponent of the Cosmological Argument propose to show us that there is something wrong with this view?

A popular but mistaken idea of how the proponent tries to show that something is wrong with the view, that every being might be dependent, is that he uses the following argument to reject it.

1. There must be a *first* being to start any causal series.
2. If every being were dependent there would be no *first* being to start the causal series.

Therefore,

3. Not every being can be a dependent being.

Although this argument is deductively valid, and its second premise is true, its first premise overlooks the distinct possibility that a causal series might be *infinite*, with no first member at all. Thus if we go back to our series of A beings, where each A is dependent, having been produced by the preceding A in the causal series, it's clear that if the series existed it would have no first member, for every A in the series there would be a preceding A which produced it, *ad infinitum*. The first premise of the argument just given assumes that a causal series must stop with a first member somewhere in the distant past. But there seems to be no good reason for making that assumption.

The eighteenth-century proponents of the Cosmological Argument recognized that the causal series of dependent beings could be infinite, without a first member to start the series. They rejected the idea that every being that is or ever was is dependent not because there would then be no first member to the series of dependent beings, but because there would then be no explanation for the fact that there are and have always been dependent beings. To see their reasoning let's return to our simplification of the supposition that the only things that exist or ever did exist are dependent beings. In our simplification of that supposition only one of the dependent beings exists at a time, each one perishing as it produces the next in the series. Perhaps the first thing to note about this supposition is that there is no individual A in the causal series of dependent beings whose existence is unexplained—A_1 is explained by A_2, A_2 by A_3, and A_n by A_{n+1}. So the first part of PSR, PSRa, appears to be satisfied. There is no particular being whose existence lacks an explanation. What, then, is it that lacks an explanation, if every particular A in the causal series of dependent beings has an explanation? It is the *series itself* that lacks an explanation. Or, as I've chosen to express it, *the fact that there are and have always been dependent beings*. For suppose we ask why it is that there are and have always been As in existence. It won't do to say that As

have always been producing other As—we can't explain why there have always been As by saying there always have been As. Nor, on the supposition that only As have ever existed, can we explain the fact that there have always been As by appealing to something other than an A—for no such thing would have existed. Thus the supposition that the only things that exist or ever existed are dependent things leaves us with a fact for which there can be no explanation; namely, the fact that there are and have always been dependent beings.

Questioning the Justification of the Second Premise

Critics of the Cosmological Argument have raised several important objections against the claim that if every being is dependent the series or collection of those beings would have no explanation. Our understanding of the Cosmological Argument, as well as of its strengths and weaknesses, will be deepened by a careful consideration of these criticisms.

The first criticism is that the proponent of the Cosmological Argument makes the mistake of treating the collection or series of dependent beings as though it were itself a dependent being, and, therefore, requires an explanation of its existence. But, so the objection goes, the collection of dependent beings is not itself a dependent being any more than a collection of stamps is itself a stamp.

A second criticism is that the proponent makes the mistake of inferring that because each member of the collection of dependent beings has a cause, the collection itself must have a cause. But, as Bertrand Russell noted, such reasoning is as fallacious as to infer that the human race (that is, the collection of human beings) must have a mother because each member of the collection (each human being) has a mother.

A third criticism is that the proponent of the argument fails to realize that for there to be an explanation of a collection of things is nothing more than for there to be an explanation of each of the things making up the collection. Since in the infinite collection (or series) of dependent beings, each being in the collection does have an explanation—by virtue of having been caused by some preceding member of the collection—the explanation of the collection, so the criticism goes, has already been given. As David Hume remarked, "Did I show you the particular causes of each individual in a collection of twenty particles of matter, I should think it very unreasonable, should you afterwards ask me, what was the cause of the whole twenty. This is sufficiently explained in explaining the cause of the parts."[2]

Finally, even if the proponent of the Cosmological Argument can satisfactorily answer these objections, he must face one last objection to his ingenious attempt to justify premise two of the Cosmological Argument. For someone may agree that if nothing exists but an infinite collection of dependent beings, the infinite collection will have no explanation of its existence, and still refuse to conclude from this that there is something wrong with the idea that every being is a dependent being. Why, he might ask, should we think that everything has to have an explanation? What's wrong with admitting that the fact that there are and have always been dependent beings is a *brute fact*, a fact having no explanation whatever? Why does everything have to have an explanation anyway? We must now see what can be said in response to these several objections.

Responses to Criticism

It is certainly a mistake to think that a collection of stamps is itself a stamp, and very likely a mistake to think that the collection of dependent beings is itself a dependent being. But the mere fact that the proponent of the argument thinks that there must be an explanation not only for each member of the collection of dependent beings but for the collection itself is not sufficient grounds for concluding that he must view the collection as itself a dependent being. The collection of human beings, for example, is certainly not itself a human being. Admitting this, however, we might still seek an explanation of why there is a collection of human beings, of why there are such things as human beings at all. So the mere fact that an explanation is demanded for the collection of dependent beings is no proof that the person who demands the explanation must be supposing that the collection itself is just another dependent being.

The second criticism attributes to the proponent of the Cosmological Argument the following bit of reasoning.

1. Every member of the collection of dependent beings has a cause or explanation.

Therefore,

2. The collection of dependent beings has a cause or explanation.

As we noted in setting forth this criticism, arguments of this sort are often unreliable. It would be a mistake to conclude that a collection of objects is light in weight simply because each object in the collection is light in weight, for if there were many objects in the collection it might be quite heavy. On the other hand, if we know that each marble weighs more than one ounce, we could infer validly that the collection of marbles weighs more than an ounce. Fortunately, however, we don't need to decide whether the inference from 1 to 2 is valid or invalid. We need not decide this question because the proponent of the Cosmological Argument need not use this inference to establish that there must be an explanation of the collection of dependent beings. He need not use this inference because he has in PSR a principle from which it follows immediately that the collection of dependent beings has a cause or explanation. For according to PSR, every positive fact must have an explanation. If it is a fact that there exists a collection of dependent beings then, according to PSR, that fact too must have an explanation. So it is PSR that the proponent of the Cosmological Argument appeals to in concluding that there must be an explanation of the collection of dependent beings, and not some dubious inference from the premise that each member of the collection has an explanation. It seems, then, that neither of the first two criticisms is strong enough to do any serious damage to the reasoning used to support the second premise of the Cosmological Argument.

The third objection contends that to explain the existence of a collection of things is the same thing as to explain the existence of each of its members. If we consider a collection of dependent beings where each being in the collection is explained by the preceding member which caused it, it's clear that no member of the collection will lack an explanation of its existence. But, so the criticism goes, if we've explained the existence of every member of a collection, we've explained the existence of the collection—there's nothing left over to be explained. This forceful criticism, originally advanced by David Hume, has gained considerable support in the modern period. But the criticism rests on an assumption that the proponent of the Cosmological Argument would not accept. The assumption is that to explain the existence of a collection of things it is *sufficient* to explain the existence of every member in the collection. To see what is wrong with this assumption is to understand the basic issue in the reasoning by which the proponent of the Cosmological Argument seeks to establish that not every being can be a dependent being.

In order for there to be an explanation of the existence of the collection of dependent beings, it's clear that the eighteenth-century proponents would require that the following two conditions be satisified:

C1. There is an explanation of the existence of each of the members of the collection of dependent beings.
C2. There is an explanation of why there are *any* dependent beings.

According to the proponents of the Cosmological Argument, if every being that exists or ever did exist is a dependent being—that is, if the whole of reality consists of nothing more than a collection of dependent beings—C1 will be satisfied, but C2 will not be satisfied. And since C2 won't be satisfied, there will be no explanation of the collection of dependent beings. The third criticism, therefore, says in effect that if C1 is satisfied, C2 will be satisfied, and, since in a collection of dependent beings each member will have an explanation in whatever it was that produced it, C1 will be satisfied. So, therefore, C2 will be satisfied and the collection of dependent beings will have an explanation.

Although the issue is a complicated one, I think it is possible to see that the third criticism rests on a mistake: the mistake of thinking that if C1 is satisfied C2 must also be satisfied. The mistake is a natural one to make for it is easy to imagine circumstances in which if C1 is satisfied C2 also will be satisfied. Suppose, for example, that the whole of reality includes not just a collection of dependent beings but also a self-existent being. Suppose further that instead of each dependent being having been produced by some other dependent being, every dependent being was produced by the self-existent being. Finally, let us consider both the possibility that the collection of dependent beings is finite in time and has a first member, and the possibility that the collection of dependent beings is infinite in past time, having no first member. Using G for the self-existent being, the first possibility may be diagramed as follows:

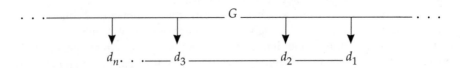

G, we shall say, has always existed and always will. We can think of d_1 as some presently existing dependent being, d_2, d_3, and so forth as dependent beings that existed at some time in the past, and d_n as the first dependent being to exist. The second possibility may be portrayed as follows:

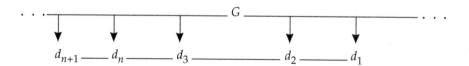

On this diagram there is no first member of the collection of dependent beings. Each member of the infinite collection, however, is explained by reference to the self-existent being G which produced it. Now the interesting point about both these cases is that the explanation that has been provided for the members of the collection of dependent beings carries with it, at least in part, an answer to the question of why there are any dependent beings at all. In both cases we may explain why there are dependent beings by pointing out that there exists a self-existent being that has been engaged in producing them. So once we have learned that the existence of each member of the collection of dependent beings has its existence explained by the fact that G produced it, we have already learned why there are dependent beings.

Someone might object that we haven't really learned why there are dependent beings until we also learn *why* G has been producing them. But, of course, we could also say that we haven't really explained the existence of a particular dependent being, say d_3, until we also learn not just that G produced it but *why* G produced it. The point we need to grasp, however, is that once we admit that every dependent being's existence is explained by G, we must admit that the fact that there are dependent beings has also been explained. So it is not unnatural that someone should think that to explain the existence of the collection of dependent beings is nothing more than to explain the existence of its members. For, as we've seen, to explain the collection's existence is to explain each member's existence and to explain why there are any dependent beings at all. And in the examples we've considered, in doing the one (explaining why each dependent being exists) we've already done the other (explained why there are any dependent beings at all). We must now see, however, that on the supposition that the whole of reality consists *only* of a collection of dependent beings, to give an explanation of each member's existence is not to provide an explanation of why there are dependent beings.

In the examples we've considered, we have gone *outside* of the collection of dependent beings in order to explain the members' existence. But if the only beings that exist or ever existed are dependent beings then each dependent being will be explained by some other dependent being, ad infinitum. This does not mean that there will be some particular dependent being whose existence is unaccounted for. Each dependent being has an explanation of its existence;

namely, in the dependent being which preceded it and produced it. So C1 is satisfied: there is an explanation of the existence of each member of the collection of dependent beings. Turning to C2, however, we can see that it will not be satisfied. We cannot explain why there are (or have ever been) dependent beings by appealing to all the members of the infinite collection of dependent beings. For if the question to be answered is why there are (or have ever been) any dependent beings at all, we cannot answer that question by noting that there always have been dependent beings, each one accounting for the existence of some other dependent being. Thus on the supposition that every being is dependent, it seems there will be no explanation of why there are dependent beings. C2 will not be satisfied. Therefore, on the supposition that every being is dependent there will be no explanation of the existence of the collection of dependent beings.

The Truth of PSR

We come now to the final criticism of the reasoning supporting the second premise of the Cosmological Argument. According to this criticism, it is admitted that the supposition that every being is dependent implies that there will be a *brute fact* in the universe, a fact, that is, for which there can be no explanation whatever. For there will be no explanation of the fact that dependent beings exist and have always been in existence. It is this brute fact that the proponents of the argument were describing when they pointed out that if every being is depen- dent, the series or collection of dependent beings would lack an explanation of *its* existence. The final criticism asks what is wrong with admitting that the universe contains such a brute, unintelligible fact. In asking this question the critic chal- lenges the fundamental principle, PSR, on which the Cosmological Argument rests. For, as we've seen, the first premise of the argument denies that there exists a being whose existence has no explanation. In support of this premise the proponent appeals to the first part of PSR. The second premise of the argument claims that not every being can be dependent. In support of this premise the proponent appeals to the second part of PSR, the part which states that there must be an explanation of any positive fact whatever.

The proponent reasons that if every being were a dependent being, then although the first part of PSR would be satisfied—every being would have an explanation—the second part would be violated; there would be no explanation for the positive fact that there are and have always been dependent beings. For first, since every being is supposed to be dependent, there would be nothing outside of the collection of dependent beings to explain the collection's existence. Second, the fact that each member of the collection has an explanation in some other dependent being is insufficient to explain why there are and have always been dependent beings. And, finally, there is nothing about the collection of dependent beings that would suggest that it is a self-existent collection. Conse- quently, if every being were dependent, the fact that there are and have always been dependent beings would have no explanation. But this violates the second part of PSR. So the second premise of the Cosmological Argument must be true: Not every being can be a dependent being. This conclusion, however, is no better than the principle, PSR, on which it rests. And it is the point of the final criticism to question the truth of PSR. Why, after all, should we accept the idea that every being and every positive fact must have an explanation? Why, in short, should we believe PSR? These are important questions, and any final judgment of the Cosmological Argument depends on how they are answered.

Most of the theologians and philosophers who accept PSR have tried to defend it in either of two ways. Some have held that PSR is (or can be) known *intuitively* to be true. By this they mean that if we fully understand and reflect on what is said by PSR we can see that it must be true. Now, undoubtedly, there are statements which are known intuitively to be true. "Every triangle has exactly three angles" or "No physical object can be in two different places in space at one and the same time" are examples of statements whose truth we can apprehend just by understanding and reflecting on them. The difficulty with the claim that PSR is intuitively true, however, is that a number of very able philosophers fail to apprehend its truth, and some even claim that the principle is false. It is doubtful, therefore, that many of us, if any, know intuitively that PSR is true.

The second way philosophers and theologians who accept PSR have sought to defend it is by claiming that although it is not known to be true, it is, nevertheless, a presupposition of reason, a basic assumption that rational people make, whether or not they reflect sufficiently to become aware of the assumption. It's probably true that there are some assumptions we all make about our world, assumptions which are so basic that most of us are unaware of them. And, I suppose, it might be true that PSR is such an assumption. What bearing would this view of PSR have on the Cosmological Argument? Perhaps the main point to note is that even if PSR is a presupposition we all share, the premises of the Cosmological Argument could still be false. For PSR itself could still be false. The fact, if it is a fact, that all of us *presuppose* that every existing being and every positive fact has an explanation does not imply that no being exists, and no positive fact obtains, without an explanation. Nature is not bound to satisfy our presuppositions. As the American philosopher William James once remarked in another connection, "In the great boarding house of nature, the cakes and the butter and the syrup seldom come out so even and leave the plates so clear."

Our study of the first part of the Cosmological Argument has led us to the fundamental principle on which its premises rest, the Principle of Sufficient Reason. Since we do not seem to know that PSR is true, we cannot reasonably claim to know that the premises of the Cosmological Argument are true. They might be true. But unless we do know them to be true they cannot *establish* for us the conclusion that there exists a being that has the explanation of its existence within its own nature. If it were shown, however, that even though we do not *know* that PSR is true we all, nevertheless, *presuppose* PSR to be true, then, whether PSR is true or not, to be consistent we should accept the Cosmological Argument. For, as we've seen, its premises imply its conclusion and its premises do seem to follow from PSR. But no one has succeeded in *showing* that PSR is an assumption that most or all of us share. So our final conclusion must be that although the Cosmological Argument might be a *sound* argument (valid with true premises), it does not provide us with good rational grounds for believing that among these beings that exist there is one whose existence is accounted for by its own nature. Having come to this conclusion, we may safely put aside the second part of the argument. For even if it succeeded in showing that a self-existent being would have the other attributes of the theistic God, the Cosmological Argument would still not provide us with good rational grounds for belief in God, having failed in its first part to provide us with good rational grounds for believing that there is a self-existent being.

Notes

1. See St. Thomas Aquinas, *Summa Theologica*, 1a. 2, 3.
2. David Hume, *Dialogues Concerning Natural Religion*, Part IX, ed. H. D. Aiken (New York: Hafner Publishing Company, 1948), pp. 59–60.

Topics for Review

1. State the first part of the Cosmological Argument and describe what is meant by a dependent being and a self-existent being.
2. Explain what is meant by the Principle of Sufficient Reason.
3. Briefly describe the several objections that have been raised against the reasoning used to justify the claim that not every being can be a dependent being. Are any of these objections successful?
4. How have philosophers sought to defend the Principle of Sufficient Reason?
5. If the Principle of Sufficient Reason is not known to be true, what conclusion must we draw about the Cosmological Argument?

Topics for Further Study

6. Discuss the following response to the Cosmological Argument:

   Perhaps we can explain the existence of the world by supposing that God exists and created it. But we are then left with the existence of God. How are we to explain that? If we say that God's existence doesn't have an explanation, we can say the same thing about the world. If we say that God's existence is self-explained, we can say the same thing about the world. Therefore, the simpler hypothesis is that either the world has no explanation or it is self-explained.

7. In human life we are constantly explaining one thing by a second thing, even though we are unable to explain the second thing. If, in all our practical affairs, explanations must come to an end, doesn't that show that the Principle of Sufficient Reason is false, or at least an impractical idea? Discuss.

3

THE ONTOLOGICAL ARGUMENT

It is perhaps best to think of the Ontological Argument not as a single argument but as a family of arguments each member of which begins with a concept of God and, by appealing only to *a priori* principles, endeavors to establish that God actually exists. Within this family of arguments, the most important historically is the argument set forth by Anselm in the second chapter of his *Proslogium* (a discourse).[1] Indeed, it is fair to say that the Ontological Argument begins with Chapter Two of Anselm's *Proslogium*. In an earlier work, *Monologium* (a soliloquy), Anselm had endeavored to establish the existence and nature of God by weaving together several versions of the Cosmological Argument. In the preface to *Proslogium* Anselm remarks that after the publication of *Monologium* he began to search for a single argument which alone would establish the existence and nature of God. After much strenuous but unsuccessful effort, he reports that he sought to put the project out of his mind in order to turn to more fruitful tasks. The idea, however, continued to haunt him until one day the proof he had so strenuously sought became clear to his mind. It is this proof which Anselm sets forth in the second chapter of *Proslogium*.

BASIC CONCEPTS

Before setting forth Anselm's argument in step-by-step fashion, it will be useful to introduce a few concepts that will help us understand some of the central ideas which figure in the argument. Suppose we draw a vertical line in our imagination and imagine that on the left side of our line are all the things which exist, while on the right side of the line are all the things which don't exist. We might then set about to make a list of some of the things on both sides of our imaginary line, a list we might start as follows:

THINGS WHICH EXIST	THINGS WHICH DON'T EXIST
The Empire State Building	The Fountain of Youth
Dogs	Unicorns
The Planet Mars	The Abominable Snowman

Now, each of the things (or sort of things) listed thus far has the following feature: it logically might have been on the other side of the line. The Fountain of Youth, for example, is on the right side of the line but *logically* there is no absurdity in the idea that it might have been on the left side of the line. Similarly, although dogs do exist, we surely can imagine without logical absurdity that they might not have existed, that they might have been on the right side of the line. Let's then record this feature of the things thus far listed by introducing the idea of a *contingent thing* as a thing that logically might have been on the other side of the line from the side it actually is on. The planet Mars and the abominable snowman are contingent things even though the former happens to exist and the latter does not.

Suppose we add to our list by writing down the phrase "the object which is completely round and completely square at the same time" on the right side of our line. The round square, however, unlike the other things thus far listed on the right side of our line, is something that *logically could not* have been on the left side of the line. Noting this, let's introduce the idea of an *impossible thing* as a thing that is on the right side of the line and logically could not have been on the left side of the line.

Looking again at our list, the question arises as to whether there is anything on the left side of our imaginary line which is such that, unlike the things thus far listed on the left side, it *logically could not* have been on the right side of the line. At this point we don't have to answer this question. But it is useful to have a concept to apply to any such things should there be any. Accordingly, let's introduce the notion of a *necessary thing* as a thing that is on the left side of our imaginary line and logically could not have been on the right side of the line.

Finally, we may introduce the idea of a *possible thing* as any thing that is either on the left side of our imaginary line or logically might have been on the left side of the line. Possible things, then, will be all those things that are not impossible things—that is, all those things that are either contingent or necessary. If there are no necessary things then all possible things will be contingent and all contingent things will be possible. If there is a necessary thing, however, then there will be a possible thing which is not contingent.

Armed with the concepts just explained we can now proceed to clarify certain important distinctions and ideas in Anselm's thought. The first of these is his distinction between *existence in the understanding* and *existence in reality*. Anselm's notion of existence in reality is the same as our notion of existence, that is, being on the left side of our imaginary line. Since the Fountain of Youth is on the right side of the line it does not exist in reality. The things which exist are, to use Anselm's phrase, the things which exist in reality. Anselm's notion of existence in the understanding, however, is not the same as any idea we normally employ. But what Anselm means by "existence in the understanding" is not particularly mysterious. When we think of a certain thing, say the Fountain of Youth, then that thing, in Anselm's view, exists in the understanding. So some of the things on both sides of our imaginary line exist in the understanding, but only those on the left side of our line exist in reality. Are there any things that don't exist in the understanding? Undoubtedly there are. For there are things, both existing and nonexisting, of which we have not really thought. Now suppose I assert that the Fountain of Youth does not exist. Since to meaningfully deny the existence of something, I must have that thing in mind, it follows on Anselm's view that whenever someone asserts that some thing does not exist, that thing does exist in the understanding.[2] So in asserting that the Fountain of Youth does not exist I imply that the Fountain of Youth does exist in the understanding. And in asserting that it doesn't exist, I have asserted (on Anselm's view) that it doesn't exist in reality. This means that my simple assertion that the Fountain of Youth doesn't exist amounts to the somewhat more complex claim that the Fountain of Youth exists in the understanding but does not exist in reality—in short, that the Fountain of Youth exists *only* in the understanding.

In view of the above we can now understand why Anselm insists that anyone who hears of God, thinks about God, or even denies the existence of God is, nevertheless, committed to the view that God exists in the understanding. Also, we can understand why Anselm treats what he calls the fool's claim that God does not exist as the claim that God exists *only* in the understanding—that is, that God exists in the understanding but does not exist in reality.

In *Monologium* Anselm sought to prove that among those beings which do exist, there is one which is the greatest, highest, and the best. But in *Proslogium* he undertakes to prove that among those things which exist, there is one which is not just the greatest among existing beings, but is such that no conceivable being is greater. We need to distinguish these two ideas: (i) a being than which *no existing being* is greater, and (ii) a being than which *no conceivable being* is greater. If the only things in existence were a stone, a frog, and a human being, the last of these, the human being, would satisfy our first idea but not our second—for we can conceive of a being (an angel or God) greater than a human. Anselm's idea of God, as he expresses it in *Proslogium*, II, is the same as (ii) above; it is the idea of "a being than which nothing greater can be conceived." It will, I think, facilitate our understanding of Anselm's argument if we make two slight changes in the way he has expressed his idea of God. For his phrase I shall substitute the following: "*the* being than which none greater *is possible*."[3] What this idea says is that if a certain being is God, then no *possible* being can be greater than it; or conversely, if a certain being is such that it is even *possible* for there to be a being greater than it, then that being is not God. What Anselm proposes to prove, then, is that the being than which none greater is possible exists in reality. If he proves this he will have proved that God, as he conceives of him, exists in reality.

But what does Anselm mean by *greatness*? Is a building, for example, greater than a man? Anselm remarks: "But I do not mean physically great, as a material object is great, but that which, the greater it is, is the better or the more worthy—wisdom, for instance."[4] Contrast wisdom with size. Anselm is saying that wisdom is something that contributes to the greatness of a thing. If a thing comes to have more wisdom than it did before (given that its other characteristics remain the same), then that thing has become a greater, better, more worthy thing than it was. Wisdom, Anselm is saying, is a great-making quality. But the mere fact that something increases in size (physical greatness) does not make that thing a better thing than it was before. So size, unlike wisdom, is not a great-making quality. By *greater than* Anselm means *better than, superior to,* or *more worthy than,* and he believes that some characteristics, like wisdom and moral goodness, are great-making characteristics in that anything which has them is a *better thing* than it would be (other characteristics of it remaining the same) were it to lack them.

We come now to what we may call the *key idea* in Anselm's Ontological Argument. Anselm believes that existence *in reality is a great-making quality.* How are we to understand this idea? Does Anselm mean that anything that exists is a greater thing than anything that doesn't? Although he doesn't ask or answer this question, it is perhaps reasonable to believe that Anselm did not mean this. For when he discusses wisdom as a great-making quality he is careful not to say that any wise thing is better than any unwise thing—for he recognizes that a just but unwise person might be a better being than a wise but unjust person.[5] I suggest that what Anselm means is that anything that doesn't exist but might have existed (is on the right side of our line but might have been on the left) would have been a greater thing than it is if it had existed (if it had been on the left side of our line). He is not comparing two different things (one existing and one not existing) and saying that the first is therefore greater than the second. Rather he is talking about one and the same thing and pointing out that if it does not exist but might have existed then *it* would have been a greater thing if it had existed. Using Anselm's distinction between existence in the understanding and existence in reality, we may express the key idea in Anselm's reasoning as follows: If something exists only in the understanding, but might have existed in reality, then it might have been greater than it is. Since the Fountain of Youth, for example, exists only in the understanding but, unlike the round square, might have existed in reality, it follows by Anselm's principle that the Fountain of Youth might have been a greater thing than it is.

DEVELOPING ANSELM'S ONTOLOGICAL ARGUMENT

Having looked at some of the important ideas at work in Anselm's Ontological Argument, we can now consider its step-by-step development. In presenting Anselm's argument I shall use the term *God* in place of the longer phrase "the being than which none greater is possible"—wherever the term *God* appears we are to think of it as simply an abbreviation of the longer phrase.

1. God exists in the understanding.

As we've noted, anyone who hears of the being than which none greater is possible is, in Anselm's view, committed to premise 1.

2. God might have existed in reality (God is a possible being).

Anselm, I think, assumes the truth of premise 2 without making it explicit in his reasoning. By asserting 2, I don't mean to imply that God does not exist in reality. All that is meant is that, unlike the round square, God is a possible being.

    3. If something exists only in the understanding and might have existed in reality, then it might have been greater than it is.

As we noted earlier this is the key idea in Anselm's Ontological Argument. It is intended as a general principle true of anything.

Steps 1–3 constitute the basic premises of Anselm's Ontological Argument. From these three items it follows, so Anselm believes, that God exists in reality. But how does Anselm propose to convince us that if we accept 1–3 we are committed by the rules of logic to accept his conclusion that God exists in reality? Anselm's procedure is to offer what is called a *reductio ad absurdum* proof of his conclusion. Instead of showing directly that the existence of God follows from 1–3, Anselm invites us to *suppose* that God does not exist (that is, that the conclusion he wants to establish is false) and then shows how this supposition when conjoined with 1–3 leads to an absurd result, a result that couldn't possibly be true because it is contradictory. In short, with the help of 1–3 Anselm shows that the supposition that God does not exist reduces to an absurdity. Since the supposition that God does not exist leads to an absurdity, that supposition must be rejected in favor of the conclusion that God does exist.

Does Anselm succeed in reducing the fool's belief that God does not exist to an absurdity? The best way to answer this question is to follow the steps of his argument.

    4. Suppose God exists only in the understanding.

This supposition, as we saw earlier, is Anselm's way of expressing the fool's belief that God does not exist.

    5. God might have been greater than he is. (2, 4, and 3)[6]

Step 5 follows from steps 2, 4, and 3. Since 3, if true, is true of anything it will be true of God. Step 3, therefore, implies that if God exists only in the understanding and might have existed in reality, then God might have been greater than he is. If so, then given 2 and 4, 5 must be true. For what 3 says when applied to God is that given 2 and 4 it follows that 5.

    6. God is a being than which a greater is possible. (5)

Surely if God is such that he logically might have been greater, then he is such than which a greater is possible.

We're now in a position to appreciate Anselm's *reductio* argument. He has shown us that if we accept 1–4 we must accept 6. But 6 is unacceptable; it is the absurdity Anselm was after. For replacing *God* in step 6 with the longer phrase it abbreviates, we see that 6 amounts to the absurd assertion:

7. The being than which none greater is possible is a being than which a greater is possible.

Now since 1–4 have led us to an obviously false conclusion, if we accept Anselm's basic premises 1–3 as true, 4, the supposition that God exists only in the understanding, must be rejected as false. Thus we have shown that

8. It is false that God exists only in the understanding.

But since premise 1 tells us that God does exist in the understanding, and 8 tells us that God does not exist only there, we may infer that

9. God exists in reality as well as in the understanding. (1, 8)

What are we to say of this argument? Most of the philosophers who have considered the argument have rejected it because of a basic conviction that from the logical analysis of a certain idea or concept we can never determine that there exists in reality anything answering to that idea or concept. We may examine and analyze, for example, the idea of an elephant or the idea of a unicorn, but it is only by our experience of the world that we can determine that there exist things answering to our first idea and not to the second. Anselm, however, believes that the concept of God is utterly unique—from an analysis of this concept he believes that it can be determined that there exists in reality a being which answers to it. Moreover, he presents us with an argument to show that it can be done in the case of the idea of God. We can, of course, simply reject his argument on the grounds that it violates the basic conviction noted above. Many critics, however, have sought to prove more directly that Anselm's argument is a bad argument and to point out the particular step in his argument that is mistaken. In what follows we shall examine the three major objections that have been advanced by the argument's critics.

Gaunilo's Criticism

The first major criticism was advanced by a contemporary of Anselm's, a monk named Gaunilo, who wrote a response entitled "On Behalf of the Fool."[7] Gaunilo sought to prove that Anselm's reasoning is mistaken by applying it to things other than God, things which we know don't exist. He took as his example the island than which none greater is possible. No such island really exists. But, argues Gaunilo, if Anselm's reasoning were correct we could show that such an island really does exist. For since it is greater to exist than not to exist, if the island than which none greater is possible doesn't exist then it is an island than which a greater is possible. But it is impossible for the island than which none greater is possible to be an island than which a greater is possible. Therefore, the island than which none greater is possible must exist. About this argument Gaunilo remarks:

If a man should try to prove to me by such reasoning that this island truly exists, and that its existence should no longer be doubted, either I should believe that he was jesting, or I know not which I ought to regard as the greater fool: myself, supposing I should allow this proof; or him, if he should suppose that he had established with any certainty the existence of this island.[8]

Gaunilo's strategy is clear. By using the very same reasoning Anselm employs in his argument, we can prove the existence of things we know don't exist. Therefore, Anselm's reasoning in his proof of the existence of God must be mistaken. In his reply to Gaunilo, Anselm insisted that his reasoning applies only to God and cannot be used to establish the existence of things other than God. Unfortunately, Anselm did not explain just why his reasoning cannot be applied to things like Gaunilo's island.

In defense of Anselm against Gaunilo's objection, we should note that the objection supposes that Gaunilo's island is a possible thing. But this requires us to believe that some finite, limited thing (an island) might have unlimited perfections. And it is not at all clear that this is possible. Try to think, for example, of a hockey player than which none greater is possible. How fast would he have to skate? How many goals would such a player have to score in a game? How fast would he have to shoot the puck? Could this player ever fall down, be checked, or receive a penalty? Although the phrase "The hockey player than which none greater is possible" seems meaningful, as soon as we try to get a clear idea of what such a being would be like, we discover that we can't form a coherent idea of it at all. For we are being invited to think of some limited, finite thing—a hockey player or an island—and then to think of it as exhibiting unlimited, infinite perfections. Perhaps, then, since Anselm's reasoning applies only to possible things, Anselm can reject its application to Gaunilo's island on the grounds that the island than which none greater is possible is, like the round square, an impossible thing.

Kant's Criticism

By far the most famous objection to the Ontological Argument was set forth by Immanuel Kant in the eighteenth century. According to this objection, the mistake in the argument is its claim, implicit in premise 3, that existence is a quality or predicate that adds to the greatness of a thing. There are two parts to this claim: (1) existence is a quality or predicate, and (2) existence, like wisdom and unlike physical size, is a greatmaking quality or predicate. Someone might accept (1) but object to (2). The objection made famous by Kant, however, is directed at (1). According to this objection, existence is not a predicate at all. Therefore, since in its third premise Anselm's argument implies that existence is a predicate, the argument must be rejected.

What is meant by the philosophical doctrine that existence is not a predicate? The central point in this doctrine concerns what we do when we ascribe a certain quality or predicate to something, as, for example, when we say of a woman next door that she is intelligent, six feet tall, or thin. In each case we seem to assert or presuppose that there *exists* a woman next door and then go on to ascribe to her a certain predicate—"intelligent," "six feet tall," or "thin." And what is claimed by many proponents of the doctrine that existence is not a predicate is that this is a *general feature* of predication. They hold that when we ascribe a quality or predicate to anything, we assert or presuppose that the thing exists and then ascribe the predicate to it. Now, if this is so, then it's clear that existence cannot be a predicate which we may ascribe to or deny of something. For if it were predicate, then when we assert of some thing that it exists we would be asserting or presupposing that it exists and then going on to predicate existence of it. For example, if existence were a predicate, then in asserting 'Tigers exist' we would be asserting or presupposing that tigers exist and then going on to predicate existence of them. Furthermore, in asserting 'Dragons do not exist' we would be asserting or presupposing, if existence were a predicate, that dragons do exist and then going on to deny that existence attaches to them. In short, if existence were a predicate, the affirmative existential statement "Tigers exist" would be a redundancy, and the negative existential statement "Dragons do not exist" would be contradictory. But clearly "Tigers exist" is not a redundancy and "Dragons do not exist" is true and, therefore, not contradictory. What this shows, according to the proponents of Kant's objection, is that existence is not a genuine predicate.

According to the proponents of the above objection, what we are asserting when we assert that tigers exist and that dragons do not is not that certain things (tigers) have and certain other things (dragons) do not have a peculiar predicate, *existence*, rather, we are saying something about the *concept* of a tiger and the *concept* of a dragon. In the first case we are saying that the concept of a tiger applies to something in the world; in the second case we are saying that the concept of a dragon does not apply to anything in the world.

Although this objection to the Ontological Argument has been widely accepted, it is doubtful that it provides us with a conclusive refutation of the argument. It may be true that existence is not a predicate, that in asserting the existence of something we are not ascribing a certain predicate or attribute to that thing. But the arguments presented for this view seem to rest on mistaken or incomplete claims about the nature of predication. For example, the argument which we stated earlier rests on the claim that when we ascribe a predicate to anything we assert or presuppose that that thing exists. But this claim appears to be mistaken. In asserting that Dr. Doolittle is an animal lover I seem to be ascribing the predicate *animal lover* to Dr. Doolittle, but in doing so I certainly am not asserting or presupposing that Dr. Doolittle actually exists. Dr. Doolittle doesn't exist but it is, nevertheless, true that he is an animal lover. The plain fact is that we can talk about and ascribe predicates to many things which do not and never did exist. Merlin, for example, no less than Houdini, was a magician, although Houdini existed but Merlin did not. If, as these examples suggest, the claim that whenever we ascribe a predicate to something we assert or presuppose that the thing exists is a false claim, then we will need a better argument for the doctrine that existence is not a predicate. There is some question, however, whether anyone has succeeded in giving a really conclusive argument for the view that existence is not a predicate.[9]

A Third Criticism

A third objection against the Ontological Argument calls into question the premise that God might have existed in reality (God is a possible being). As we saw, this premise claims that "the being than which none greater is possible" is not an impossible object. But is this true? Consider the series of positive integers—1, 2, 3, 4 and so on. We know that any integer in this series, no matter how large, is such that a larger than it is possible. Therefore, "the positive integer than which none larger is possible" is an impossible object. Perhaps this is also true of "the being than which none greater is possible." That is, perhaps no matter how great a being may be, it is possible for there to be a being greater than it. If this were so, then, like "the integer than which none larger is possible," Anselm's God would not be a possible object. The mere fact that there are degrees of greatness, however, does not entitle us to conclude that Anselm's God is like "the integer than which none larger is possible." There are, for example, degrees of size in angles—one angle is larger than another—but it is not true that no matter how large an angle is it is possible for there to be an angle larger than it. It is logically impossible for an angle to exceed four right angles. The notion of an angle, unlike the notion of a positive integer, implies a degree of size beyond which it is impossible to go. Is Anselm's God like a largest integer, and therefore impossible, or like a largest angle, and therefore possible? Some philosophers have argued that Anselm's God is impossible.[10] But the arguments for this conclusion are not very compelling. Perhaps, then, this objection is best construed not as proving that Anselm's God is impossible, but as raising the question whether any of us is in a position to know that "the being than which none greater is possible" is a possible object. For Anselm's argument cannot be a successful proof of the existence of God unless its premises are not just true, but are really *known* to be true. Therefore, if we don't know that Anselm's God is a possible object, then his argument cannot prove the existence of God to us, cannot enable us to know that God exists.

A Final Critique

We've had a look at both Anselm's argument, and the three major objections philosophers have raised against it. In this final section I want to present a somewhat different critique of the argument, a critique suggested by the basic conviction noted earlier: namely, that from the mere logical analysis of a certain idea or concept, we can never determine that there exists in reality anything answering to that idea or concept.

Suppose someone comes to us and says:

> I propose to define the term *God* as *an existing, wholly perfect being*. Now since it can't be true that an existing, wholly perfect being does not exist, it can't be true that God, as I've defined him, does not exist. Therefore, God must exist.

This argument appears to be a very simple Ontological Argument. It begins with a particular idea or concept of God and ends by concluding that God, so conceived, must exist. What can we say in response? We might start by objecting to this definition of *God*, claiming (1) that only predicates can be used to define a term, and (2) that existence is not a predicate. But suppose our friend is not impressed by this response—either because he thinks no one has fully explained what a predicate is or proved that existence isn't one, or because he thinks that anyone can define a word in whatever way he pleases. Can we allow our friend to define the word *God* in any way he pleases and still hope to show that it will not follow from that definition that there actually exists something to which this concept of God applies? I think we can. Let's first invite him, however, to consider some concepts other than this peculiar concept of God.

Earlier we noted that the term *magician* may be applied both to Houdini and Merlin, even though the former existed whereas the latter did not. Noting that our friend has used *existing* as part of this definition of *God*, suppose we agree with him that we can define a word in any way we please, and, accordingly, introduce the following words with the following definitions:

A *magican* is defined as an *existing magician*.
A *magico* is defined as a *nonexisting magician*.

Here we have introduced two words and used *existing* or *nonexisting* in their definitions. Now something of interest follows from the fact that *existing* is part of our definition of a magican. For while it's true that Merlin was a *magician* it isn't true that Merlin was a *magican*. And something of interest follows from our including *nonexisting* in the definition of a magico. For while it's true that Houdini was a *magician* it isn't true that Houdini was a *magico*. Houdini was a *magician* and a *magican*, but not a *magico*, whereas Merlin was a *magician* and a *magico*, but not a *magican*.

What we have just seen is that introducing *existing* or *nonexisting* into the definition of a concept has a very important implication. If we introduce *existing* into the definition of a concept, it follows that no nonexisting thing can exemplify that concept. And if we introduce *nonexisting* into the definition of a concept, it follows that no existing thing can exemplify that concept. No nonexisting thing can be a *magican* and no existing thing can be a *magico*.

But must some existing thing exemplify the concept *magican*? No! From the fact that *existing* is included in the definition of *magican* it does not follow that some existing thing is a *magican*—all that follows is that no nonexisting thing is a *magican*. If there were no magicians in existence there would be nothing to which the term *magican* would apply. This being so, it clearly does not follow merely from our definition of *magican* that some existing thing is a *magican*. Only if magicians exist will it be true that some existing thing is a *magican*.

We are now in a position to help our friend see that, from the mere fact that God is defined as an existing, wholly perfect being, it will not follow that some existing being is God. Something of interest does follow from his definition: namely, that no nonexisting being can be God. But whether some existing thing is God will depend entirely on whether some existing thing is a wholly perfect being. If no wholly perfect being exists there will be nothing to which this concept of God can apply. This being so, it clearly does not follow merely from this definition of *God* that some existing thing is God. Only if a wholly perfect being exists will it be true that God, as our friend conceives of him, exists.

Implications for Anselm's Argument

The implications of these considerations for Anselm's ingenious argument can now be traced. Anselm conceives of God as a being than which none greater is possible. He then claims that existence is a greatmaking quality, something that has it is greater than it would have been had it lacked existence. Clearly then, no nonexisting thing can exemplify Anselm's concept of God. For if we suppose that some nonexisting thing exemplifies Anselm's concept of God and also suppose that that nonexisting thing might have existed in reality (is a possible thing), then we are supposing that that nonexisting thing (1) might have been a greater thing, and (2) is, nevertheless, a thing than which a greater is not possible. Thus far Anslem's reasoning is, I believe, impeccable. But what follows from it? All that follows from it is that no nonexisting thing can be God (as Anselm conceives of God). All that follows is that given Anselm's concept of God, the proposition "Some nonexisting thing is God" cannot be true. But, as we saw earlier, this is also the case with the proposition "Some nonexisting thing is a magican." What remains to be shown is that some existing thing exemplifies Anselm's concept of God. What really does follow from his reasoning is that the only thing that logically could exemplify his concept of God is something which actually exists. And this conclusion is not without interest. But from the mere fact that nothing but an existing thing could exemplify Anselm's concept of God, it does not follow that some existing thing actually does exemplify his concept of God—no more than it follows from the mere fact that no nonexisting thing can be a magican that some existing thing is a magican.[11]

There is, however, one major difficulty in this critique of Anselm's argument. This difficulty arises when we take into account Anselm's implicit claim that God is a possible thing. To see just what this difficulty is, let's return to the idea of a possible thing. A possible thing, we determined, is any thing that either is on the left side of our imaginary line or logically might have been on the left side of the line. Possible things, then, will be all those things that, unlike the round square, are not impossible things. Suppose we concede to Anselm that God, as he conceives of him, is a possible thing. Now, of course, the mere knowledge that something is a possible thing doesn't enable us to conclude that that thing is an existing thing. For many possible things, like the Fountain of Youth, do not exist. But if something is a possible thing, then it is either an existing thing or a nonexisting thing. The set of possible things can be exhaustively divided into those possible things which actually exist and those possible things which do not exist. Therefore, if Anselm's God is a possible thing, it is either an existing thing or a nonexisting thing. We have concluded, however, that no nonexisting thing can be Anselm's God; therefore, it seems we must conclude with Anselm that some actually existing thing does exemplify his concept of God.

To see the solution to this major difficulty we need to return to an earlier example. Let's consider again the idea of a magican, an existing magician. It so happens that some magicians have existed—Houdini, The Great Blackstone, and others. But, of course, it might have been otherwise. Suppose, for the moment, that no magicians have ever existed. The concept "magician" would still have application, for it would still be true that Merlin was a magician. But what about the concept of a "magican?" Would any possible object be picked out by that concept? No! For no nonexisting thing could exemplify the concept "magican." And on the supposition that no magicians ever existed, no existing thing would exemplify the concept "magican."[12] We then would have a coherent concept "magican" which would not be exemplified by any possible object at all. For if all the possible objects which are magicians are nonexisting things, none of them would be a magican and, since no possible objects which exist are magicians, none of them would be a magican. We then would have a coherent, consistent concept "magican", which in fact is not exemplified by any possible object at all. Put in this way, our result seems paradoxical. For we are inclined to think that only contradictory concepts like "the round square" are not exemplified by any possible things. The truth is, however, that when *existing* is included in or implied by a certain concept, it may be the case that no possible object does in fact exemplify that concept. For no possible object that doesn't exist will exemplify a concept like "magican" in which *existing* is included; and if there are no existing things which exemplify the other features included in the concept—for example, "being a magician" in the case of the concept "magican"—then no possible object that exists will exemplify the concept. Put in its simplest terms, if we ask whether any possible thing is a magican, the answer will depend entirely on whether any existing thing is a magician. If no existing things are magicians, then no possible things are magicans. Some possible object is a magican just in case some actually existing thing is a magician.[13]

Applying these considerations to Anselm's argument we can find the solution to our major difficulty. Given Anselm's concept of God and his principle that existence is a great-making quality, it really does follow that the only thing that logically could exemplify his concept of God is something which actually exists. But, we argued, it doesn't follow from these considerations alone that God actually exists, that some existing thing exemplifies Anselm's concept of God. The difficulty we fell into, however, is that when we add the premise that God is a possible thing, that some possible object exemplifies his concept of God, it really does follow that God actually exists, that some actually existing thing exemplifies Anselm's concept of God. For if some possible object exemplifies his concept of God, that object is either an existing thing or a nonexisting thing. But since no nonexisting thing could exemplify Anselm's concept of God, it follows that the possible object which exemplifies his concept of God must be a possible object that actually exists. Therefore, given (1) Anselm's concept of God, (2) his principle that existence is a great-making quality, and (3) the premise that God, as conceived by Anselm, is a possible thing, it really does follow that Anselm's God actually exists.

A Too Generous Grant

I think we now can see that in granting Anselm the premise that God is a possible thing we have granted far more than we intended to grant. All we thought we were granting is that Anselm's concept of God, unlike the concept of a round square, is not contradictory or incoherent. But without realizing it we were in fact granting much more than this, as became apparent when we considered the idea of a "magican." There is nothing contradictory in the idea of a magican, an existing magician. But in asserting that a magican is a possible thing, we are, as we saw, directly implying that some existing thing is a magician. For if no existing thing is a magician, the concept of a magican will apply to no possible object whatever. The same point holds with respect to Anselm's God. Since Anselm's concept of God logically cannot apply to some nonexisting thing, the only possible objects to which it could apply are possible objects which actually exist. Therefore, in granting that Anselm's God is a possible thing, we are granting far more than that his idea of God isn't incoherent or contradictory. Suppose, for example, that every existing being has some defect which it might not have had. Without realizing it, we were denying this when we granted that Anselm's God is a possible being. For if every existing being has a defect it might not have had, then every existing being might have been greater. But if every existing being might have been greater, then Anselm's concept of God will apply to no possible object whatever. Therefore, if we allow Anselm his concept of God and his principle that existence is a great-making quality, then in granting that God, as Anselm conceives of him, is a possible being, we will be granting much more than that his concept of God is not contradictory. We will be granting, for example, that some existing thing is as perfect as it can be. For the plain fact is that Anselm's God is a possible thing only if some *existing* thing is as perfect as it can be.

Our final critique of Anselm's argument is simply this. In granting that Anselm's God is a possible thing, we are in fact granting that Anselm's God actually exists. But since the purpose of the argument is to prove to us that Anselm's God exists, we cannot be asked to grant as a premise a statement which is virtually equivalent to the conclusion that is to be proved. Anselm's concept of God may be coherent and his principle that existence is a great-making quality may be true. But all that follows from this is that no nonexisting thing can be Anselm's God. If we add to all of this the premise that God is a possible thing it will follow that God actually exists. But the additional premise claims more than that Anselm's concept of God isn't incoherent or contradictory. It amounts to the assertion that some existing being is supremely great. And since this is, in part, the point the argument endeavors to prove, the argument begs the question: it assumes the point it is supposed to prove.

If the above critique is correct, Anselm's argument fails as a proof of the existence of God. This is not to say, however, that the argument isn't a work of genius. Perhaps no other argument in the history of thought has raised so many basic philosophical questions and stimulated so much hard thought. Even if it fails as a proof of the existence of God, it will remain as one of the high achievements of the human intellect.

Notes

1. Some philosophers believe that Anselm sets forth a different and more cogent argument in Chapter Three of his *Proslogium*. For this viewpoint see Charles Hartshorne, *Anselm's Discovery* (La Salle, Illinois: Open Court Publishing Co., 1965) and Norman

Malcolm, "Anselm's Ontological Arguments," *The Philosophical Review*, LXIX, No. 1 (1960), pp. 41–62. For an illuminating account both of Anselm's intensions in *Proslogium*, II and III and of recent interpretations of Anselm, see Arthur C. McGill's essay "Recent Discussions of Anselm's Argument" in *The Many-faced Argument*, eds. John Hick and Arthur C. McGill (New York: The Macmillan Co., 1967), pp. 33–110.

2. Anselm does allow that someone may assert the sentence "God does not exist" without having in his understanding the object or idea for which the word *God* stands (See *Proslogium*, IV in *Saint Anselm: Basic Writings*, tr. Sidney N. Deane). But when a person does understand the object for which a word stands, then when he uses that word in a sentence denying the existence of that object, he must have that object in his understanding. It is doubtful, however, that Anselm thought that incoherent or contradictory expressions like *round square* stand for objects which may exist in the understanding.

3. Anselm speaks of *a being* rather than *the being* than which none greater can be conceived. His argument is easier to present if we express his idea of God in terms of *the being*. Secondly, to avoid the psychological connotations of *can be conceived* I have substituted *possible*.

4. St. Anselm, *Monologium*, II in *Saint Anselm, Basic Writings*, tr. Sidney N. Deane.

5. See *Monologium*, XV in *Saint Anselm, Basic Writings*, tr. Sidney N. Deane.

6. The numbers in parentheses refer to the earlier steps in the argument from which the present step is derived.

7. Gaunilo's brief essay, Anselm's reply, and several of Anselm's major works, as translated by S. N. Deane, are collected together in *Saint Anselm: Basic Writings* (LaSalle, Illinois: Open Court Publishing Co., 1962).

8. Deane, *Saint Anselm: Basic Writings*, p. 151.

9. Perhaps the most sophisticated presentation of the objection that existence is not a predicate is William P. Alston's "The Ontological Argument Revisited" in *The Philosophical Review*, LXIX (1960), pp. 452–74.

10. See, for example, C. D. Broad's discussion of the Ontological Argument in *Religion, Philosophy, and Psychical Research* (New York: Harcourt, Brace & Co., 1953).

11. An argument along the lines just presented may be found in J. Shaffer's illuminating essay, "Existence, Predication and the Ontological Argument," *Mind* LXXI (1962), pp. 307–25.

12. I am indebted to Professor William Wainwright for bringing this point to my attention.

13. In the language of possible worlds, we can say that some object x is a *magican* in a possible world w, provided (i) x is a magician in w, and (ii) x is a magician in whatever world happens to be actual. For more on this matter, as well as a critical discussion of some other versions of the Ontological Argument, see my essay "Modal Versions of the Ontological Argument" in *Philosophy of Religion*, ed. Louis Pojman (Belmont, CA: Wadsworth, 1987), pp. 69–73.

Topics for Review

1. What is meant by an impossible being, a possible being, a contingent being, and a necessary being? Give an example of each of the first three.
2. What is Anselm's distinction between existence in the understanding and existence in reality?
3. What is the key idea in the Ontological Argument?
4. What, briefly, are the three traditional objections to the Ontological Argument?
5. Explain the final objection, which claims that the Ontological Argument begs the question.

Topics for Further Study

6. In Chapter Three of his *Proslogium*, Anselm introduces the principle that if a being exists in such a way that it could not fail to exist, it is greater than a being which exists but could fail to exist. Compare and contrast this principle with the key idea in the Ontological Argument. Try to formulate a second version of the Ontological Argument by using the principle of *Proslogium*, Chapter Three.

7. Which of the several objections to the Ontological Argument strikes you as most plausible? Which strikes you as least plausible? For what reasons?

4

THE TELEOLOGICAL ARGUMENT

The Teleological Argument has as its starting point our sense of wonder not that things exist, but that so many things that exist in our universe exhibit order and design. Beginning from this sense of wonder, the argument endeavors to convince us that whatever produced the universe must be an intelligent being. Perhaps the best-known statement of the argument is given in David Hume's *Dialogues Concerning Natural Religion:*

> Look round the world: contemplate the whole and every part of it: You will find it to be nothing but one great machine, subdivided into an infinite number of lesser machines, which again admit of subdivisions to a degree beyond what human senses and faculties can trace and explain. All these various machines, and even their most minute parts, are adjusted to each other with an accuracy which ravishes into admiration all men who have ever contemplated them. The curious adapting of means to ends, throughout all nature, resembles exactly, though it much exceeds, the productions of human contrivance; of human design, thought, wisdom, and intelligence. Since therefore the effects resemble each other, we are led to infer, by all the rules of analogy, that the causes also resemble; and that the Author of Nature is somewhat similar to the mind of man, though possessed of much larger faculties, proportioned to the grandeur of the work which he has executed. By this argument *a posteriori,* and by this argument alone, do we prove at once the existence of a Deity, and his similarity to human mind and intelligence.[1]

ARGUMENT BY ANALOGY

There is an *analogy,* this passage tells us, between many things in nature and things produced by human beings, for example, machines. Since we know that machines (watches, cameras, typewriters, automobiles, and so forth) have been produced by intelligent beings, and since many things in nature so closely resemble machines, we are justified "by all the rules of analogy" in concluding that whatever produced those things in nature is an intelligent being. The Teleo-logical Argument, then, as expressed in this passage, is an *argument from analogy*, and for our purposes may be set forth as follows:

1. Machines are produced by intelligent design.
2. The universe resembles a machine.

Therefore,

3. Probably the universe was produced by intelligent design.

The critical questions we must consider in assessing the Teleological Argu-ment spring mainly from the fact that it employs *analogical reasoning*. To better understand such reasoning, let's consider the following example in which it is used. Suppose you are working in a chemical laboratory and somehow manage to produce a new chemical compound. It occurs to you that this chemical might have some very beneficial results if you were to swallow a bit of it. On the other hand, since its properties are not well understood, it also occurs to you that the chemical might harm you considerably. Being both cautious and curious, you seek some way of finding out whether the chemical will benefit you or harm you, short of actually swallowing some of it. It occurs to you that you might surrepti-tiously place some in the food of your dinner guests that evening and simply sit back and observe what happens. It they all die within an hour of ingesting the chemical, you then have exceptionally strong evidence that the chemical would harm you. For obvious reasons, however, you feel it improper to try out an unknown chemical on other human beings, particularly your dinner guests. Instead, you expose some monkeys or rats to the chemical and conclude from its effect on them what its likely effect on you will be.

Reflecting on this example will help us understand both what analogical reasoning is and why we sometimes must employ it in trying to discover some-thing about ourselves and our world. If you had given the chemical to a number of human beings, say your dinner guests, then from the effect of the chemical on them you could have inferred its effect on you. Such reasoning would not have been analogical since your dinner guests are exactly like you; they belong to the same natural class to which you belong, the class of human beings. As it was, you could not engage in such straightforward reasoning because the immediate natural class—the class of human beings—to which you belong could not be examined in connection with the chemical. You then did the next best thing: you picked a natural class, the class of monkeys, to which you don't belong, but whose members you *resemble* in certain ways. You resemble monkeys in having a nervous system, being warm blooded, and in numerous other respects. Moreover, the ways in which you resemble monkeys are *relevant* to finding out the likely effect of the chemical on you. Creatures that have a central nervous system, are warm blooded, and are otherwise similar, tend to have similar responses to chemical substances. So although the analogical reasoning you end up employing is somewhat weaker than the straightforward reasoning you would have used if you could have tried out the chemical on human beings, it is, nevertheless, good reasoning and provides you with evidence concerning the likely effect of the chemical on you.

The Teleological Argument endeavors to answer the question of whether our universe results from intelligent design. If we had observed the origin of many universes other than our universe and also observed that all or most of them resulted from intelligent design, we then could have reasoned in a straightforward fashion that our universe likely arose from intelligent design. This would not have been analogical reasoning since we would have reasoned from things (other universes) that are exactly the same as the subject of our investigation, our universe. But since we have no knowledge or experience of universes other than our own, we must employ analogical reasoning; we must start with things that resemble, but are not the same as, our universe and infer that because these other things arose from intelligent design, it is likely that our universe arose from intelligent design. Such an argument, being an analogical argument based on resemblance of different things, is bound to be weaker than a straightforward argument from things exactly the same (that is, other universes), but it is clearly the best we can do if we are seeking knowledge about whatever it is that produced our universe. Of course, the strength of the argument will depend on the features in terms of which these other things resemble our universe and on the relevance of these features to the question of whether our universe arose from intelligent design. We must now pursue these larger questions. We must ask: (1) What are the features in terms of which our universe is said to resemble a machine? and (2) Are these features relevant to the question of whether the universe arose from intelligent design?

The Universe as Machine

In what way or ways is the universe like a machine? The eighteenth-century English theologian, William Paley, one of the major exponents of the Teleological Argument, compared the universe to a watch and claimed that every manifestation of design which exists in a watch also exists in the works of nature. And, in the passage quoted earlier from Hume's *Dialogues Concerning Natural Religion,* we are reminded that there is "a curious adaptation of means to ends" throughout all nature. Apparently, then, the way in which the universe is supposed to resemble a machine is that parts of nature are seen to be related to one another in the *same way* as parts of a machine are related to one another. If we can get a clearer picture of just how the parts of machines are related to one another, we can then see whether the proponents of the Teleological Argument are correct in thinking that there are many things in nature whose parts are related to one another in exactly the same way.

If we examine a watch that is in good working order, we will note rather quickly that its parts are so connected that when one part moves, other parts are caused to move as well—gears, for example, are so arranged that the movement of one causes another to move. This is a common feature of machines with moving parts, and it is also a feature to be found within the universe. Our solar system, for example, is composed of parts, the sun, planets, and their moons, which move, and in their moving cause, by gravitational force, other parts to move. While all this is true, however, it is not the full story of how the parts of machines are related to one another. For if we look again at our watch, we discover not only that its parts are so arranged that they work together, but that under proper conditions they work together to serve a certain *purpose*. The parts of a watch are so arranged that under proper conditions they work together to enable us to tell the time of day. So too with the parts of other machines—automobiles, cameras, or typewriters. The parts of these machines are all so related to one another that under proper conditions they work together to serve some purpose.

Let's capture this interesting feature of machines by introducing the idea of a *teleological system*. A teleological system, we shall say, is any system of parts in which the parts are so arranged that under proper conditions they work together to serve a certain purpose. Most machines are clearly teleological systems. Moreover, a somewhat complex machine may well have parts that are themselves teleological systems. An automobile, for example, is a teleological system; its parts are so arranged that under proper conditions, they work together to enable someone to be transported quickly from one place to another. But various parts of an automobile are also teleological systems. The carburetor, for example, is a system of parts so arranged to provide the proper mixture of fuel and air for combustion.

What the proponents of the Teleological Argument claim as the basis for the analogy between the universe and machines is that in the world of nature, we find many things, and parts of things, that are teleological systems. The human eye, for example, is clearly a teleological system. Its parts exhibit an intricate order and are so arranged that under proper conditions they work together for the purpose of enabling a person to see. Other organs in humans and animals are undoubtedly also teleological systems, each serving some reasonably clear purpose. Indeed, it seems reasonable to believe that the plants and animals which compose a great part of the world of nature are teleological systems. As the twentieth-century philosopher C. D. Broad has remarked:

> The most superficial knowledge of organisms does make it look as if they were very complex systems designed to preserve themselves in face of varying and threatening external conditions and to reproduce their kind. And, on the whole, the more fully we investigate a living organism in detail the more fully does what we discover fit in with this hypothesis. One might mention, e. g., the various small and apparently unimportant glands in the human body whose secretions are found to exercise a profound influence over its growth and well-being. Or again we might mention the production in the blood of antitoxins when the body is attacked by organisms likely to injure it.[2]

We can now see, I think, the force with which this argument strikes the imagination of its supporters. Once we understand what a watch is, how it works and for what purpose, it would be utterly absurd to suppose that its origin is due to some accident rather than to intelligent design. But if we look carefully at many things in nature, plants and animals, for example, we discover that their parts exhibit an orderly arrangement fitted to a purpose (survival of the organism and the reproduction of its kind) that, if anything, exceeds the purposeful arrangement of parts in the watch. How absurd, then, to suppose that the world of nature arose from accident rather than intelligent design. Something of the force of the argument on the human imagination is conveyed in the following observation by the seventeenth-century philosopher, Henry More:

> For why have we three joints in our legs and arms, as also in our fingers, but that it was much better than having two or four? And why are our fore-teeth sharp like chisels to cut, but our inward teeth broad to grind (instead of) the fore-teeth broad and the other sharp? But we might have made a hard shift to have lived through in that worser condition. Again, why are the teeth so luckily placed, or rather, why are there not teeth in other bones as well as in the jaw-bones? for they might have been as capable as these. But the reason is nothing is done foolishly or in vain; that is, there is a divine Providence that orders all things.[3]

We have been trying to answer the first of two critical questions directed at the Teleological Argument: What are the features in terms of which our universe is said to resemble machines? What we have seen is that in the world of nature, there are many things (plants and animals, for example) that appear to share with machines the interesting and important feature of being *teleological systems*. Before we turn to our second critical question, however, we need to recognize exactly what we have acknowledged about our universe if we accept the claim that plants and animals, no less than machines, are teleological systems.

It is one thing to believe that the universe contains many *parts* which are teleological systems, and quite another thing to believe that the *universe itself* is a teleological system. Nothing we have considered thus far would show that the universe itself is a teleological system. For, to show that, we would have to claim that the universe itself has a purpose and that its parts are so arranged that they work together toward the realization of that purpose. But can we, by just looking at the small fragment of our universe available to us, hope to discern the purpose of the universe itself? It seems clear that we cannot. If we know that God created the universe and also why he created it, we might reasonably infer that the universe itself is a teleological system. But since the Teleological Argument is an argument for the existence of God, it cannot presuppose his existence and purposes without assuming what it is trying to prove. At best, then, what we can say is that the universe contains many parts (other than objects made by human beings, like machines), parts which are teleological systems. And this means that we aren't justified in saying that the *universe itself* is like a machine. What we are perhaps justified in saying is that the universe contains many natural parts (that is, parts that are not made by human beings) that resemble machines; they resemble machines because, like machines, they are teleological systems. Accepting this limitation, we can revise our statement of the Teleological Argument as follows:

1. Machines are produced by intelligent design.
2. Many natural parts of the universe resemble machines.

Therefore,

3. Probably the universe (or at least many of its natural parts) was produced by intelligent design.

Evidence of Intelligent Design

The second critical question we must raise concerning the Teleological Argument is whether the feature in terms of which many natural parts of the universe resemble machines is *relevant* to the question of whether the universe (or many of its natural parts) arose from intelligent design. To this question it is clear that the answer is *yes*. We know that intelligent design accounts for the fact that machines are teleological systems. We then discover that the world of nature is populated with many teleological systems. What more plausible account can we give of their origin than to suppose that they too arose from intelligent design? And since it's clear that no human being could have been the intelligent designer of the universe (or its natural parts which are teleological systems), it seems reasonable to suppose that some suprahuman being intelligently designed the universe as a whole, or at least many of its parts.

Although intelligent design is a plausible hypothesis by which to account for the many teleological systems in the world of nature, is it the only hypothesis available to us? Until Darwin (1809–1882) and the theory of evolution, it is doubtful that anyone had a naturalistic explanation of teleological systems in nature that could seriously compete with the hypothesis of intelligent design. But since the development of the theory of evolution, the Teleological Argument has lost some of its persuasive force, for we now possess a fairly well-developed naturalistic hypothesis by which the teleological systems in nature can be explained, a hypothesis that makes no mention of intelligent design. Briefly put, the Darwinian theory of natural selection purports to explain why nature contains so many organisms whose various parts are so well-fitted to their survival. According to this theory, animals and plants undergo variations or changes that are inherited by their descendants. Some variations provide organisms with an advantage over the rest of the population in the constant struggle for life. Since plants and animals produce more offspring than the environment will support, those in which favorable variations occur tend to survive in greater numbers than those in which unfavorable variations occur. Thus, it happens that over great periods of time there slowly emerge large populations of highly developed organisms whose parts are so peculiarly fitted to their survival.

Whether the Darwinian theory of natural selection is true or false, it must be admitted that it stands in competition with the intelligent-designer hypothesis as a possible explanation of the fact that the world of nature contains so many highly developed teleological systems. The implication of this for the Teleological Argument is that it no longer has the persuasive force it once enjoyed. Although it undoubtedly provides us with some grounds for thinking that many parts of the world of nature arose from intelligent design, we now have reason to question the *strength* of the inference from teleological systems in nature to an intelligent-designer, for in the theory of natural selection we possess a competing hypothesis by which to explain those teleological systems.[4]

HUME'S CRITICISMS OF THE TELEOLOGICAL ARGUMENT

Although David Hume's *Dialogues Concerning Natural Religion* was written before the advent of the Darwinian theory, it has long been recognized as the classical attack on the Teleological Argument. For our purposes, Hume's criticisms can be divided into two groups: criticisms of the claim that the universe is like a machine, and criticisms of the claim that the Teleological Argument provides us with adequate grounds for belief in the theistic God. We can best conclude our study of the Teleological Argument by considering some of Hume's main objections.

Hume points out first that the vastness of the universe weakens the claim that it resembles a machine or some other human creation such as a house or a ship. Secondly, he notes that although design and order exist in the part of the universe we inhabit, for all we know there are vast reaches of the universe in which absolute chaos reigns. And, finally, although admitting that intelligent design is observed to be a cause in the production of things within the small fragment of the universe we can observe, he argues that it is an unreasonable leap to conclude that intelligent design is the productive force throughout the entire universe. "A very small part of this great system, during a very short time, is very imperfectly discovered to us; and do we thence pronounce decisively concerning the origin of the whole?"[5]

These objections are aimed at the second premise of our original formulation of the Teleological Argument, the premise that the universe as a whole resembles a machine. The objections, however, do not affect so directly our revised version of the argument in which the second premise reads, "Many natural parts of the universe resemble machines." For in the revised version no claim is made about the universe as a whole or about those parts of the universe that we are unable to observe. Hence, since it is the revised version that now concerns us, we may safely put aside the first group of Hume's criticisms.

The second group of criticisms is directed not at the argument as we have formulated it, but at any attempt to construe the argument as providing adequate grounds for theistic belief, for believing that there exists a supremely perfect being who created the universe. And on this score, there can be little doubt that Hume is right. From inspecting the universe, we may perhaps conclude that it arose from intelligent design, but beyond that point the Teleological Argument is unable to go; it provides us with no rational grounds for thinking that whatever produced the universe is *perfect, one* or *spiritual*. We can't infer that what produced the universe is supremely wise or good because, for all we know, the universe is a very imperfect production, more like an Edsel or a Corvair than a Rolls Royce. And even if the world in its vastness were known to be a very fine piece of work, still, for all we know, this world might be the last in a series of worlds, many of which are botched and bungled creations, before the Deity finally managed to learn the art of world making.

It is part of theistic belief that there is a single being who produced the world, but since we know that many machines, buildings, automobiles, and other devices result from the combined efforts of many designers, the universe, for all we know, might be the product of the work of many minor deities, each possessed of limited intelligence and skill.

It is part of theistic belief that the Deity is incorporeal (lacking a body), a purely spiritual being. But, again, if we infer from the similarity between the world of nature and a machine to a similarity of their causes, then, since in the case of machines we know of no cause (human being) that is incorporeal, we have no grounds to infer that whatever produced the world is an incorporeal being.

Hume sums up this second group of objections by noting that anyone who limits his grounds for religious belief to the Teleological Argument "is able perhaps to assert, or conjecture, that the universe, sometime, arose from something like design: but beyond that position he cannot ascertain one single circumstance; and is left afterwards to fix every point of his theology by the utmost license of fancy and hypothesis."[6]

The implication of Hume's second set of criticisms is clear. Theism cannot be established by means of the Teleological Argument alone. Many theists would accept this implication. They would contend, however, that the several major arguments for the existence of God, *taken together*, do provide rational grounds for believing in the theistic God. So the second set of criticisms advanced by Hume, although clearly showing the limitations of the Teleological Argument, do not touch the more general claim that the traditional arguments for God, taken together, provide rational grounds for theism.

ACCEPTABLE ARGUMENTS

In this and the preceding two chapters, we have wrestled with the three major arguments for God's existence. We've tried to understand these arguments as well as the major objections that have been advanced against them. In each case, I've suggested that the arguments fail to provide us with compelling rational grounds for believing that the theistic God exists. The Cosmological Argument, although perhaps sound, cannot enable us to know that there is a self-existent being because it rests on a principle, the Principle of Sufficient Reason, which none of us knows to be true. The Ontological Argument, although a thing of beauty and genius, does not prove that there exists an unsurpassably great being because it begs the question—we would have to know the conclusion to be true in order to know that its premises are true. And, finally, the Teleological Argument at best provides us with some grounds for thinking that some natural parts of the universe arose from intelligent design. But, as we noted, the hypothesis of intelligent design must compete with other hypotheses, particularly the hypothesis of natural selection.

What if we put the arguments together, trying to justify theism not by each one separately but by the three taken as one? This would be helpful *if* each of the arguments really succeeded in providing solid rational grounds for some aspect of the theistic God. But, as we've seen, neither the Cosmological nor the Ontological argument succeeds in doing this. Our final judgment of the arguments, then, is that taken singly or together, they fail to establish theistic belief. As the American philosopher and psychologist William James remarked: "The arguments for God's existence have stood for hundreds of years with the waves of unbelieving criticism breaking against them, never totally discrediting them in the ears of the faithful, but on the whole slowly and surely washing out the mortar from between their joints."[7]

Our conclusion that the three traditional arguments fail to prove the existence of God should not be taken to mean that they are intellectually or religiously worthless. For they have been judged against an exceptionally high standard. We have asked whether they succeed as *demonstrations* or *proofs* of the existence of God; and we have seen that they fall short of this high standard. But not many important philosophical arguments manage to satisfy this high standard. Some contemporary philosophers and theologians, therefore, have been content to view the arguments not as *proving* the existence of God, but as showing that the existence of God is a *plausible hypothesis* by which we might account for the world and our experience. The arguments, on this view, provide us with reasons for defending belief in God as *rational*. They are *acceptable* arguments in the sense that they advance considerations in favor of the hypothesis that God exists.

Although we cannot here pursue this last point in much detail, it is important to recognize that an argument may be an *acceptable* argument for its conclusion even though it fails as a *proof* of its conclusion. The Cosmological Argument, for example, is not a proof of its conclusion because it rests on a principle (PSR) which we don't *know* and can't prove to be true. But PSR, nonetheless, may be a plausible principle, a principle which someone might reasonably judge to be worthy of belief. Insofar as this is so, the Cosmological Argument may lend weight to theistic belief, while still falling short of proving it. To some extent, similar remarks may be made about both the Ontological Argument and the Teleological Argument. Hence, although the traditional claim that these arguments *prove* the existence of God has been seen to be mistaken, this does not rule out the possibility that one or more of the arguments may play a significant role in the intellectual defense of theism.[8]

Notes

1. David Hume, *Dialogues Concerning Natural Religion,* Part II, ed. H. D. Aiken (New York: Hafner Publishing Company, 1948), p. 17.
2. C. D. Broad, *The Mind and Its Place in Nature* (London: Routledge & Kegan Paul, Ltd., 1925), p. 83.
3. Quoted by J. J. C. Smart in "The Existence of God," *New Essays in Philosophical Theology,* eds. Antony Flew and Alasdair MacIntyre (London: SCM Press Ltd., 1955), p. 43.
4. Some philosophers and theologians have developed versions of the Teleological Argument in which Darwinian evolution is treated not as a rival hypothesis to theism, but as one of the general mechanisms in the world which may be best explained by the theistic hypothesis. F. R. Tennant, for example, in chapter four of the second volume of *Philosophical Theology* (Cambridge and New York: Cambridge University Press, 1930) takes the view that the force of the Teleological Argument does not lie in the attempt to account for "particular cases of adaptedness in the world." All such particular cases, he thought, might be explained by natural mechanisms. Tennant, therefore, sought to widen the base of the Teleological Argument by suggesting that the hypothesis of intelligent design be advanced as a plausible explanation of the innumerable forces and mechanisms in the world—of which evolution is but one—that support a general order

of nature including aesthetic and moral values. For a critical discussion of this and other restatements of the traditional Teleological Argument see John Hick's *Arguments for the Existence of God* (New York: Herder and Herder, 1971), Chapters One and Two, pp. 18–36.

5. Hume, *Dialogues,* Part II, ed. H. D. Aiken (New York: Hafner Publishing Company, 1948), pp. 22–23.

6. Hume, *Dialogues,* Part V, ed. H. D. Aiken (New York: Hafner Publishing Company, 1948), p. 40.

7. William James, *The Varieties of Religious Experience* (New York: The Modern Library, 1936), p. 427.

8. For an account of the arguments along this line see George F. Thomas, *Philosophy and Religious Belief* (New York: Charles Scribner's Sons, 1970), Chapter 6.

Topics for Review

1. Explain why the Teleological Argument must use analogical reasoning. What two critical questions must we raise about the Teleological Argument?
2. Explain what is meant by a teleological system. Is it reasonable to believe that many things in nature are teleological systems?
3. What criticisms does Hume raise against the claim that the universe resembles a machine? Do these criticisms tell against the revised form of the argument?
4. Is the Teleological Argument an adequate foundation for theism? Explain.
5. What general conclusions can we draw concerning the three major arguments for the existence of God?

Topics for Further Study

6. Describe the kind of world which would make the following views (each in turn) probable.
   a. There are many finite deities.
   b. There is one God, omnipotent, and wholly good.
   c. There is one God, omnipotent, but not wholly good.
   d. There is one God, wholly good, but not omnipotent.
7. Develop a version of the Teleological Argument in which evolution is viewed as evidence in support of an intelligent designer, rather than viewed as a competing hypothesis. See Note 4 of this chapter for useful references.

5

RELIGIOUS AND MYSTICAL EXPERIENCE

Before Robinson Crusoe actually saw the man Friday, his justification for believing that some person other than himself existed on the island consisted in traces left by Friday, such as footprints. The believer who bases a belief in God solely on arguments for God's existence, like the Cosmological and Teleological arguments, is in a position something like Crusoe's before actually seeing Friday. Belief in God rests on a conviction that the world and the way things are interrelated in the world are traces of God's activity, testifying to the existence of some sort of supreme being. Once Crusoe actually saw Friday, however, his grounds for believing that he was not alone on the island were not limited to traces left by Friday, they included a direct personal awareness of Friday himself. Analogously, religious and mystical experience is often viewed by those who undergo such experience as a direct, personal awareness of God himself, and, consequently, as exceptionally strong justification for the belief in God. In this chapter we shall consider religious and mystical experience with the aim of assessing the extent to which they may provide rational justification for theistic belief.

TOWARDS A DEFINITION OF RELIGIOUS EXPERIENCE

Our first task is to try to understand what religious experience is. How are we to characterize religious experience? This question is exceptionally difficult, and any characterization we arrive at will likely be inadequate, perhaps even somewhat arbitrary. But we need to have some idea, however vague and inadequate it may turn out to be, of what it is we hope to examine. Let's begin by considering a clear example of a religious experience—the experience of Saul on the road to Damascus. Then we can have a look at how some of the ablest students of religious experience have tried to characterize it.

Now as he journeyed he approached Damascus, and suddenly a light from heaven flashed about him. And he fell to the ground and heard a voice saying to him, "Saul, Saul, why do you persecute me?" And he said, "Who are you, Lord?" And he said, "I am Jesus, whom you are persecuting; but rise and enter the city, and you will be told what you are to do." The men who were traveling with him stood speechless, hearing the voice but seeing no one. Saul arose from the ground; and when his eyes were opened, he could see nothing; so they led him by the hand and brought him into Damascus. And for three days he was without sight, and neither ate nor drank.[1]

In this experience, which proved to be the turning point in Saul's life, transforming him from Saul the persecutor into Paul the Apostle, there is an awareness on Saul's part of a divine figure, "Who are you, Lord?", accompanied by a good bit of fear and trembling, and an awareness of his own insignificance. It is somewhat unclear as to what Saul actually saw with his eyes, perhaps only a dazzling light which left him temporarily blind. He did hear a voice and understood what it said to him.

Although Saul's experience is clearly religious, it doesn't tell us what a religious experience is, nor does it give us a characterization by which we can distinguish religious from nonreligious experience. You don't have to see a dazzling light to have a religious experience, nor do you have to hear a voice. Moreover, just seeing a dazzling light and hearing a voice isn't enough to make a religious experience. How then are we to characterize religious experience?

Dependence, Otherness and Union

In his important book, *The Idea of the Holy*, the German theologian Rudolf Otto (1896–1937) endeavored to get at the essential element in religious experience by critically examining the characterization of religious experience given by the nineteenth-century theologian, Friedrich Schleiermacher. According to Schleiermacher, what distinguishes religious experience is that in such an experience one is overcome by *the feeling of absolute dependence*. Of course, we often are aware of ourselves as dependent—on our friends, or on the whims of professors in grading papers. Such feelings of dependence are not distinctly religious, and Schleiermacher did not think they were. They are only instances of the feeling of *relative* dependence. In religious experience, however, the central element is the feeling of *absolute* dependence, the consciousness of one's self as absolutely dependent.

Otto suggests a name, "creature-feeling," for that element in religious experience which Schleiermacher sought to describe as an awareness of one's self as absolutely dependent. His basic objection is not that Schleiermacher has failed to pick out an important element in religious experience, for Otto readily admits that the sense of one's self as creature is an element in religious experience. His objection is that *creature-feeling* is not the most basic element in religious experience, and by making it the basic element, Schleiermacher was led into two errors. The first of these error is subjectivism, making the essence of religious experience to be an awareness, not of another, but of one's own *self* as absolutely dependent. The second error is that on Schleiermacher's account God is reached only by inference. For by making the essence of religious experience to consist of a certain awareness of one's self, Schleiermacher was led to regard God not as something of which one is immediately aware, but as something that must be reached as the result of an inference, as the cause of one's absolute dependence, which alone is immediately experienced.

In place of Schleiermacher's account of the essence of religious experience as consisting in the awareness of one's self as absolutely dependent, Otto claimed that the essential element is the awareness of *another* (something outside the self) as holy or divine. Thus, for Otto, the immediate awareness of God is the really essential element, and the sense of one's self as absolutely dependent (creature-feeling) is an immediate result of the essential element, the awareness of another as holy. Otto then entered into a penetrating analysis of the elements (such as awe, mystery, dread) which are contained in the awareness of something as *holy*.

Following Otto's lead we might tentatively characterize a religious experience as an experience in which one is directly aware of another (something outside the self) as holy (divine). And perhaps this is as adequate a characterization of religious experience as can be given. There is, however, one difficulty with it. In Otto's characterization one is aware of something else, something *distinct from* and *outside* one's self. Undoubtedly, many religious experiences are like this. But the highest form of mystical experience seems to be an experience in which there is no awareness of another as distinct from the self. What religious mystics seem to strive for is an experience in which the awareness of one's self as *distinct from* the object of the experience is obliterated, destroyed. The highest form of mystical experience is one of absolute union with the divine, an experience in which one's self enters into and becomes one with the divine, so that there is, in the experience, no awareness of *another* (something distinct from the self) at all.

Consider, for example, the following two passages by the German mystical theologian Meister Eckhart (1260–1328). ". . . we are not wholly blessed, even though we are looking at divine truth; for while we are still looking at it, we are not in it. As long as a man has an object under consideration he is not one with it."[2] "In this barren Godhead, activity has ceased and therefore the soul will be most perfect when it is thrown into the desert of the Godhead, where both activity and forms are no more, so that it is sunk and lost in this desert where its identity is destroyed."[3] In these two passages Eckhart clearly indicates that the soul is in its most blessed or perfect state when it experiences the divine so intensely that it loses its own identity and becomes one with the divine. In this state there is no awareness of the divine as object and the soul as subject, distinct from the divine. As the mystical philosopher Plotinus (A.D. 205–270) remarked: "We should not speak of seeing, but instead of seen and seer, speak boldly of a simple Unity for in this seeing we neither distinguish nor are there two."[4] The difficulty with Otto's characterization of religious experience is that it excludes experiences of the sort described by Eckhart and Plotinus, experiences which have been prized by religious mystics as the highest form of direct encounter with the divine that it is possible to achieve.

The Presence of the Divine

In the interest, then, of not excluding such experiences from the category of *religious experience,* I suggest that we amend Otto's characterization as follows. A religious experience, we shall say, is *an experience in which one senses the immediate presence of the divine.* Several clarifying comments need to be made about this characterization of religious experience.

First, I mean this characterization to include those experiences of the divine in which there is no sense of otherness (the experiences of the religious mystics, for example), rather a sense of union or identity with the divine, as well as those experiences in which there is a clear sense of otherness, of encountering a divine figure, as, for example, in the experience of Saul on the road to Damascus. Second, we must be careful not to confuse *believing* that the divine is present with *sensing the presence* of the divine. A Catholic partaking of communion may well believe that the divine is present, having been taught that the substance of the bread becomes divine when it is consecrated by the priest. But he or she may not have a direct experience of the divine, and may not have a sense of the immediate presence of the divine when partaking of communion. To sense the immediate presence of the divine is to have a particular experience which one takes to be a direct experience of the divine. One may believe that the divine is present without having a direct experience of the divine. Third, by characterizing a religious experience as an experience in which one senses the immediate presence of the divine, we are narrowing the idea of a religious experience in two important ways. We are excluding from consideration religious experiences that are not of the divine—for example, feeling penitent for having sinned—and we are excluding experiences of the divine, if such there be, in which one has no awareness of the object of the experience as divine. Perhaps a person sometimes has an experience of God but has no sense of the presence of God because he fails to recognize that it is God who is appearing to him. Cases like this occur in ordinary sense perception. Someone may directly perceive a walnut tree but have no sense of the presence of a walnut tree because the person thinks (mistakenly) that what he or she is experiencing is a maple tree. The person may even later declare (mistakenly) that he or she has never seen a walnut tree. So, too, we cannot preclude someone's actually perceiving God but having no sense of the presence of God because the person is mistaken about what he or she is experiencing. If such experiences occur, they will not fit under our characterization of what is a religious experience. Fourth, by "the divine" I don't mean simply the theistic God. For there are many conceptions of the divine other than the God of theism. By "the divine" I mean whatever would be recognized as deity by some religious group, including nontheistic religious groups. Admittedly, this leaves our characterization of religious experience somewhat vague and imprecise. But this is unavoidable, given the fact that there are diverse religious traditions with various conceptions of the divine, some of which are themselves quite vague and imprecise. Finally, we need to recognize that in saying that someone has had a religious experience, we are not prejudicing the question of whether the divine she or he has experienced exists or does not exist. One may have a sense of the presence of a certain object even when there is no such object actually present to be sensed. For example, one may be sitting quietly at a desk writing and, quite suddenly, be overcome by the sense of the presence of another person in the room, only to turn around and discover that no one is there. Thus, the mere fact that one senses the immediate presence of something (whether divine or not) does not in itself imply that the something in question exists. Macbeth really did have an experience in which he sensed the immediate presence of a dagger, even though the dagger did not exist. In saying, therefore, that Saul had a religious experience on the road to Damascus we leave open the question of whether the experience was *delusory,* as was Macbeth's experience of the dagger, or *veridical,* as when, for example, we directly experience something that actually exists independently of us. The question we must ultimately raise, then, is not whether people really have religious experiences—they most certainly do—but whether it is reasonable to believe that their experiences are veridical, rather than delusory.

Thus far we have characterized religious experience so as to include both experiences in which one senses the presence of the divine as a being distinct from oneself and experiences in which one senses one's own union with a divine presence. The first sort we may think of as *ordinary religious experiences;* the second are best characterized as *mystical religious experiences.* Our aim here is to look at religious experiences, both ordinary and mystical, with a view to determining the extent to which the existence of such experiences provides rational grounds for belief in God (or some divine reality).

ORDINARY RELIGIOUS EXPERIENCES

Experiences in which one senses the immediate presence of a divine being may include some visual and auditory content. Saul's religious experience, for example, included sensory content—a blinding light, a voice, and so on. But other experiences of the divine do not contain sensory content. Here is a report of one such experience.

> all at once I . . . felt the presence of God—I tell of the thing just as I was conscious of it—as if his goodness and his power were penetrating me altogether. . . . Then, slowly, the ecstasy left my heart; that is, I felt that God had withdrawn the communion which he had granted, . . . I think it well to add that in this ecstasy of mine God had neither form, color, odor, nor taste; moreover, that the feeling of his presence was accompanied with no determinate localization. . . . At bottom the expression most apt to render what I felt is this: God was present, though invisible; he fell under no one of my senses, yet my consciousness perceived him.[5]

The question before us is whether the existence of such experiences as these provide us (or at least those who have them) with a *good reason* to believe that God (or some sort of divine being) exists. Initially, one might be tempted to think that they do not on the grounds that reports of religious experiences may be nothing more than reports of certain *feelings* (joy, ecstasy, etc.) that now and then come over some people who already believe in God and are perhaps all too eager to feel themselves singled out for a special appearance by the divine. Against such an objection, however, we should note that a number of those who report having ordinary religious experiences are keenly aware of the difference between experiences of one's own feelings (joy, sadness, peacefulness, etc.) and experiences that involve a sense of the presence of some other being. They are also aware of the fact that wanting a certain experience may lead one to mistake some other experience for it. Unless we have some very strong reason not to, we should take their reports as sincere, careful efforts to express the contents of their experiences. And those reports are not primarily reports of subjective psychological states; they are reports of encounters with what is taken to be an independently existing divine being.

But still, even if we acknowledge that the experiences cannot fairly be described as reports of nothing more than one's feelings, why should we think they are veridical perceptions of what they seem to be? Macbeth's experience of a dagger isn't fairly described as Macbeth having a certain feeling; it is an experience which purports to be of some object apart from himself. But the experience was a hallucination. Why shouldn't we think that experiences in which one senses the immediate presence of God (or some divine figure) are all hallucinatory? The answer given by those who think religious experiences constitute a good reason to believe God exists is that we should dismiss them as delusory only if we have some special reason to think that they are delusory. And in the absence of such special reasons, the rational thing to do is to view them as probably veridical. It will help us to look at this line of argument in some detail.

If a person has an experience which he or she takes to be of some particular object, is the fact that he or she has that experience a *good reason* to think that particular object exists? Our first reaction is to say no. We are inclined to say no because we all can think of experiences which seem to be of some particular object, when in fact no such object exists. Consider two examples. You walk into a room and have a visual experience that you take to be a perception of a red wall. Unknown to you there are red lights shining on the white wall you are looking at, thus making it appear red. Here you are experiencing an actually existing wall that happens to be white, but there is no red wall for you to perceive. How then can the fact that you have an experience which clearly seems to be a perception of a red wall be a good reason for thinking that there actually is a red wall? Again, unknown to you someone puts a powerful hallucinogenic drug in your coffee resulting in your having an experience which you take to be a perception of a large, coiled snake in front of the chair in which you are sitting. Unlike our first example (there is a wall, it's just not red), there is no snake at all that you are seeing. Others in the room who have no reason to deceive you assure you that there is no snake in the room. Your experience of the snake is entirely delusory. So, how can the fact that you have an experience which clearly seems to be a perception of a coiled snake be a good reason for thinking that the coiled snake exists?

For an experience to be a good reason for believing a claim to be true is for that experience to rationally justify you in believing that claim *provided that you have no reasons for thinking otherwise*. Reasons for thinking otherwise are either (a) reasons for thinking that claim to be false or (b) reasons for thinking that, given the circumstances in which it occurs, the experience is not sufficiently indicative of the truth of the claim. Consider again our second example. Since we know that actually existing physical things (including snakes) would be seen by the other people in the room if they are really there, you come to have a Type A reason for thinking otherwise. That is, when others who are in a position to see it say there is no snake, you come to have some reason for thinking that the snake does not actually exist. In our first example, if we suppose that all you come to know is that red lights are shining on the wall and that such lights would make the wall appear red even if it is white, then our reason to think otherwise is not itself a reason to think that there is no red wall. It is a Type B reason. What it tells us is that, whether the wall is red or not, in the circumstances that exist (red lights are shining on the wall) your experience is not sufficiently indicative of its being true that the wall is red. For you now know that you could be having that experience even if the wall is white.

What we've seen is that we must distinguish an experience being a good reason for a claim from that experience justifying that claim *no matter what else we know.* Those who think that having an experience that one takes to be of some particular object is a *good reason* to think that particular object exists recognize that we may know or come to know Type A or Type B reasons to think otherwise. All they insist is that in the *absence* of such defeating reasons, one who has such an experience is rationally justified in believing that the particular object exists. One prominent philosopher has argued that what is at stake here is a basic principle of rationality, a principle he calls the Principle of Credulity.[6] According to this principle, if a person has an experience which seems to be of x, then, unless there is some reason to think otherwise, it is rational to believe that x exists. If we grant this principle, it would seem arbitrary to refuse to apply it to religious experiences, experiences in which one senses the immediate presence of the divine. So, unless we have some reason to question these experiences, it would seem rational to believe that God or some divine being exists.

Before we turn to consider mystical religious experiences, we should note two difficulties in the view that the Principle of Credulity renders it rational for us to accept ordinary religious experiences as veridical. The first difficulty is that the Principle of Credulity presupposes that we have some understanding of what reasons there might be for questioning our experiences and some way of telling whether or not these reasons are present. Consider again our example of your experience which you take to be a perception of a large, coiled snake. Like other physical objects that make up the world we perceive by our five senses, snakes are public objects that are observable by others who satisfy certain conditions. That is, we can predict that people with good eyesight will see a snake (if one is there) provided there is good light and they look in the right direction. It is because physical objects are subject to such predictions that we can understand what reasons there might be for questioning an experience which seems to be a perception of a snake and can often tell whether such reasons are present. In the case of divine beings, however, matters are quite different. Presumably, it is entirely up to God whether to reveal his presence to some human being. If God does so, he may or may not disclose himself to others who are in a similar situation. What this means is that it is quite difficult to discover reasons for thinking that someone's ordinary religious experience is delusive. But since the Principle of Credulity supposes that we understand what reasons there might be to question an experience, some doubt exists as to whether the principle can be fairly applied to experiences whose subjects take them to be perceptions of the presence of a divine being. Of course, since God is a perfectly good being, we can from that fact alone discover some reason for thinking an experience that purports to be of God is delusive. For suppose someone reports an experience which he takes to be a perception of God commanding him to kill all those who sincerely seek to live a moral and holy life. We can be confident that God did not reveal that message and thus have a reason for thinking the experience to be delusive. Some doubt remains, however, whether there is an adequate range of reasons for questioning religious experiences to warrant much confidence in the application of the Principle of Credulity to them. Thus, once we come to learn that a presumption of the Principle of Credulity is not adequately satisfied by religious experiences, it is at least doubtful that the principle justifies us in holding religious experiences to be genuine perceptions of reality.

Suppose someone who has not had religious experiences examines various reports of those who have enjoyed them. One salient feature of these experiences is that most of them are embedded in one or another of a plurality of religious traditions, traditions that cannot all be true. For example, Saul's experience on the road to Damascus is embedded in Christianity as an experience of Jesus as a divine being. No such experience is a part of Judaism or Islam. Indeed, within these religious traditions Jesus is not a divine being at all. Experiences of Allah in Islam or God in Judaism are not experiences of a divine being who is a trinity of persons, as is the Christian God. In Hinduism one may have an experience of Krishna, but not Jesus, as a divine being. Moreover, Hinduism also includes a strain in which the divine presence, Brahman, is experienced as something other than a person. It seems unlikely that all of these religious experiences can be veridical perceptions of a divine presence. These experiences are embedded in and support rival religious traditions that contradict one another. Realizing this, what view should be held by a person who has not had any religious experiences? If the Principle of Credulity works for any, it will work equally well for all. But they can hardly all be veridical perceptions of a divine presence. Faced with this situation, it would appear that the rational thing for this person to do is not to accept any one of these religious experiences as veridical. So, even if we agree to continue applying the Principle of Credulity to religious experiences, it may well be that the person who has not had a religious experience is rationally justified in not accepting such experiences as veridical perceptions of reality. For the fact that these experiences are embedded in and support conflicting religious traditions may provide that person with a reason for not accepting any particular religious experience as veridical.

MYSTICAL RELIGIOUS EXPERIENCES

Students of mysticism usually distinguish two broad types of mystical religious experience: the *extrovertive* and the *introvertive*. The extrovertive way looks outward through the senses into the world around us and finds the divine reality there. The introvertive way turns inward and finds the divine reality in the deepest part of the self. The introvertive way is the more important of the two types of mystical experience, but it will be helpful to examine each type in some detail.

Extrovertive Experience

In the extrovertive way, the mystics use their senses to perceive the same world of trees, hills, brooks, and streams that we all perceive. But in a mystical experience they see these ordinary objects transfigured and transformed—they see an inner essence in all these things and may feel their deeper selves to be one with this inner essence, an essence that seems to be the same in the different objects perceived. W. T. Stace reports an experience of this type, an experience of an American whom Stace calls "N. M." N. M.'s experience occurred as he was looking out onto the back yard of an old apartment building.

> The buildings were decrepit and ugly, the ground covered with boards, rags, and debris. Suddenly every object in my field of vision took on a curious and intense kind of existence of its own; that is, everything appeared to have an "inside"—to exist as I existed, having inwardness, a kind of individual life, and every object seen under this aspect, appeared exceedingly beautiful. There was a cat out there, with its head lifted, effortlessly watching a wasp that moved without moving just above its head. Everything was *urgent* with life which was the same in the cat, the wasp, the broken bottles, and merely manifested itself differently in these individuals (which did not therefore cease to be individuals however). All things seemed to glow with a light that came from within them.[7]

Stace reports that in conversation with N. M. he was told that not only did all those external objects seem to share one and the same life, but that that life was also the same with the life which was and is in himself. N. M.'s account continues:

> I experienced a complete certainty that at that moment I saw things as they really were, and I was filled with grief at the realization of the real situation of human beings, living continuously in the midst of all this without being aware of it. This thought filled my mind and I wept. But I also wept over the things themselves which we never saw and which we made ugly in our ignorance, and I saw that all ugliness was a wounding of life. . . . I became aware that whatever it was that had been happening had now ceased to happen. I began to be aware of time again, and the impression of entering time was as marked as though I had stepped from air into water from a rarer into a thicker element.[8]

Experiences somewhat like N. M.'s have been reported by a number of mystics in various religious traditions.[9] Stace suggests, for example, that N. M.'s experience parallels the experience of Meister Eckhart:

> Here (i.e. in this experience) all blades of grass, wood, and stone, all things are One. . . . When is a man in mere understanding? When he sees one thing separated from another. And when is he above mere understanding? When he sees all in all, then a man stands above mere understanding."[10]

Reflecting on mystical experience of the extrovertive type, we can list the following features as characteristic of the experience.

1. Looks outward through the senses
2. Sees the inner essence of things, an essence which appears to be alive, beautiful, and the same in all things
3. Sense of union of one's deeper self with this inner essence
4. Feeling that what is experienced is divine
5. Sense of reality, that one sees things as they really are
6. Sense of peace and bliss
7. Timelessness, no awareness of the passage of time during the experience

Introvertive Experience

In introvertive mystical experience one looks within and finds the divine in the core of the soul. It's not that you just think about yourself. According to the mystics you must enter into the deepest and darkest part of yourself. And this is an extraordinarily hard thing to do. For to do this you must first detach yourself from your ordinary state of consciousness. What is the ordinary state of consciousness? It is one in which you may be conscious of any of a number of contents of consciousness: sensations, desires, feelings, images, wishes, memories, thoughts. So long as you are occupied with any of these—even noble thoughts of God—you cannot enter into the deepest part of the self, where there is nothing but silence. All the great mystics agree on this point. The ordinary state of consciousness must be set aside; you must empty consciousness of all these contents. Eckhart, using the phrase "the birth of Christ in the soul" for the mystical experience of the introvertive type, notes the importance and difficulty of detaching oneself from the ordinary state of consciousness.

> The birth is impossible without a complete withdrawal of the sense . . . and great force is required to repress all the agents of the soul and cause them to cease functioning. It takes much strength to gather them all in, and without that strength it cannot be done.[11]

Perhaps in recognition of the extreme difficulty in achieving detachment, mystics have developed various "exercises" to help one accomplish this task. There are the Yoga techniques of India, for example, in which breathing exercises are undertaken as a way of obtaining mastery over the conscious life. And the Christian mystics in Catholic monasteries developed the technique of "prayer," not in the usual sense of asking God for things, but in the sense of meditation, practiced with the intent of removing obstacles to achieving union with God.

Suppose, somehow, one were to achieve detachment, to remove the activity of the senses and the activity of the intellect from consciousness. What would happen? Instead of losing consciousness or falling asleep, you may experience the core of your soul which is empty of all content. Mystics describe this experience as one of emptiness, a sense of nothingness. Metaphors such as "darkness," "a wilderness," "the desert" are used to characterize this experience of emptiness. The point on which the mystics insist is that only as the self loses awareness of itself and of other things can it be empty and ready for God to enter. As Eckhart notes:

> The genuine word of eternity is spoken only in that eternity of the man who is himself a wilderness, alienated from self and all multiplicity.[12]

Similarly, the Spanish mystic, St. John of the Cross (1542–1591), says,

> Now the soul must be emptied of all these imagined forms, figures, and images, and it must remain in darkness with respect to these senses if it is to attain Divine Union, . . .[13]

Apparently, if, when the soul reaches this state of complete emptiness and darkness, God does enter in, one experiences a sense of encountering ultimate reality, experiences a oneness with this reality, and has a sense of complete peace and bliss. In the Catholic mystical tradition, the experience is called the beatific vision, and however difficult it may be for those who have attained this vision to describe it, it is abundantly clear that for the mystics this experience is the pearl of great price. For them it transcends all else that life on earth has to offer.

Reflecting on mystical experience of the introvertive type we can list the following features as characteristic of the experience:

1. A state of consciousness devoid of its ordinary contents: sensations, images, thoughts, desires, and so forth
2. An experience of absolute oneness, with no distinctions or divisions
3. Sense of reality, that one is experiencing what is ultimately real
4. Feeling that what is experienced is divine
5. Sense of complete peace and bliss
6. Timelessness, no awareness of the passage of time during the experience

Having characterized mystical religious experience, we come now to the question of whether such experiences provide rational grounds for believing in the reality of the divine. In discussing this question it will be helpful to confine ourselves to the major strand of religious mystical experience, mystical experience of the introvertive type.

THE UNANIMITY THESIS

One difficulty we encountered with ordinary religious experiences is that they appear to be of distinctly different divine beings—Jesus, Krishna, Allah, Brahman, and others. We call this a difficulty because the experiences are embedded in and support rival religious traditions that cannot all be true. To some extent, then, to accept one of these experiences as veridical is to raise doubts about the ordinary religious experiences in some rival religious tradition. In contrast, a number of philosophers and religious thinkers have contended that mystical religious experiences of the introvertive type are fundamentally the same, a claim that is sometimes called "the unanimity thesis." William James expressed the point in the following way:

> The overcoming of all usual barriers between the individual and the Absolute is the great mystic achievement. In mystic states we both become one with the Absolute and we become aware of our oneness. This is the everlasting and triumphant mystical tradition, hardly altered by differences of clime or creed. In Hinduism, in Neoplatonism, in Suffism, in Christian mysticism, in Whitmanism, we find the same recurring note, so that there is about mystical utterances an eternal unanimity which ought to make a critic stop and think, and which brings it about that the mystical classics have, as has been said, neither birthday nor native land.[14]

A number of commentators on mystical experience—W. T. Stace, Aldous Huxley, Bertrand Russell, and C. D. Broad, to name but a few—agree with James that there is among mystics of various cultures and religious traditions a unanimity, whether partial or complete, concerning what is encountered in the mystical experience. And they also agree that the unanimity among the mystics is a point in favor of the view that mystical experience is a *veridical* perception of reality, and, therefore, may provide rational grounds for belief in the reality of the divine.

Why should the fact—assuming for the moment that it is a fact—that the unanimity thesis is true be a point in the mystic's favor, a reason, perhaps, for judging her or his experience to be *veridical* rather than delusory? Well, suppose that while teaching a course in philosophy of religion I suddenly have an experience in which a voice speaks to me, a voice seeming to come from somewhere above, and the voice says: "Rowe, the CIA is watching you." I manage somehow to finish the lecture, but immediately afterwards report my rather extraordinary experience to some of my colleagues in the university. Suppose that they then undertake to determine, as best they can, whether my experience was veridical, whether, that is, there actually was a voice independent of me conveying the message I heard, or whether my experience was delusory, the voice being but a projection of some internal disturbance within me, as was the dagger experienced by Macbeth. One very natural thing for them to do would be to inquire of the students who were in my class at the time I had the experience in the hope of finding out whether any of them also heard the voice. Clearly, if a sufficient number of them heard a voice saying roughly what I reported, this would count on the side of regarding my experience as veridical. Whereas, if none of them reported hearing the voice, my colleagues would have some grounds for regarding my experience as delusory, perhaps due to some form of paranoia on my part. So the fact that a number of people have the very same experience normally counts as a point in favor of the experience being veridical. Of course, the fact that someone in Chicago did not hear the voice I reported is not relevant because that person was not in the position (being in the classroom) to hear the voice. Nor is the fact relevant that the voice was not heard by some of my students who were in the classroom but sound asleep. For although they were in the position to hear the voice, they failed to satisfy another condition (being awake) that is necessary for hearing the voice, if a voice was really there to be heard.

Turning to mystical experience, we can now see the importance of the unanimity thesis to the question of whether the mystic's experience is veridical or delusory. The fact that numerous individuals have essentially the same experience is relevant to the question of whether the experience is veridical, provided that it is reasonable to think that there are conditions such that when satisfied one would have the experience if it were veridical, and not have the experience if it were delusory. Mystics do seem to undertake to satisfy certain conditions (detachment, for example) and often have the experience when those conditions are satisfied. But there is no clear or sure way of telling when someone has really satisfied the conditions required for the mystical experience. Moreover, it may be that the object of the experience, if a divine being, may or may not choose to reveal itself even when the necessary conditions are satisfied. For these reasons it is difficult to know when the fact that someone who has endeavored to satisfy the conditions for the experience, but failed to have the experience, should be counted against the claim that mystical experience is veridical. Nevertheless, it does seem reasonable to take the fact that mystics everywhere have the *same* experience as a point in favor of the mystic's experience being veridical.

But is the unanimity thesis true? Do mystics everywhere have basically the same experience? If we are thinking of individuals who enjoy experiences of the introvertive type, it might seem that the answer must be yes. For in being introvertive mystical experiences, their experiences will possess the features 1–6 in terms of which introvertive mystical experience was characterized. We must remember, however, that item 4 mentions the sense that one is encountering "the divine," and that we have purposely allowed the expression "the divine" to stand for *whatever* would be recognized as such by some religious group. Thus when Meister Eckhart describes his experience as one in which his self is lost in the *godhead*, the divine nature common to the three persons of the trinity—God the Father, God the Son, and God the Holy Ghost—and when a Hindu mystic describes his experiences as union with *Brahman*, the universal self, we have two quite different conceptions of the divine, but both experiences are examples of mystical experience of the introvertive type.

Since mystics from differing religious traditions—Christian, Jewish, Islamic, Hindu, and others—use quite different conceptions of the divine to characterize the reality they encounter in their respective mystical experiences, why should we believe that they all enjoy the very *same* experience? In some forms of Hinduism the divine is conceived as an impersonal reality, whereas when Saint Teresa characterizes her experience as "union with God," she employs the Christian conception of the divine as a supreme, loving, personal being. Confronted with these facts, how can the proponent of the unanimity thesis continue to hold that the Christian, Jewish, Islamic, Hindu, and Buddhist mystics all have the very same experience? They can do so by distinguishing between an *experience* and its *interpretation* and by suggesting that the differences that appear in the mystics' descriptions of the reality they encounter are largely due to different interpretations of the same experience rather than to direct descriptions of different experiences. In his useful book, *The Teachings of the Mystics*, Stace introduces the distinction in the following way:

> On a dark night out of doors one may see something glimmering white. One person may think it a ghost. A second person may take it for a sheet hung out on a clothesline. A third person may suppose that it is a white-painted rock. Here we have a single experience with three different interpretations. The experience is genuine, but the interpretations may be either true or false. If we are to understand anything at all about mysticism, it is essential that we should make a similar distinction between a mystical experience and the interpretations which may be put upon it either by mystics themselves or by nonmystics. For instance, the same mystical experience may be interpreted by a Christian in terms of Christian beliefs and by a Buddhist in terms of Buddhistic beliefs.[15]

Armed with this distinction, Stace and others have taken the experience of the mystic as essentially an encounter with a reality that is one and devoid of all distinctions, an experience accompanied by feelings of exalted peace, blessedness, and joy. The mystic's identification of the reality encountered with some form of the divine—God, the Brahman, the universal self, the void, or Nirvana—is viewed as not part of the experience itself but as an interpretation of the experience in accordance with the doctrines of the religious tradition to which the mystic belongs. And it is by pressing this view that Stace and other students of mysticism have been able to defend the unanimity thesis against the objection we've considered.

Suppose we grant that mystics from various religious traditions enjoy pretty much the same experience. Stace, Broad, Huxley, Russell, and others who do grant this note that unanimity is not a *proof* that mystical experience is veridical. Stace, for example, notes that there is unanimity on the part of all persons who take the drug santonin that white things appear yellow, and Broad remarks: "Persons of all races who habitually drink alcohol to excess eventually have perceptual experiences in which they seem to themselves to see snakes or rats crawling about their rooms or beds."[16] But neither Stace's example nor Broad's is a case of veridical perception. Nevertheless, the unanimity of the mystics concerning their experience remains a point in favor of their experience being veridical. How, then, are we to decide the matter?

Mystical Experience: Veridical or Delusory?

In judging whether an experience is veridical or delusory we also take into account the state of the persons having the experience. The use of santonin and the excessive use of alcohol bring about abnormal states in the users, states which make for distorted and delusory experiences of the world. And it is precisely for this reason that Russell argues that the mystic's experience should be judged delusory. For, unlike the scientist, who requires of us only normal eyesight and other perceptions, the mystic, Russell argues, "demands changes in the observer, by fasting, by breathing exercises, and by a careful abstention from external observation."[17] The mystic, like the drunkard, produces abnormal bodily and mental states within himself or herself. Such states, Russell argues, lead to abnormal, unreliable perceptions, perceptions which are more than likely delusory. With characteristic wit and style he concludes: "From a scientific point of view, we can make no distinction between the man who eats little and sees heaven and the man who drinks much and sees snakes. Each is in an abnormal physical condition, and therefore has abnormal perceptions."[18] Although the mystic's feeling-state of peace and bliss is something Russell values greatly, the mystic's experience, so far as it purports to be an encounter with objective reality, is rejected by Russell as more than likely delusive.

There is, I think, an unstated assumption in Russell's rejection of mystical experience, an assumption that must be called into question. What we know about abnormal bodily and mental states is that they make for distorted and delusory perceptions of the physical world, the world of our ordinary experience. It must be remembered, however, that the mystic claims to perceive a realm which transcends the world of ordinary experience, a spiritual realm altogether different from the physical world. The hidden assumption in Russell's argument is that bodily and mental states that interfere with reliable perceptions of the physical world also interfere with reliable perceptions of a spiritual world beyond the physical, if there is such a spiritual world to be perceived. Perhaps this assumption is reasonable, but it certainly is not obviously true. Indeed, there may be reasons for thinking that just the reverse of this assumption is more than likely true. As C. D. Broad has written:

> Suppose, for the sake of argument, that there is an aspect of the world which remains altogether outside the ken of ordinary persons in their daily life. Then it seems very likely that some degree of mental and physical abnormality would be a necessary condition for getting sufficiently loosened from the objects of ordinary sense-perception to come into cognitive contact with this aspect of reality. Therefore the fact that those persons who claim this peculiar kind of cognition generally exhibit certain mental and physical abnormalities is rather what might be anticipated if their claims were true. One might need to be slightly "cracked" in order to have some peep-holes into the super-sensible world.[19]

Although a religious skeptic, Broad argues forcibly for the view that mystical experiences are more than likely veridical. He summarizes his position as follows:

> Finally I come to the argument for the existence of God which is based on the occurrence of specifically mystical and religious experiences. I am prepared to admit that such experiences occur among people of different races and social traditions, and that they have occurred at all periods of history. I am prepared to admit that, although the interpretations which have been put on them have differed still more, there are probably certain characteristics which are common to all of them which suffice to distinguish them from all other kinds of experience. In view of this I think it more likely than not that in religious and mystical experience men come into contact with some Reality or some aspect of Reality which they do not come into contact with in any other way.[20]

In view of his point, noted earlier, that unanimity does not itself show an experience to be veridical, and in view of the fact that in the passage just cited no support for his positive view of mystical experience over and above unanimity is mentioned, we need to ask what leads Broad to this assessment of mystical experience. His reasons, expressed as an argument, are as follows:

1. There is considerable agreement among mystics concerning the reality they have experienced.
2. When there is considerable agreement among observers as to what they take themselves to be experiencing, it is reasonable to conclude that their experiences are veridical, unless there be some positive reason to think them delusive.
3. There are no positive reasons for thinking that mystical experiences are delusive.

Therefore,

4. It is reasonable to believe that mystical experiences are veridical.

The key premise in this argument is number 2, which Broad argues is the practical postulate we go by in our dealings with non-mystical experiences.[21] In the case of the unanimity among drunkards who see rats and snakes, Broad argues that we do have a positive reason for thinking their experiences delusive.

> Since these (rats and snakes) are the sort of things which we could see if they were there, the fact that we cannot see them makes it highly probable that they are not there. . . . It therefore seems reasonable to conclude that the agreement among drunkards is a sign, not of a revelation but of a delusion.[22]

The claims made by the mystics, however, are not such that they conflict with what we can perceive in our ordinary state of consciousness. So Broad concludes that given the application to mystical experience of the practical postulate we employ everywhere else, it is reasonable to regard mystical experience as veridical.

Although Russell does not discuss Broad's practical postulate, there is nothing in his remarks about mystical experience to suggest that he would reject the postulate or refuse to apply it to mystical experience. His disagreement with Broad concerns premise 3. For, as we saw, Russell thinks that the fact that the mystics often are in an abnormal bodily or mental state when they have their mystical experiences is a positive reason for thinking them delusive. We have, however, noted a questionable assumption Russell makes in rejecting premise 3, and have considered Broad's reasons for refusing to accept that assumption.

So far as the disagreement between Russell and Broad over premise 3 is concerned, my inclination is to side with Broad. It is reasonable to believe (1) that the nature of the reality the mystics encounter would perhaps require some significant changes in us if we were to perceive it, changes which might well interfere with accurate observations of the ordinary physical world, and (2) that were mystical experience veridical it would bring about rather extraordinary changes in those who enjoy the experience. So the mere fact that mystics undergo certain alterations of body and mind does not constitute a positive reason for thinking mystical experience delusive.

A Middle Path

Should we then conclude with Broad that mystical experience is probably veridical? My reservation about doing so concerns the application of Broad's practical postulate to mystical experience. When we are confronted with a fair degree of unanimity among those who enjoy a certain experience there is, I think, an important difference between (1) knowing how to proceed to find positive reasons for rejecting their experience as delusory, if there should be any, and (2) not knowing how to proceed to find such positive reasons if there should be any. When we are in situation 1, as we clearly are in the case of experiences of rats and snakes by those who habitually drink alcohol to excess, the application of Broad's postulate is undoubtedly warranted. But when we are in situation 2, as we nonmystics do seem to be with regard to mystical experience, the application of Broad's postulate is perhaps unwarranted. In which case the question of whether mystical experience is veridical or delusory seems to end in something like a stalemate.

Over ninety years ago William James ended his brilliant study of mysticism by drawing three conclusions:

1. Mystical states, when well developed, usually are, and have the right to be, absolutely authoritative over the individuals to whom they come.
2. No authority emanates from them which should make it a duty for those who stand outside of them to accept their revelations uncritically.
3. They break down the authority of the nonmystical or rationalistic consciousness, based upon the understanding and the senses alone. They show it to be only one kind of consciousness.[23]

It is unlikely that the studies of mysticism over the intervening years have invalidated these conclusions. The third conclusion simply notes that mystical experiences establish that there is a mode of consciousness other than the ordinary state of consciousness. In contrast to Russell (we have good reason to think mystical experiences are delusive) and Broad (we have good reasons to think mystical experiences are veridical), James takes a middle course in his second conclusion, suggesting that we nonmystics have no good reasons for regarding mystical experiences as veridical and no good reasons for regarding them as delusory. He adds to this, in his first conclusion, that the mystics themselves not only generally do regard their experiences as veridical but are *justified* in doing so. Although we have not discussed James' first conclusion, the considerations we have advanced in this chapter do point in the directions taken in his second and third conclusions.

Earlier we discussed two difficulties for the view that the Principle of Credulity renders it rational for us to accept ordinary religious experiences as veridical. We may now summarize our conclusions concerning the question of whether mystical religious experiences provide rational grounds for believing in the reality of the divine. Since we have concluded with James that nonmystics do not have good reasons for accepting mystical experiences as veridical, the fact that mystical experiences occur does not provide nonmystics with rational grounds for believing in the reality of the divine. Moreover, even if nonmystics were to follow Broad in regarding mystical experiences as probably veridical, the fact that different mystics employ different conceptions of the divine in interpreting their respective experiences would make it difficult to determine whether, and in what sense, the reality apprehended by the mystics is divine. Broad himself is careful to remark that he does not think there is any good reason to suppose that the Reality encountered by the mystics is personal. Therefore, so far as the theistic God is concerned, it seems reasonably clear that mystical experiences provide very little in the way of rational grounds for believing in the existence of such a being. And this conclusion may well hold for the mystics themselves, as well as for nonmystics. For although we may admit with James that the mystics themselves are justified in regarding their experiences as veridical, to the extent that the experience itself is an encounter with absolute oneness, devoid of distinctions, the experience would not itself justify belief in the theistic God. The theistic mystic, already believing in the theistic God, may interpret this experience as an encounter with some aspect of that being. But this is quite different from holding that the *experience itself* justifies the mystic in believing in the reality of the theistic God.

Notes

1. Acts 9:3-9 (Revised Standard Version).
2. R. B. Blakney, *Meister Eckhart: A Modern Translation* (New York: Harper & Row Publishers, 1941), p. 200.
3. Blakney, *Meister Eckhart: A Modern Translation,* pp. 200–201.
4. Quoted by Walter T. Stace in *Mysticism and Philosophy* (New York: J. B. Lippincott Co., 1960), p. 233.
5. Quoted in William James, *The Varieties of Religious Experience* (New York: The Modern Library, 1936), pp. 67–68.
6. Richard Swinburne, *The Existence of God* (Oxford: The Clarendon Press, 1979), p. 254.
7. Stace, *Mysticism and Philosophy,* pp. 71–72.
8. Stace, *Mysticism and Philosophy,* pp. 71–72.
9. N. M. had the experience he describes after taking the hallucinogenic drug mescalin. The question of the relationship between certain drug induced experiences and mystical experiences has been much discussed in recent years. For a brief, interesting account of the subject see Huston Smith, "Do Drugs Have Religious Import?" *The Journal of Philosophy,* LXI, No. 18 (1964), pp. 517–530.
10. Quoted by Stace in *Mysticism and Philosophy,* p. 63.
11. Blakney, *Meister Eckhart: A Modern Translation,* p. 109.
12. Blakney, *Meister Eckhart: A Modern Translation,* p. 120.
13. St. John of the Cross, *The Dark Night of the Soul,* trans. and ed. K. F. Reinhardt (New York: Ungar Publishing Co., 1957), p. 51.
14. William James, *The Varieties of Religious Experience* (New York: The Modern Library, 1936), p. 410.

15. W. T. Stace, *The Teachings of the Mystics* (New York: New American Library, 1960), p. 10.

16. C. D. Broad, "Arguments for the Existence of God. II," *The Journal of Theological Studies,* XL (1939), p. 161.

17. Bertrand Russell, *Religion and Science* (London: Oxford University Press, 1935), p. 187.

18. Russell, *Religion and Science,* p. 188.

19. Broad, "Arguments for the Existence of God. II," p. 164.

20. C. D. Broad, *Religion, Philosophy, and Physical Research* (New York: Humanities Press, 1969), pp. 172–73.

21. Broad, "Arguments for the Existence of God, II," p. 163. Broad's principle is similar to the Principle of Credulity discussed earlier. The chief difference is that Broad's principle takes an experience to be veridical (unless there are positive reasons for thinking it delusive) when there are a number of experiences that agree with it. The Principle of Credulity does not require agreeing experiences.

22. Broad, "Arguments for the Existence of God, II," p. 162.

23. James, *The Varieties of Religious Experience,* p. 414.

Topics for Review

1. Explain what is meant by a religious experience. How are ordinary religious experiences different from mystical religious experience?

2. What is the Principle of Credulity? How does it help to show that ordinary religious experiences are veridical?

3. What basic argument does Broad give in support of the view that it is reasonable to think that mystical experience is veridical?

4. Explain the difference between the views of Russell and Broad concerning whether it is reasonable to regard mystical experience as veridical.

5. Does mystical experience provide good grounds for belief in theistic God? Discuss.

Topics for Further Study

6. Critically discuss the following argument.
   Ordinary religious experiences do not prove the existence of God. But the fact that such experiences occur does need to be explained. And the simplest explanation is that there exists a God who causes people to experience him. Therefore, it is very probable that God exists.

7. James says that mystical states have the *right* to be absolutely authoritative over those to whom they come. Is James correct, or should those who have these experiences view them as delusory? Discuss.

6

THE PROBLEM OF EVIL

Thus far we have been engaged in acquainting ourselves with the major idea of God that has emerged in western civilization, the theistic idea of God as a supremely good being, creator of but separate from and independent of the world, omnipotent, omniscient, eternal, and self-existent (Chapter One), and in examining some of the major attempts to justify belief in the existence of the theistic God (Chapters Two–Five). In Chapters Two through Four we considered the three major arguments for the existence of God (Cosmological, Teleological, and Ontological), arguments which appeal to facts supposedly available to any rational person, whether religious or not, and in Chapter Five we examined religious and mystical experience as a source and justification for belief in God. It is now time to turn to some of the difficulties for theistic belief, some of the sources which have been thought to provide grounds for atheism, for the belief that the theistic God does not exist. The most formidable of these difficulties is the problem of evil.

The existence of evil in the world has been felt for centuries to be a problem for theism. It seems difficult to believe that a world with such a vast amount of evil as our world contains could be the creation of, and under the sovereign control of, a supremely good, omnipotent, omniscient being. The problem has confronted the human intellect for centuries and every major theologian has attempted to offer a solution to it.

There are two important forms of the problem of evil which we must be careful to distinguish. I shall call these two forms the *logical* form of the problem of evil, and the *evidential* form of the problem of evil. Although the important difference between these two forms of the problem will become fully clear only as they are discussed in detail, it will be useful to have a brief statement of each form of the problem set before us at the beginning of our enquiry. The logical form of the problem of evil is the view that the existence of evil in our world is *logically inconsistent* with the existence of the theistic God. The evidential form of the problem of evil is the view that the variety and profusion of evil in our world, although perhaps not logically inconsistent with the existence of the theistic God, provides, nevertheless, *rational support* for atheism, for the belief that the theistic God does not exist. We must now examine each of these forms of the problem in some detail.

THE LOGICAL PROBLEM

The logical form of the problem implies that theism is internally inconsistent, for the theist accepts each of two statements which are logically inconsistent. The two statements in question are:

1. God exists and is omnipotent, omniscient, and wholly good.

and

2. Evil exists.

These two statements, so the logical form of the problem insists, are logically inconsistent in the same way as

3. This object is red.

is inconsistent with

4. This object is not colored.

Suppose, for the moment, that the proponent of the logical form of the problem of evil were to succeed in proving to us that statements 1 and 2 are logically inconsistent. We would then be in the position of having to reject either 1 or 2; for, if two statements are logically inconsistent, it is impossible for both of them to be true; if one of them is true then the other *must* be false. Moreover, since we could hardly deny the reality of evil in our world, it seems we would have to reject belief in the theistic God; we would be driven to the conclusion that atheism is true. Indeed, even if we should be tempted to reject 2, leaving us the option of believing 1, this temptation is not one to which most theists could easily yield. For most theists adhere to religious traditions which emphasize the reality of evil in our world. In the Judeo-Christian tradition, for example, murder is held to be an evil, sinful act, and it can hardly be denied that murder occurs in our world. So, since theists generally accept and emphasize the reality of evil in our world, it would be something of a disaster for theism if the central claim in the logical form of the problem of evil were established: that 1 is logically inconsistent with 2.

To Establish Inconsistency

How can we establish that two statements are inconsistent? Sometimes nothing needs to be established since the two statements are *explicitly contradictory*, as, for example, the statements "Elizabeth is over five feet tall" and "Elizabeth is not over five feet tall." Often, however, two inconsistent statements are not explicitly contradictory. In such cases we can establish that they are inconsistent by deriving from them two statements that are explicitly contradictory. Consider statements 3 and 4, for example. It's clear that these two statements are logically inconsistent, they cannot both be true. But they are not explicitly contradictory. If asked to prove that 3 and 4 are inconsistent, we can do this be deriving explicitly contradictory statements from them. To derive the explicitly contradictory statements we need to add another statement to 3 and 4.

 5. Whatever is red is colored.

From 3, 4, and 5 we can then easily derive the explicitly contradictory pair of statements, "This object is colored" (from 3 and 5) and "This object is not colored" (repetition of 4). This, then, is the procedure we may follow if we are asked to establish our claim that two statements are logically inconsistent.

Before we consider whether the proponent of the logical form of the problem of evil can *establish* the claim that statements 1 and 2 are logically inconsistent, one very important point about the procedure for establishing that two statements are logically inconsistent needs to be clearly understood. When we have two statements which are not explicitly contradictory, and want to establish that they are logically inconsistent, we do this by adding some further statement or statements to them and then deriving from the entire group (the original pair and the additional statement or statements) a pair of statements that are explicitly contradictory. Now the point that needs very careful attention is this: in order for this procedure to work, the statement or statements we add must be not just true but *necessarily true*. Notice, for example, that the statement we added to 3 and 4 in order to establish that they are inconsistent is a necessary truth—it is logically impossible for something to be red but not colored. If, however, the additional statement or statements used in order to deduce the explicitly contradictory statements are true, but not necessarily true, then although we may succeed in deducing explicitly contradictory statements, we will *not* have succeeded in showing that the original pair of statements are logically inconsistent.

To see that this is so let's consider the following pair of statements.

 6. The object in my right hand is a coin.

and,

 7. The object in my right hand is not a dime.

Clearly, 6 and 7 are *not* logically inconsistent, for both of them might be, or might have been, true. They aren't logically inconsistent because there is nothing logically impossible in the idea that the coin in my right hand should be a quarter or a nickel. (Contrast 6 and 7 with 3 and 4. Clearly there is something logically impossible in the idea that this object be red and yet not colored.) But notice that we can add a statement to 6 and 7 such that from the three of them explicitly contradictory statements can be derived.

8. Every coin in my right hand is a dime.

From 6, 7, and 8 we can derive the explicitly contradictory pair of statements, "The object in my right hand is a dime" (from 6 and 8) and "The object in my right hand is not a dime" (repetition of 7). Now suppose 8 is true, that in fact every coin in my right hand is a dime. We will have succeeded, then, in deducing explicitly contradictory statements from our original pair, 6 and 7, with the help of the *true* statement 8. But, of course, by this procedure we won't have established that 6 and 7 are logically inconsistent. Why not? Because 8—the additional statement— although true, is not necessarily true. Statement 8 is not a necessary truth because I might (logically) have had a quarter or a nickel in my right hand. Statement 8 is in fact true, but since it logically could have been false, it is not a necessary truth. We must, then, keep clearly in mind that to *establish* two statements to be logically inconsistent by adding a statement and then deriving explicitly contradictory statements, the additional statement must be not just true, but necessarily true.

Application to the Logical Problem of Evil

Since (1) "God exists and is omnipotent, omniscient, and wholly good," and (2) "Evil exists" are not explicitly contradictory, those who hold that 1 and 2 are logically inconsistent need to make good this claim by adding a necessarily true statement to 1 and 2 and deducing explicitly contradictory statements. But what statement might we add? Suppose we begin with

9. An omnipotent, omniscient, good being will prevent the occurrence of any evil whatever.

From 1, 2, and 9 we can derive the explicitly contradictory statements, "No evil exists" (from 1 and 9) and "Evil exists" (repetition of 2). So if we can show that statement 9 is necessarily true we will have succeeded in establishing the thesis of the logical form of the problem of evil: that 1 and 2 are logically inconsistent. But is 9 necessarily true? Well, recalling our discussion of omnipotence, it would seem that God would have the power to prevent any evil whatever, for "preventing the occurrence of an evil" does not appear to be a logically contradictory task like "making a round square." But it is no easy matter to establish that 9 is necessarily true. For in our own experience we know that evil is sometimes connected with good in such a way that we are powerless to achieve the good without permitting the evil. Moreover, in such instances, the good sometimes outweighs the evil, so that a good being might intentionally permit the evil to occur in order to realize the good which outweighs it.

Leibniz gives the example of a general who knows that in order to achieve the good of saving the town from being destroyed by an attacking army he must order his men to defend the town, with the result that some of his men will suffer and die. The good of saving the women and children of the town outweighs the evil of the suffering and death of a few of the town's defenders. Although he could have prevented their suffering and death by ordering a hasty retreat of his forces, the general cannot do so without losing the good of saving the town and its inhabitants. It certainly does not count against the general's goodness that he permits the evil to occur in order to achieve the good which outweighs it. Perhaps, then, some evils in our world are connected to goods which outweigh them in such a way that even God cannot achieve the goods in question without permitting the evils to occur that are connected to those goods. If this is so, statement 9 is not necessarily true.

Of course, unlike the general's, God's power is unlimited, and it might be thought that no matter how closely evil and good may be, God could always achieve the good and prevent the evil. But this overlooks the possibility that the occurrence of some evils in our world is *logically necessary* for the achievement of goods which outweigh them, so that the task of bringing about those goods without permitting the evils that are connected to them to occur is as impossible a task as making a round square. If so, then, again, while being omnipotent God could prevent the evils in question from occurring, he could not, even though omnipotent, achieve the outweighing goods while preventing the evils from occurring.[1] Therefore, since (i) omnipotence is not the power to do what is logically impossible, and (ii) it may be logically impossible to prevent the occurrence of certain evils in our world and yet achieve some very great goods that outweigh those evils, we cannot be sure that statement 9 is necessarily true, we can't be sure that an omnipotent, wholly good being will prevent the occurrence of any evil whatever.

What we have just seen is that the attempt to establish that 1 and 2 are inconsistent by deducing explicitly contradictory statements from 1, 2, and 9 is a failure. For although 1, 2, and 9 do yield explicitly contradictory statements, we are not in a position to know that 9 is necessarily true.

The suggestion that emerges from the preceding discussion is that we replace 9 with

10. A good, omnipotent, omniscient being prevents the occurrence of any evil that is not logically necessary for the occurrence of a good which outweighs it.

Statement 10, unlike 9, takes into account the possibility that certain evils might be so connected to goods which outweigh them that even God cannot realize those goods without permitting the evils to occur. Statement 10, then, appears to be not only true, but necessarily true. The problem now, however, is that from 1, 2, and 10, explicitly contradictory statements cannot be derived. All that we can conclude from 1, 2, and 10 is that the evils which do exist in our world are logically necessary for the occurrence of goods which outweigh them, and that statement is not an explicit contradiction.

The general difficulty affecting attempts to establish that 1 and 2 are logically inconsistent is now apparent. When we add a statement, such as 9, which allows us to derive explicitly contradictory statements, we cannot be sure that the additional statement is necessarily true. On the other hand, when we add a statement, such as 10, which does seem to be necessarily true, it turns out that explicitly contradictory statements cannot be derived. No one has succeeded in producing a statement which is both known to be necessarily true and such that when added to 1 and 2 enables us to derive explicitly contradictory statements. In view of this, it is reasonable to conclude that the logical form of the problem of evil is not much of a problem for theism, for its central thesis, that 1 and 2 are logically inconsistent, is a thesis that no one has been able to establish by a convincing argument.

"The Free Will Defense"

Before turning to the evidential form of the problem of evil, it is important to understand the bearing of one traditional theistic defense on the logical form of the problem of evil. According to this defense—"The Free Will Defense"—God, even though omnipotent, *may not have been able* to create a world in which there are free human creatures without, thereby, permitting the occurrence of considerable evil. The basic assumption in this defense is that it is logically impossible for a person both *freely* to perform some act and to have been *caused* to perform that act. Without this assumption, the Free Will Defense collapses. For if it is possible for a person to be caused to do an act and yet to perform that act freely, then clearly God could have created a world in which there are free human creatures who only do what is right, who never do evil—for he, being omnipotent, could simply create the creatures and cause them to do only what is right.

Let's suppose that the basic assumption of the Free Will Defense is true, that it is logically impossible to be caused to do an act and yet to do that act freely. What this assumption means is that although God can cause there to be creatures and cause them to be free with respect to a certain act, he *cannot* cause them freely to perform the act and he cannot cause them freely to refrain from performing the act—whether the person performs the act or refrains from performing it will be up to that person, and not up to God, if the performing or refraining is to be freely done. Now suppose God creates a world with free human creatures, creatures who are free to do various things, including good and evil. Whether the free human creatures he creates will exercise their freedom to do good or evil will be up to them. And it is logically possible that no matter what free creatures God causes to exist, each of them will use his freedom on some occasion to do evil. Since this is so, it is *possible* that God could not have created a world with free creatures who do only what is right; it is possible that any world that God can create containing creatures free to do good or evil is a world in which these creatures sometimes do evil.

What the above line of argument endeavors to establish is that it is logically possible that the following statement is true.

11. God, although omnipotent, cannot create a world in which there are free human creatures and no evil.

But if it is possible that 11 is true, and also possible that a world with free human creatures is a better world than a world without free human creatures, then it follows that 1 and 2 are not inconsistent at all. For consider the following group of statements:

1. God exists and is omnipotent, omniscient, and wholly good.
11. God, although omnipotent, cannot create a world in which there are free human creatures and no evil.
12. A world with free human creatures and some evil is a better world than a world with no free human creatures.
13. God creates the best world he can.

From 1, 11, 12, and 13 it follows that 2 "Evil exists." But if 1, 11, 12, and 13 imply 2 and there is no inconsistency in 1, 11, 12, and 13, then there can be no inconsistency between 1 and 2. If a group of statements is not inconsistent, then no statement that follows from that group can be inconsistent with any or all statements in the group.

We can now see the relevance of the Free Will Defense to the logical form of the problem of evil. We objected to the logical form of the problem of evil because no one has succeeded in establishing its central thesis, that (1) "God is omnipotent, omniscient, and wholly good" is inconsistent with (2) "Evil exists." But, of course, from the fact that no one has *proved* that 1 and 2 are inconsistent, it doesn't follow that they aren't inconsistent. What the Free Will Defense endeavors to do is to go the final step, to *prove* that 1 and 2 are really consistent. It does this by trying to establish that it is *possible* (logically) that both 11 and 12 are true and that there is no logical inconsistency in the group of statements, 1, 11, 12, and 13. Whether the Free Will Defense is successful in its aim of showing that 1 and 2 are logically consistent is a matter too complicated and controversial for us to pursue here.[2] Even if it is unsuccessful, however, the theist need not be unduly troubled by the logical form of the problem of evil, for, as we've seen, no one has established that 1 and 2 are inconsistent.

THE EVIDENTIAL PROBLEM

I turn now to the evidential form of the problem of evil: the form of the problem which holds that the variety and profusion of evil in our world, although perhaps not logically inconsistent with the existence of God provides, nevertheless, *rational support* for the belief that the theistic God does not exist. In developing this form of the problem of evil, it will be useful to focus on some particular evil that our world contains in considerable abundance. Intense human and animal suffering, for example, occurs daily and in great plenitude in our world. Such intense suffering is a clear case of evil. Of course, if the intense suffering leads to some greater good, a good we could not have obtained without undergoing the suffering in question, we might conclude that the suffering is *justified*, but it remains an evil nevertheless. For we must not confuse the intense suffering in and of itself with the good things to which it sometimes leads or of which it may be a necessary part. Intense human or animal suffering is *in itself* bad, an evil, even though it may sometimes be justified by virtue of being a part of, or leading to, some good which is unobtainable without it. What is evil in itself may sometimes be good *as a means* because it leads to something which is good in itself. In such a case, while remaining an evil in itself, the intense human or

animal suffering is, nevertheless, an evil which someone might be morally justified in permitting.

Taking human and animal suffering as a clear instance of evil which occurs
with great frequency in our world, the evidential form of the problem of evil can
be stated in terms of the following argument for atheism.

1. There exist instances of intense suffering which an omnipotent,
   omniscient being could have prevented without thereby preventing the
   occurrence of any greater good.
2. An omniscient, wholly good being would prevent the occurrence of any
   intense suffering it could, unless it could not do so without thereby
   preventing the occurrence of some greater good.

Therefore,

3. There does not exist an omnipotent, omniscient, wholly good being.

What are we to say about this argument for atheism, an argument based on the
profusion of one sort of evil in our world? The argument is valid; therefore, if we
have rational grounds for accepting its premises, to that extent we have rational
grounds for accepting atheism. Do we, however, have rational grounds for
accepting the premises of this argument?

The second premise of the argument expresses a belief about what a morally
good being would do under certain circumstances. According to this belief, if a
morally good being knew of some intense suffering that was about to occur and
he was in a position to prevent its occurrence, he would prevent it *unless* he could
not do so without thereby losing some greater good of which he was aware. This
belief (or something very close to it) is, I think, held in common by theists and
nontheists. Of course, there may be disagreement about whether something is
good, and whether, if it is good, one would be morally justified in permitting
some intense suffering to occur in order to obtain it. Someone might hold, for
example, that no good is great enough to justify permitting an innocent child to
suffer terribly. To hold such a view, however, is not to deny premise 2 which
claims only that *if* an omniscient, wholly good being permits intense suffering
then there must be some greater good (a good which outweighs the suffering in
question) which the good being could not obtain without permitting the intense
suffering. So stated, 2 seems to express a belief that accords with our basic moral
principles, principles shared by both theists and nontheists. If we are to fault this
argument, therefore, we must find some fault with its first premise.

Suppose in some distant forest lightning strikes a dead tree, resulting in a
forest fire. In the fire a fawn is trapped, horribly burned, and lies in terrible agony
for several days before death relieves its suffering. So far as we can see, the fawn's
intense suffering is pointless, leading to no greater good. Could an omnipotent,
omniscient being have prevented the fawn's apparently pointless suffering? The
answer is obvious, as even the theist will insist. An omnipotent, omniscient being
could easily have prevented the fawn from being horribly burned, or, given the
burning, could have spared the fawn the intense suffering by quickly ending its

life, rather than allowing the fawn to lie in terrible agony for several days. Since no greater good, so far as we can see, would have been lost had the fawn's intense suffering been prevented, doesn't it appear that premise 1 of the argument is true, that there do exist instances of intense suffering which an omnipotent, omniscient being could have prevented without thereby preventing the occurrence of any greater good?

It must be acknowledged that the case of the fawn's apparently pointless suffering does not *prove* that premise 1 is true. For even though we cannot see how the fawn's suffering leads to any greater good, it hardly follows that it does not do so. After all, we are often surprised by how things we thought to be unconnected turn out to be intimately connected. Perhaps, then, there is some familiar good outweighing the fawn's suffering to which that suffering is connected in a way we do not see. Furthermore, there may well be unfamiliar goods, goods we haven't dreamed of, to which the fawn's suffering is inextricably connected. Indeed, it would seem to require something like omniscience on our part before we could lay claim to *knowing* that there is no greater good to which the fawn's suffering leads which an omnipotent, omniscient being could not have achieved without permitting that suffering. So the case of the fawn's suffering does not enable us to *establish* the truth of premise 1.

The truth is that we are not in a position to *prove* that 1 is true. We cannot *know* with certainty that instances of suffering of the sort described in 1 do occur in our world. But it is one thing to *know* or *prove* that 1 is true and quite another thing to have *rational grounds* for believing 1 to be true. We are often in the position where in the light of our experience and knowledge it is rational to believe that a certain statement is true, even though we are not in a position to prove or to know with certainty that the statement is true. In the light of our past experience and knowledge it is, for example, very reasonable to believe that neither Goldwater nor McGovern will ever be elected president, but we are scarcely in the position of knowing with certainty that neither will ever be elected president. So, too, with 1, although we cannot know with certainty that it is true, it perhaps can be rationally supported, shown to be a rational belief.

Consider again the case of the fawn's suffering. There are two distinct questions we need to raise: "Does the fawn's suffering lead to some greater good?" and "Is the greater good to which it might lead such that an omnipotent, omniscient being could not obtain it without permitting the fawn's suffering?" It may strike us as unlikely that the answer to the first question is yes. And it may strike us as quite a bit more unlikely that the answer to the second question is yes. But even if we should think it is reasonable to believe that the fawn's suffering leads to a greater good unobtainable without that suffering, we must then ask whether it is reasonable to believe that *all* the instances of profound, seemingly pointless human and animal suffering lead to greater goods. And, if they should somehow all lead to greater goods, is it reasonable to believe that an omnipotent, omniscient being *could not* have brought about *any* of those goods without permitting the instances of suffering which supposedly lead to them? When we consider these more general questions in the light of our experience and knowledge of the variety and profusion of human and animal suffering occurring daily in our world, it seems that the answer must be *no*. It seems quite unlikely that all the instances of intense human and animal suffering occurring daily in our world lead to greater goods, and even more unlikely that if they all do, an omnipotent, omniscient being could not have achieved at least some of those goods without permitting the instances of suffering that lead to them. In the light of our experience and knowledge of the variety and scale of human and animal suffering in our world, the idea that none of those instances of suffering could have been prevented by an omnipotent being without the loss of a greater good seems an extraordinary, absurd idea, quite beyond our belief. It seems then that although we cannot *prove* that premise 1 is true, it is, nevertheless, altogether *reasonable* to believe that 1 is true, that it is a *rational* belief.

Returning now to our argument for atheism, we've seen that the second premise expresses a basic belief common to theists and nontheists. We've also seen that our experience and knowledge of the variety and profusion of suffering in our world provides *rational support* for the first premise. Seeing that the conclusion, "There does not exist an omnipotent, omniscient, wholly good being" follows from these two premises, it does seem that we have *rational support* for atheism, that it is reasonable for us to believe that the theistic God does not exist.

RESPONSES TO THE EVIDENTIAL PROBLEM

Of the two forms of the problem of evil we've considered, the first (the *logical* form) was seen to be not a serious difficulty for theistic belief. The second form (the *evidential* form), has been seen to be a significant problem for theistic belief, for its basic thesis—that the variety and profusion of evil in our world provides rational support for atheism—has been shown to be plausible. It is time now to see how the theist might best respond to the evidential form of the problem of evil. The responses can best be explained in terms of the basic argument for atheism by means of which the evidential form of the problem of evil was presented. Indeed, the responses challenge either the first premise of that argument or the considerations advanced in support of it. We will consider two responses before looking at what is probably the best response open to the theist.

Fallacious Reasoning

The first response does not try to give any reasons for thinking that premise 1 is false. Instead, the theist here contends only that no good reasons have been given for thinking that premise 1 is true. Against the reasoning that was presented above in behalf of 1, the theist may endeavor to argue that the reasoning is fallacious, engaging in a faulty inference from "we don't know of any good that would justify an omnipotent being in permitting instances of suffering like the fawn's" to "there is no good that would justify an omnipotent being in permitting instances of suffering like the fawn's." Indeed, the theist might go on to argue that given the immense degree to which God's knowledge would exceed our own, it is somewhat likely that any good that would justify God in permitting instances of suffering like the fawn's would be beyond our ken, something that we shouldn't expect to comprehend.[3]

Theodicies

The second sort of response consists in presenting a *theodicy*, an attempt to explain what God's purposes might be for permitting the profusion of evil in our world. Unlike the first response, a theodicy endeavors to provide some reasons for thinking that premise 1 may be false. Rather than providing very brief comments about various theodicies—evil is punishment for sin, evil is due to free will, evil is necessary for us to appreciate good, etc.—it will be more helpful for us to look in some depth at one of the more promising theodicies, one developed and defended by a prominent contemporary philosopher, John Hick, and referred to as a theodicy of "soul-making."[4]

Before giving a synopsis of the soul-making theodicy, it will be helpful to reflect on the general bearing of theodicies on the evidential problem of evil. Just what does a theodicy endeavor to do? Does it propose to tell us in some detail just what good it is that justifies God in permitting the fawn's suffering? No. Such an account would presume a knowledge of God's specific purposes, a knowledge that it would be unreasonable to expect we would have without some detailed revelation from God. What a theodicy does endeavor to do is to fasten on some good (real or imaginary) and argue that achieving it would justify an omnipotent being in permitting evils like the fawn's suffering. Whether obtaining the good in question is God's actual reason for permitting evils like the fawn's suffering is not really part of what a theodicy tries to establish. It only hopes to show that *if* obtaining the good in question were God's aim in permitting evils like the fawn's suffering, then (given what we know) it would be reasonable to believe that an omnipotent being would be justified in permitting such evils. In this way, then, a theodicy endeavors to cast doubt on premise 1 in our argument from evil.

The fawn's suffering is an instance of *natural* evil, evil that results from natural forces. When a person tortures and kills an innocent child, the suffering of the child is an instance of *moral* evil, evil that results from the conscious decision of some personal agent. What goods does Hick think are served by the profusion of natural and moral evil in our world? There are two goods that figure in Hick's theodicy. The first is the state in which all human beings develop themselves through their free choices into moral and spiritual beings. The second is the state in which such beings enter into an eternal life of bliss and joy in fellowship with God. Let's begin our synopsis by considering the first of these states, the state in which all human beings develop themselves through their free choices into moral and spiritual beings. How might the obtaining of such a good justify an omnipotent, omniscient being in permitting evils like the fawn's suffering and the suffering of the innocent child who is brutally tortured and killed?

Since the fawn's suffering and the child's suffering are instances of natural and moral evil, different answers may be required. Let's begin with horrendous moral evils like the child's suffering while being tortured. Hick's first step is to argue that if moral and spiritual development through free choices is the good in question, then an environment in which there is no significant suffering, no occasion for significant moral choices, would not be one in which moral and spiritual growth would be possible. In particular, a world in which no one can harm another, in which no pain or suffering results from any action, would not be a world in which such moral and spiritual growth could occur.

I think we can concede to Hick that a pain-free paradise, a world in which no one could be injured and no one could do harm, would be a world devoid of significant moral and spiritual development. But what are we to make of the fact that the world we live in is so often inimical to such moral and spiritual development? For clearly, as Hick is careful to note, much of the pain and suffering in our world frustrates such development.

> The overall situation is thus that, so far as we can tell, suffering occurs haphazardly, uselessly, and therefore unjustly. It appears to be only randomly related either to past desert or to future soul-making. Instead of serving a constructive purpose, pain and misery seem to fall upon men patternlessly and meaninglessly, with the result that suffering is often underserved and often occurs in amounts exceeding anything that could have been morally planned.[5]

Hick's response to this point is to ask us what would happen were our world one in which suffering occurred " . . . not haphazardly and therefore unjustly, but on the contrary justly and therefore non-haphazardly."[6] In such a world, Hick reasons that people would avoid wrongdoing out of fear rather than from a sense of duty. Moreover, once we saw that suffering was always for the good of the sufferer, human misery would no longer " . . . evoke deep personal sympathy or call forth organized relief and sacrificial help and service. For it is presupposed in those compassionate reactions both that the suffering is not deserved and that it is *bad* for the sufferer."[7] Hick then concludes:

> It seems, then, that in a world that is to be the scene of compassionate love and self-giving for others, suffering must fall upon mankind with something of the haphazardness and inequity that we now experience. It must be apparently unmerited, pointless, and incapable of being morally rationalized. For it is precisely this feature of our common human lot that creates sympathy between man and man and evokes the unselfishness, kindness and goodwill which are among the highest values of personal life.[8]

Let's assume with Hick that an environment fit for human beings to develop the highest qualities of moral and spiritual life must be one that includes real suffering, hardships, disappointments, failure, and defeat. For moral and spiritual growth presuppose these. Let's also assume that such an environment must operate, at least for the most part, according to general and dependable laws, for only on the basis of such general laws can a person engage in the purposeful decision making essential to rational and moral life. And given these two assumptions it is, I think, understandable how an omniscient, omnipotent being may be morally justified in permitting the occurrence of evils, both moral and natural. Moreover, it is important, as Hick stresses, that it not be apparent to us that all the instances of suffering that occur are required for and result in the good of moral and spiritual growth. For then we would cease to strive to eliminate these evils and thereby diminish the very human struggles that so often bring about moral and spiritual development.

Our excursion into John Hick's theodicy has shown us, perhaps, how a theodicy may succeed in justifying God's permission of both natural and moral evil. But so far we haven't been given any justification for the permission of the fawn's awful suffering, nor have we a justification for the intense suffering of the innocent child who is brutally tortured and killed by an adult human being. In the case of the fawn's suffering we can say that given the existence of the animals in our world and the operation of the world according to natural laws, it is unavoidable that instances of intense and prolonged animal suffering would occur. In the case of the suffering of that particular innocent child we can say that on their way toward moral and spiritual development, it is perhaps unavoidable that human beings will sometimes seriously harm others through a bad use of freedom. But neither of these points will morally justify an omnipotent, omniscient being in permitting the suffering of that particular fawn or the suffering of that particular innocent child. It is simply unreasonable to believe that if the adult acted freely in brutally beating and killing that innocent child, his moral and spiritual development would have been permanently frustrated had he been prevented from doing what he did. And it is also unreasonable to believe that permitting such an act is morally justified even if preventing it would somehow diminish the perpetrator's moral and spiritual odyssey. And in the case of the fawn, it is simply unreasonable to believe that preventing its being severely burned, or mercifully ending its life so that it does not suffer intensely for several days, would so shake our confidence in the orderliness of nature that we would forsake our moral and spiritual development. Hick seems not unaware of this limitation to his theodicy, at least with respect to natural evils. With respect to human pain due to sources independent of the human will, he remarks:

> In response to it, theodicy, if it is wisely conducted, follows a negative path. It is not possible to show positively that each item of human pain serves God's purpose of good; on the other hand, it does seem possible to show that the divine purpose, [. . .] could not be forwarded in a world that was designed as a permanent hedonistic paradise.[9]

What we've seen is that Hick's theodicy fails if it is intended to provide a good that would justify an omnipotent, omniscient being in permitting the fawn's intense suffering or the innocent child's intense suffering. The best that Hick can do is to argue that a world *utterly devoid* of natural and moral evil would preclude the realization of the goods he postulates as justifying an omnipotent, omniscient being in permitting evil. However, since the prevention of the fawn's suffering or the innocent child's suffering would not leave our world utterly devoid of natural or moral evil, his all-or-nothing argument provides no answer to our question. Nor will it do to say that if an omnipotent, omniscient being were to prevent the suffering of the fawn or the innocent child it would thereby be obligated to prevent all such evils. For were it to do so it may well be, as Hick has argued, that we would cease to engage in very significant soul-making. The problem Hick's theodicy leaves us is that it is altogether reasonable to believe that some of the evils that occur could have been prevented without either diminishing our moral

and spiritual development or undermining our confidence that the world operates according to natural laws. Hick's theodicy, therefore, does not succeed in
providing a reason to reject premise 1, that there exist instances of suffering that
an omnipotent, omniscient being could have prevented without thereby preventing the occurrence of any greater good.

The "G. E. Moore Shift"

The best procedure for the theist to follow in rejecting premise 1 is an *indirect*
procedure. This procedure I shall call "the G. E. Moore shift," so called in honor
of the twentieth-century philosopher, G. E. Moore, who used it to great effect in
dealing with the arguments of the skeptics. Skeptical philosophers such as David
Hume have advanced ingenious arguments to prove that no one can know of the
existence of any material object. The premises of their arguments employ plausible principles, principles which many philosophers have tried to reject directly,
but only with questionable success. Moore's procedure was altogether different.
Instead of arguing directly against the premises of the skeptic's arguments, he
simply noted that the premises implied, for example, that he (Moore) did not
know of the existence of a pencil. Moore then proceeded indirectly against the
skeptic's premises by arguing:

I do know that this pencil exists.
If the skeptic's principles are correct I cannot know of the existence of this
    pencil.
Therefore,
The skeptic's principles (at least one) must be incorrect.

Moore then noted that his argument is just as valid as the skeptic's, that both of
their arguments contain the premise "If the skeptic's principles are correct Moore
cannot know of the existence of this pencil," and concluded that the only way to
choose between the two arguments (Moore's and the skeptic's) is by deciding
which of the first premises it is more rational to believe—Moore's premise "I do
know that this pencil exists" or the skeptic's premise asserting that certain
skeptical principles are correct. Moore concluded that his own first premise was
the more rational of the two.[10]

Before we see how the theist may apply the G. E. Moore shift to the basic
argument for atheism, we should note the general strategy of the shift. We're
given an argument: p, q, therefore, r. Instead of arguing *directly* against p, another
argument is constructed—not-r, q, therefore, not-p—which begins with the denial of the conclusion of the first argument, keeps its second premise, and ends
with the denial of the first premise as its conclusion. Let's compare these two:

I. p II. not-r
   q q
   r not-p

Now it is a truth of logic that if I is valid II must be valid as well. Since the
arguments are the same so far as the second premise is concerned, any choice

between them must concern their respective first premises. To argue against the first premise *p* by constructing the counterargument II is to employ the G. E. Moore shift.

Applying the G. E. Moore shift against the first premise of the basic argument for atheism, the theist can argue as follows:

not-3. There exists an omnipotent, omniscient, wholly good being.
2. An omniscient, wholly good being would prevent the occurrence of any intense suffering it could, unless it could not do so without thereby preventing the occurrence of some greater good.

Therefore,

not-1. It is not the case that there exist instances of intense suffering which an omnipotent, omniscient being could have prevented without thereby preventing the occurrence of any greater good.

We have now two arguments: the basic argument for atheism from 1 and 2 to 3, and the theist's best response, the argument from not-3 and 2 to not-1. What the theist then says about 1 is that he or she has rational grounds for believing in the existence of the theistic God not-3, accepts 2 as true, and sees that not-1 follows from not-3 and 2. The theist concludes, therefore, that he or she has rational grounds for rejecting 1. Having rational grounds for rejecting 1, the theist concludes that the basic argument for atheism is mistaken.

Argument and Response: An Assessment

It is now time to assess the relative merits of the basic argument for atheism as well as the theist's best response to it. Suppose that someone is in the position of having no rational grounds for thinking that the theistic God exists. Either this person has not heard of the arguments for the existence of God or has considered them but finds them altogether unconvincing. Perhaps, too, he or she has not had any visions of God and is rationally convinced that the religious experiences of others fail to provide any good grounds for theistic belief. Contemplating the variety and scale of human and animal suffering in our world, however, this individual concludes that it is altogether reasonable to accept premise 1 as true. It must be admitted, I think, that such a person is rationally justified in accepting atheism. Suppose, however, that another person has had religious experiences which justify her or him in believing that the theistic God exists. Perhaps, too, this person has carefully examined the Ontological Argument and found it rationally coercive. It must be admitted, I think, that such a person has some rational grounds for accepting theism. But what if this individual is aware of the basic argument for atheism and the considerations advanced in support of its first premise? In that case she or he will have some rational grounds for believing that theism is true and some rational grounds for believing that 1 is true, and, therefore, that theism is false. This person must then weigh the relative strength of his or her grounds for theism against his or her grounds for 1 and atheism. If the grounds for theism seem rationally stronger than the grounds for 1, this individual may reasonably reject 1, since its denial is implied by theism and 2. Of course, assessing the relative merit of competing rational grounds is no easy matter, but it seems clear that someone may be rationally justified in accepting theism and concluding that 1 and the basic argument for atheism are mistaken.

In terms of our own response to the basic argument for atheism and the theist's counter argument against 1, each of us must judge in the light of personal experience and knowledge whether our grounds for believing 1 are stronger or weaker than our grounds for believing that the theistic God exists. What we have seen is that since our experience and knowledge may differ it is possible, indeed likely, that some of us may be justified in accepting 1 and atheism, while others of us may be rationally justified in accepting theism and rejecting 1.

The conclusion to which we have come is that the evidential form of the problem of evil is a serious but not insurmountable problem for theism. To the extent that she or he has stronger grounds for believing that the theistic God exists than for accepting 1, the theist, on balance, may have more reason to reject 1 than she or he has for accepting it. However, in the absence of good reasons for believing that the theistic God exists, our study of the evidential form of the problem of evil has led us to the view that we rationally justified in accepting atheism.

We must not confuse the view that someone may be rationally justified in accepting theism, while someone else is rationally justified in accepting atheism, with the *incoherent* view that both theism and atheism may be true. Since theism (in the narrow sense) and atheism (in the narrow sense) express contradictory claims, one must be true and the other false. But since the evidence one possesses may justify one in believing a statement which, in the light of the total evidence, is a false statement, it is possible for different people to be rationally justified in believing statements which cannot both be true. Suppose, for example, a friend of yours takes a flight to Hawaii. Hours after takeoff you learn that the plane has gone down at sea. After a twenty-four hour search, no survivors have been found. Under these circumstances it is rational for you to believe that your friend has perished. But it is hardly rational for your friend to believe that while bobbing up and down in a life vest and wondering why the search planes have failed to spot her. Theism and atheism cannot both be true. But because of differing experience and knowledge, someone may be rationally justified in accepting theism while someone else is rationally justified in believing atheism.

Earlier we characterized a theist as someone who believes that the theistic God exists, and an atheist as someone who believes that the theistic God does not exist. In the light of our study of the problem of evil, perhaps we should introduce further distinctions. A *friendly atheist* is an atheist who believes that someone may well be rationally justified in believing that the theistic God exists. An unfriendly atheist is an atheist who believes that no one is rationally justified in believing that the theistic God exists. Similar distinctions are to be made with respect to theism and agnosticism. An *unfriendly agnostic*, for example, is an agnostic who thinks that no one is rationally justified in believing that the theistic God exists and no one is rationally justified in believing that the theistic God does not exist. Again, we must note that the friendly atheist (theist) does not believe that the theist (atheist) has a *true* belief, only that he or she may well be rationally justified in holding that belief. Perhaps the final lesson to be drawn from our study of the problem of evil is that the *friendly* versions of theism, agnosticism, and atheism are each preferable to their respective unfriendly versions.

Notes

1. Suppose, for example, that there are occasions when the act of *forgiving someone for an evil deed* is a good that outweighs the evil deed that is forgiven. Clearly, even an omnipotent being could not bring about this good without permitting the evil deed it outweighs. Again, *courageously bearing pain* might be a good that on occasion outweighs the evil of the pain that is courageously borne. But it is logically impossible for someone to bear courageously an evil pain, without the occurrence of an evil pain.
2. A more elaborate account of the Free Will Defense can be found in Alvin Plantinga, *God, Freedom, and Evil* (New York: Harper & Row, Publishers, 1974).
3. For some discussion of this first response see Steven Wykstra, "The Humean Obstacle to Evidential Arguments From Suffering: On Avoid the Evils of 'Appearance,'" *International Journal for the Philosophy of Religion* 16 (1984): pp. 73–93.
4. See *Evil and the God of Love* (New York: Harper and Row, 1966), particularly Ch. XVII of the revised edition, published in 1978, *God and the Universe of Faiths* (New York: St. Martin's Press, 1973), and Chapter Four of *Philosophy of Religion,* 3rd edition (Englewood Cliffs, New Jersey: Prentice-Hall, 1983).
5. *God and the Universe of Faiths,* p. 58.
6. *Ibid.*
7. *Ibid.,* p. 60.
8. *Ibid.*
9. *Philosophy of Religion,* p. 46.
10. See, for example, the two chapters on Hume in G. E. Moore, *Some Main Problems of Philosophy* (London: George Allen & Unwin Ltd., 1953).

Topics for Review

1. Explain the difference between the logical form of the problem of evil and the evidential form of the problem of evil.
2. What is the major difficulty with the central thesis of the logical form of the problem of evil?
3. How does the Free Will Defense bear on the logical form of the problem of evil?
4. Explain the basic argument for atheism that expresses the evidential form of the problem of evil. What responses might the theist make to this argument?
5. Explain the difference between friendly atheism (theism) and unfriendly atheism (theism). Why might the friendly versions be preferable to the unfriendly versions?

Topics for Futher Study

6. Discuss the central issue between the theist and the atheist concerning the evidential form of the problem of evil. Which do you think has the better argument? Explain.
7. Discuss the following argument:
   The fact of suffering in the world doesn't constitute a genuine problem for Christianity because, according to Christianity, no real comparison can be made between the momentary misery experienced in this life and the eternal joy and bliss that Christianity promises in the life to come.

Chapter

7

THE MEANINGFULNESS OF RELIGIOUS LANGUAGE

When theists assert that God created the heavens and the earth, that he loves his creatures, that he knows whatever will come to pass, they believe that what they assert is true. As we have seen, critics of theism have generally held that the claims of theists are either false or groundless in the sense that there are no good reasons for thinking them to be true. In recent times, however, some critics have challenged the meaningfulness of the claims of theism. They have argued that the assertions of theism are meaningless and, therefore, neither true nor false. In this chapter we shall consider this more recent attack on theism and have a look at some attempts to explain how religious assertions are meaningful.

LOGICAL POSITIVISM

The charge that religious assertions are meaningless, mere nonsense, was forcefully made by the proponents of a philosophical movement called *Logical Positivism*. Logical Positivism began in the 1920s with a group of philosophers meeting in Vienna, a group known as "the Vienna Circle."[1] But its most popular spokesman was the English philosopher A. J. Ayer, who in 1936 wrote the major manifesto of the movement, *Language, Truth, and Logic.* In this book Ayer set forth the basic thesis of Logical Positivism and drew its implications for theology and much of traditional philosophy. The implications were quite alarming: theology and much of traditional philosophy were found to be *literally meaningless.* The thesis that led to this staggering judgment is called "The Verifiability Principle of Meaning." Since this principle lies behind so many of the recent attacks against the meaningfulness of religious assertions, it will be useful to examine it briefly.

The Verifiability Principle of Meaning

The Verifiability Principle of Meaning says that a statement is literally meaningful just in case it is either analytic or empirically verifiable. Analytic statements are all those statements whose truth or falsehood follows from the meaning of the words used in making the statements. "All bachelors are unmarried," "Either Mary is over six feet tall or Mary is not over six feet tall," "Some triangles have more than three angles" are all analytic statements. Once we understand the meaning of the words used in these statements we see immediately that the first two must be true, whereas the last must be false. "Smith is a bachelor," "Joan is over six feet tall," "God exists," "Columbus discovered America," are statements which aren't analytic. And what the principle says about all such statements (nonanalytic statements) is that they are literally meaningful only if they are empirically verifiable.

What does it mean to say of a statement that it is empirically verifiable? As we shall see, this question became a major stumbling block for Logical Positivism. But for the moment we can answer the question in an informal way as follows: A statement is empirically verifiable just in case some possible sense-experience is relevant to the determination of its truth or falsehood. Consider, for example, the statement "There are flowers growing on the planet Neptune." This statement is certainly not analytic. According to the verifiability principle of meaning, therefore, it is literally meaningful only if it is logically possible that we should have some sense-experience that would count for its truth or falsehood. Although it is perhaps technically impossible—we don't have the physical means of going to Neptune or seeing it up close—to have some sense-experience that would tend to confirm the presence or absence of flowers on Neptune, there is no logical impossibility, no contradiction in the idea that a human being should be present on Neptune and have visual experiences of flowers growing there. So the statement "There are flowers growing on the planet Neptune" is literally meaningful, for it is empirically verifiable, even though we cannot now in fact verify it.

The idea of empirical verification seems, on the surface at least, to be quite liberal. It is not required that any human being has verified a statement in order for it to be meaningful. Nor is it required that the statement be confirmed or disconfirmed throughout the course of human history. All that is required is that it be *logically possible* for some human being to have some sense-experience that is relevant to determining whether the statement is true or false. If this is not logically possible, if it is inconceivable that any sense experience should count for or against the statement, then, according to the principle, the statement is literally meaningless, it is neither true nor false.

Implications for Philosophy and Theology

As liberal as the idea of empirical verification may seem to be, the logical positivists argued that the statements of theology and many of the cherished doctrines of traditional philosophy fail to qualify as empirically verifiable and, therefore, are literally meaningless. Consider, for example, the statement "The Absolute enters into, but is itself incapable of, evolution and progress," a statement which Ayer tells us he has taken at random from *Appearance and Reality*, the major work of the English idealist philosopher F. H. Bradley (1846–1924).[2] As Ayer notes, this statement "is not even in principle verifiable. For one cannot conceive of an observation which would enable one to determine whether the

Absolute did, or did not, enter into evolution and progress."[3] Since the statement is clearly not analytic, Ayer concludes that it is nonsense, literally meaningless.

Ayer draws a similar conclusion about such basic theological assertions as "There exists a transcendent god."[4] For no possible sense experience could show that such a statement is true or false. So the basic statements of theology, like those of much traditional philosophy, are void of literal meaning. What meaning they do possess may be poetic or emotional, but they cannot convey any information about the nature of reality. Only statements that are literally meaningful are capable of truth or falsehood. And only statements that are true can convey information about the nature of reality.

Ayer is careful to point out that the logical positivist's position concerning theism is not to be confused with either atheism or agnosticism.

It is important not to confuse this view of religious assertions with the view that is adopted by atheists, or agnostics. For it is characteristic of an agnostic to hold that the existence of a god is a possibility in which there is no good reason either to believe or disbelieve; and it is characteristic of an atheist to hold that it is at least probable that no god exists. And our view that all utterances about the nature of God are nonsensical, so far from being identical with, or even lending any support to, either of these familiar contentions, is actually incompatible with them. For if the assertion that there is a god is nonsensical, then the atheist's assertion that there is no god is equally nonsensical, since it is only a significant proposition that can be significantly contradicted. As for the agnostic, although he refrains from saying either that there is or that there is not a god, he does not deny that the question whether a transcendent god exists is a genuine question. He does not deny that the two sentences "There is a transcendent god" and "There is no transcendent god" express propositions one of which is actually true and the other false. All he says is that we have no means of telling which of them is true, and therefore ought not to commit ourselves to either. But we have seen that the sentences in question do not express propositions at all. And this means that agnosticism also is ruled out.[5]

OBJECTIONS TO LOGICAL POSITIVISM

Although Logical Positivism attracted many disciples and fellow travelers, at least among Anglo-American philosophers, it has not survived as a viable philosophical position. Indeed, from the very beginning serious objections were raised concerning its basic thesis, the verifiability principle of meaning, objections which were never satisfactorily answered. Among these objections, three are worth noting.

The question was raised as to whether the verifiability principle of meaning passes its own test for being literally meaningful. The statement "A statement is literally meaningful just in case it is either analytic or empirically verifiable" is not an analytic statement. Is it then empirically verifiable? Can we gather evidence for its truth or falsehood? To admit that we can is to imply that it is a general claim about meaningful statements, and not itself the *test* by which we are to determine whether a statement is meaningful or not. Moreover, since many people profess to find the statement "God exists" a meaningful statement, then if "God exists" is neither analytic nor empirically verifiable, it may well be that the positivist's thesis is false. In response to this objection the positivists took the view that the verifiability principle of meaning is not itself a statement at all. It is, they responded, more like a rule or proposal that we should follow or adopt. But then, the objection continues, why should we adopt this proposal rather than some other proposal that allows theological statements to be meaningful? To this, the positivists were able to give a reply that convinced no one other than those already committed to the verification principle.

A second objection concerned what appeared to many to be an arbitrary limitation of experience to sense experience: tasting, touching, smelling, seeing, and hearing. Mystical experience, for example, is not sense experience. Why is it excluded from those experiences which might confirm or refute a statement?

Perhaps the most serious objection to be raised concerned the notion of empirical verifiability. We gave an informal explanation of this notion in terms of the *relevance* of some possible sense experience to the determination of a statement's truth or falsehood. But how are we to spell out this test more exactly? In the first edition of *Language, Truth, and Logic,* Ayer tried to clarify the test by stating that a statement S is empirically verifiable just in case some sense experience statement could be deduced from S "in conjunction with certain other premises without being deducible from those other premises alone."[6] Within a very short time, however, it was pointed out by Isaiah Berlin that Ayer's criterion allows meaning to any statement whatever.[7] Take any statement S, say, "The Absolute is lazy." According to Ayer's criterion "The Absolute is lazy" is empirically verifiable and, therefore, literally meaningful if some sense experience statement can be deduced from it in conjunction with some other premise without being deducible from that premise alone. But if we accept "This ball is red" as a sense experience statement we can easily satisfy Ayer's criterion by taking as our other premise "If the Absolute is lazy then this ball is red." Our sense experience statement "This ball is red" is deducible from "The Absolute is lazy" in conjunction with our other premise "If the Absolute is lazy then this ball is red," without being deducible from that premise alone.

In the introduction to the second edition of *Language, Truth, and Logic,* published in 1946, Ayer acknowledged the difficulty and offered a second, far more complicated explanation of the criterion for determining whether a statement is empirically verifiable.[8] In a review of the second edition of this famous book, however, the logician Alonzo Church was able to show that Ayer's revised criterion still allowed meaning to any statement whatever.[9] And since then the fortunes of the verifiability principle of meaning have not substantially improved. Either the principle has been stated in so restricted a form as to deprive significant scientific hypotheses of literal meaning or it has been stated in such a way that critics like Berlin and Church have been able to show that it allows literal meaning to any statement whatever.[10]

LINGERING DOUBTS

As a result of the above objections, as well as other criticisms, Logical Positivism is largely a thing of the past. There has remained, however, a feeling that the statements of theology and much of traditional philosophy are somehow suspect, that if they yield no empirical consequences they are not really meaning-ful at all. This feeling surfaced in the 1950s with the publication of "Theology and Falsification," a discussion initiated by the English philosopher Antony Flew.[11] Flew began his discussion by relating a parable.

> Once upon a time two explorers came upon a clearing in the jungle. In the clearing were growing many flowers and many weeds. One explorer says, "Some gardener must tend this plot." The other disagrees. "There is no gardener." So they pitch their tents and set a watch. No gardener is ever seen. "But perhaps he is an invisible gardener." So they set up a barbed-wire fence. They electrify it. They patrol with bloodhounds. . . . But no shrieks ever suggest that some intruder has received a shock. No movements of the wire ever betray an invisible climber. The bloodhounds never give cry. Yet still the Believer is not convinced. "But there is a gardener, invisible, intangible, insensible to electric shocks, a gardener who has no scent and makes no sound, a gardener who comes secretly to look after the garden which he loves." At last the Sceptic despairs. "But what remains of your original assertion? Just how does what you call an invisible, intangible, eternally elusive gardener differ from an imaginary gardener or even from no gardener at all?"[12]

The point of Flew's parable is that what appears to be a significant assertion, "There is a gardener who tends this plot," turns out on inspection to be quite empty of content, for nothing that happens is allowed to count as evidence against it. But if an assertion is held to be compatible with whatever happens, it's clear that it makes no significant assertion at all. Flew then applies the point to the claims of religion.

> Now it often seems to people who are not religious as if there was no conceivable event or series of events the occurrence of which would be admitted by sophisticated religious people to be a sufficient reason for conceding "There wasn't a God after all" or "God does not really love us then." Someone tells us that God loves us as a father loves his children. We are reassured. But then we see a child dying of inoperable cancer of the throat. His earthly father is driven frantic in his efforts to help, but his Heavenly Father reveals no obvious sign of concern. Some qualification is made—God's love is "not merely human love" or it is "an inscrutable love", perhaps—and we realize that such sufferings are quite compatible with the truth of the assertion that "God loves us as a father (but, of course, . . .)". We are reassured again. But then perhaps we ask: what is this assurance of God's (appropriately qualified) love worth, what is this apparent guarantee really a guarantee against? Just what would have to happen not merely (morally and wrongly) to tempt but also (logically and rightly) to entitle us to say "God does not love us" or even "God does not exist"? . . . "What would have to occur or to have occurred to constitute for you a disproof of the love of, or of the existence of God?"[13]

What is Flew's argument against the meaningfulness of religious assertions like "God loves his creatures"? Perhaps it goes as follows:

1. If religious people deny (or would deny) that any conceivable event or series of events would count against the assertion "God loves his creatures" then "God loves his creatures" is not a meaningful assertion.

2. Religious people deny (or would deny) that any conceivable event or series of events would count against the assertion "God loves his creatures."

Therefore,

3. "God loves his creatures" is not a meaningful assertion.[14]

Assertions and Bliks

Before we examine Flew's argument in detail, there is one rather "radical" response to it that merits attention. The English philosopher R. M. Hare took the view in response to Flew that Flew had missed the whole point about religion in general and Christianity in particular. In saying "God loves his creatures," the religious person, Hare contended, is not trying to make an *assertion* at all, so it should not be in the least surprising that nothing is allowed to count against what he or she says. What then is the religious individual doing? To answer this question, Hare introduced the word *blik* and replies that in saying "God loves his creatures" the religious person is not making an *assertion*, but giving voice to a *blik*. *Bliks* are not assertions, for whereas what happens in the world can count against an assertion, nothing is allowed to count against a *blik*. To illustrate his point Hare relates another parable.

> A certain lunatic is convinced that all dons want to murder him. His friends introduce him to all the mildest and most respectable dons that they can find, and after each of them has retired, they say, "You see, he doesn't really want to murder you; he spoke to you in a most cordial manner; surely you are convinced now?" But the lunatic replies "Yes, but that was only his diabolical cunning; he's really plotting against me the whole time, like the rest of them; I know it I tell you". However many kindly dons are produced, the reaction is still the same.[15]

Hare notes that since there is no behavior of the dons that the lunatic will allow to count against "All the dons want to murder me," if we apply Flew's test it will follow that the lunatic isn't asserting anything at all. But granting Flew this point, it is still very important to recognize the profound difference between what the lunatic thinks about the dons and what his friends think about them. If there were no such difference, we would not call him a lunatic and the dons would have no reason to be uneasy about him.

> Let us call that in which we differ from this lunatic, our respective *bliks*. He has an insane *blik* about dons; we have a sane one. It is important to realize that we have a sane one, not no *blik* at all; for there must be two sides to any argument—if he has a wrong *blik*, then those who are right about dons must have a right one. Flew has shown that a *blik* does not consist in an assertion or system of them; but nevertheless it is very important to have the right *blik*.[16]

Summarizing Hare's remarks about *bliks*, we can note four points:

1. *Bliks are not assertions.*
   Events can count against an assertion, but nothing is allowed to count against a *blik*.

2. *There is a right and a wrong blik.*
   The lunatic has a wrong *blik.* It is not that his friends have no *blik;* they have a *blik* too, only they have the right *blik.*
3. *It makes an enormous difference to your feelings, attitudes, and behavior as to which blik you have.*
4. *Differences between bliks cannot be settled by observation of what happens in the world.*

Hare thinks Flew has misunderstood the purpose of sentences like "God exists" and "God loves his creatures." Flew is right in pointing out that religious people allow nothing to count against them. He is also right in concluding that, if in uttering these sentences religious people were engaged in making *assertions,* the fact that they allow nothing to count against them would show their assertions to be meaningless. Where Flew goes wrong, according to Hare, is in thinking that the sentences are used to make assertions; instead, they are used to express a religious *blik* about the world.

The chief difficulty with Hare's view is that his notion of a *blik,* attractive as it otherwise may be, does not seem to be coherent. The difficulty is due to Hare's need to make some judgment about *bliks,* to sort out insane or wrong *bliks* from sane or right *bliks.* Thus the lunatic has an insane *blik,* whereas his friends have a sane *blik.* But on what grounds is one *blik* said to be insane and the other sane?

> Surely this, that the graduate holds to his theory in the face of any and all observations that can be made concerning the behavior of dons (this is why he is said to be a lunatic), whereas his friends *do* allow the behaviour of dons to count. And if the behavior of dons had been other than it was (if dons had been creeping around after dark with guns and knives and pots of poison) then the opinion of the lunatic's friends would have been other than it was. This is why they are said to be sane. But then what *they* say about dons is *falsifiable,* and if *that* is so, then they, unlike the lunatic, haven't a "blik" about dons at all. They make factual claims. The right "blik" turns out not to be a "blik" at all.[17]

In a response to Hare, Flew insists "that any attempt to analyse Christian religious utterances as expressions or affirmations of a *blik* rather than as (at least would-be) assertions about the cosmos is fundamentally misguided."[18] His basic reason for saying this is that such an interpretation is quite opposed to the interpretation Christians generally give of their own religious utterances. "If Hare's religion really is a *blik,* involving no cosmological assertions about the nature and activities of a supposed personal creator, then surely he is not a Christian at all?"[19]

Evaluating the Doubts

Having taken a look at a somewhat "radical" attempt to answer Flew's argument against the meaningfulness of religious claims, we can now examine his argument more directly, probing it for weaknesses and hidden assumptions. For a start, we might challenge the second premise of his argument, pointing out that religious people would regard certain events, should they occur, as counting rather decisively against "God loves his creatures." Suppose, for example, God suddenly began to hate us, or to feel extremely jealous of his creatures. Surely most religious people would view such a turn of events as counting rather decisively against "God loves his creatures." Still, it might be objected, many religious thinkers hold that God's love for his creatures is *necessary*, so that it really is *inconceivable* that God should suddenly begin to hate us. And what Flew's second premise asserts is that religious people would deny that any *conceivable* event counts against "God loves his creatures." But either "God loves his creatures" is viewed as necessarily true or it is not. If it is not, then God's hating us is a *conceivable* event and would be regarded as counting against "God loves his creatures." If "God loves his creatures" is thought to be *necessarily true*, and "God exists" is viewed as having the same status, then perhaps no *conceivable* event would be allowed to count against "God loves his creatures." But the fact that no conceivable event counts against "$2 + 2 = 4$" does not rob that statement of meaning, so why should we worry about the meaningfulness of "God loves his creatures?"

In the face of this straight-forward rejection of the second premise of his argument, it's clear how Flew would respond. "God hates us" is as much in jeopardy as "God loves his creatures." The point is not whether absolutely *any* event would count against "God loves his creatures" but whether any *empirical* event would do so—an event that happens in our everyday world. If nothing that happens in the world of everyday human experience counts against "God loves his creatures," if God's love for us is compatible with absolutely any series of empirical happenings, if the supposed fact that God loves us rules out no conceivable developments in the world we live in, then the claim that God loves us seems empty of any real significance at least so far as our life in this world goes.

Our first probe of Flew's argument has shown that his view is closer to the positivist's empirical verification criterion of meaning than our original statement of his argument suggested. And we had best recognize this explicitly by inserting *empirical* between *conceivable* and *event* in both premises of the argument. The second premise will now read:

2a. Religious people deny (or would deny) that any conceivable, empirical event would count against the assertion "God loves his creatures."

We will then have two interpretations of Flew's view. If 2a is true then Flew holds either that "God loves his creatures" is *absolutely meaningless* (first view) or that "God loves his creatures" has *no significance so far as our lives in this world go* (second view). On the second view Flew may allow that "God loves his creatures" is meaningful and, hence, either true or false. But his point would be that it has no significance in terms of what happens to us during our earthly lives—whatever happens in the daily world of human experience is compatible with the truth or falsehood of "God loves his creatures," nothing counts for or against it. For our purposes, we need not trouble ourselves with which of these two is the view Flew actually holds. The weaker of the two views, the second, is more defensible than the first and is still troublesome for theology, so we shall concern ourselves with it. What we shall say, however, applies equally well to the first view.

Many religious thinkers, I think, would deny the second premise of Flew's argument, both in its original (2) and in its revised (2a) form. They would insist that God's love for his creatures does have implications for how things go in the world of everyday human experience. God is not an absentee landlord who has set the world in motion and forgotten about it. They would insist, therefore, that there are conceivable events or developments in the world that, should they occur, would count against God's love for his creatures.

Again, then, it seems that Flew's argument falters on a false premise, premise 2a. Flew's response undoubtedly would be to ask religious thinkers to *specify* exactly what empirical happenings are ruled out by God's love for his creatures. Is another Vietnam ruled out, an all-out nuclear war, another political leader like Hitler? If the religious person cannot say precisely what conceivable events are actually ruled out, then the claim that some such events are ruled out is insignificant.

But here, I think, Flew and the theists are locked in battle over an issue that cannot easily be decided in Flew's favor. For we need to distinguish between

  i) the claim that there are some conceivable empirical events that are ruled out by God's love for his creatures.

and,

  ii) the claim that we can *specify* what empirical events are ruled out by God's love for his creatures.

Theists, holding as they do that God exercises providential care over his creation, are prepared to assent to (i). They believe that God's love for us is *not* compatible with absolutely any conceivable empirical happenings in the world. But they also hold that it is not given to us in this life to understand fully the workings of God's providence. They believe that only in the next life will we understand how and why the things that have happended to us in this life are manifestations of God's providence and loving care. Therefore, theists are not able to assent to (ii). They cannot *specify* exactly what those empirical events are that, should they occur, would give us grounds for concluding that God does not love us. Is this position unreasonable? It hardly seems to be. But it does seem clear that Flew's second premise, in both its original and revised form, is incorrect. Perhaps, then, Flew's argument is best formulated as follows:

  1c. If religious people are unable to *specify* exactly what conceivable, empirical event or series of events would count against the assertion "God loves his creatures" then "God loves his creatures" is not a meaningful assertion.
  2c. Religious people are unable to *specify* exactly what conceivable, empirical event or series of events would count against the assertion "God loves his creatures."

Therefore,

3. "God loves his creatures" is not a meaningful assertion.

Concerning this final version of Flew's argument, I've already indicated that the theist will accept 2c but reject 1c. Is 1c true? It seems to me unlikely that it is. What can be said, I suppose, is that the theist has a fuller grasp of human love than he or she has of divine love. For in the case of human love the theist has a better grasp of just what the empirical events are that would count against the claim that some particular human being loves us. But this hardly implies that "God loves his creatures" is empty of significance, and it is a position that theists themselves have long held. I conclude, therefore, that neither the basic thesis of Logical Positivism nor the somewhat less stringent line of argument proposed by Flew has succeeded in showing either that theological statements such as "God loves his creatures" are meaningless or without any implications concerning life in this world.

THE CONTINUING EFFORT TO ESTABLISH MEANINGFULNESS

If the major attempts to show that religious language is meaningless are unsuccessful, as they seem to be, there remains the problem of explaining how they are meaningful and what, in particular, they mean. In the final part of this chapter we shall have a look at this problem and consider one of the theories concerning the meaning of religious discourse that has arisen in response to it.

"God made the heavens and the earth," "God loves his creatures," "God forgives the sins of those who truly turn unto him" and a host of other sentences constitute an essential part of religious discourse, particularly within theistic religions. The problem of explaining how these sentences are meaningful and what, in particular, they mean arises mainly from two features thought to be essential features of the theistic God. The first of these is that God is an *eternal* being. (Actually, the problem arises only in connection with the second sense of *eternal*: that God is timeless, outside of time. But since so many traditional theologians have held that God is eternal in the sense of timeless, we can accurately say that for a number of traditional theologians *timelessness* is an essential feature of the theistic God.) If God is eternal in the sense of being outside of time, what can possibly be meant by ascribing action terms like *making* or *forgiving* to God? For surely the activities expressed by these terms take *time* for their performance. If someone has forgiven you, it makes sense to ask *when* he or she performed this act. But if God is timeless, it makes no sense to ask *when* he performed some act. The clear implication, then, of the idea that God is timeless is that action terms like *making* and *forgiving* cannot be used with their primary or literal meaning when they are ascribed to God. If so, then what do they mean when we ascribe them to God?

The second essential feature of the theistic God that gives rise to the need for explaining how our talk about God is meaningful is that he is a *purely spiritual, immaterial* being. In recognition of this, a number of traditional theologians have distinguished between predicate expressions which in their primary meaning refer either to parts of a body (for example, *hand* or *face*) or to activities impossible without a body (for example, *walking* or *drinking*) and predicate expressions which in their primary meaning refer to properties of the mind or to mental activities (for example, *wise, just, merciful*, or *loving*). Expressions of the first kind cannot be predicated *properly* (that is, with their primary meaning) of God. For since God does not have a body, to apply them properly to him would result either in contradiction or nonsense. Thus, such expressions may be predicated of God only metaphorically. Expressions of the second kind, it is felt, can be predicated properly of God.

One major difficulty with the view that terms which seem to designate mental activities (*forgiving* or *loving*) can be applied to God in their primary or literal sense is that the ways in which we tell whether an individual is forgiving or just do include *bodily behavior*—what she or he says and how she or he behaves. How then does one determine that a purely immaterial being has performed an act of forgiveness?[20]

Among the theories which endeavor to explain how predicates, whose primary meaning is acquired in relation to human beings (*loving, forgiving*, and so forth), are to be understood when applied to God, perhaps the major theory is the theory of Analogy, a theory found in the writings of Aquinas and his commentator Cajetan.[21] According to this theory, predicate expressions like *just* and *merciful* do not have the same meaning when applied to creatures as they do when applied to God. Nor are they used in an entirely different sense, as, for example, the term *bank* is used to mean both a financial institution and the ridge of earth bordering a river. That is, terms like *just* and *merciful* when used of God and creatures are used neither *univocally* (with the same meaning) nor *equivocally* (with a purely different meaning); they are, according to the theory, used *analogously*.

The two sorts of analogous predication most important for this theory of religious language are analogy of attribution and analogy of proportionality. A classical example of the former is the application of the term *healthy* to both a person and his or her complexion. The same term is applied to both the person and the complexion because of a certain relation between a healthy human being and a healthy complexion; namely, the latter is a sign of the former. Health belongs primarily to the person and only secondarily to the complexion. But when we say "God lives" and "that person lives," what is the relation between the life of God and life of a human being? According to this traditional theory the analogy is based on the causal relation. Since God causes life in his creatures, he has life in whatever way he must in order to create life in human beings. The difficulty with this view is that it leaves us in the dark as to the nature of the Divine Life, for all it strictly implies is that God causes life in people. Another difficulty is that the term *cause* as applied to both finite things and to God presumably would have to be elucidated by the theory as well. And we could not use the causal relation between causal activity in God and causal activity in people in order to explain how the term *cause* is meaningfully applied to God.

The analogy of attribution supposes that just as *healthy* belongs primarily to a person and only secondarily to one's complexion, so *life* belongs primarily to God and only in a derivative sense to his creatures. The analogy of proportionality, however, supposes that *life* belongs properly to both God and humans. But *life* does not denote in God what it denotes in humans, for the sort of life God has is determined by the kind of being he is and the sort of life people have is determined by the kind of beings they are. Thus we have an analogy of proportionality: God's life is to his being as an individual's life is to her or his being. The major difficulty with this view, however, is that since God's nature or being is so little understood by us, we are unable to understand very well the kind of life God has. Some modern exponents of the theory of analogy have suggested that a satisfactory theory of religious meaning would require a combination of both the analogy of attribution and the analogy of proportionality.[22]

Clearly a major task for theologians and philosophers of religion is to develop a satisfactory theory explaining how predicates taken from the human, finite realm can be meaningfully applied to an infinite, timeless, purely spiritual being.

Notes

1. For an excellent, brief account of Logical Positivism, as well as other developments in English philosophy in this century, see G. J. Warnock, *English Philosophy Since 1900* (New York: Oxford University Press, 1966).
2. A. J. Ayer, *Language, Truth, and Logic*, 2d ed. (New York: Dover Publication, Inc., 1946), p. 36.
3. Ayer, *Language, Truth, and Logic*, p. 36.
4. Ayer, *Language, Truth, and Logic*, pp. 114–20.
5. Ayer, *Language, Truth, and Logic*, pp. 115–16.
6. Ayer, *Language, Truth, and Logic*, p. 39.
7. Isaiah Berlin, "Verifiability in Principle," *Proceedings of the Aristotelian Society*, XXXIX. (1938–1939), pp. 225–248.
8. Ayer, *Language, Truth, and Logic*, p. 13.
9. Alonzo Church, "Review of 2nd edition of *Language, Truth, and Logic*," *Journal of Symbolic Logic*, XIV (1949), p. 53.
10. For a more detailed account of the difficulties affecting the verifiability principle of meaning see Alvin Plantinga, *God and Other Minds* (Ithaca, New York: Cornell University Press, 1967), pp. 156–68.
11. Antony Flew, "Theology and Falsification," in *New Essays in Philosophical Theology*, eds. Antony Flew and Alasdair MacIntyre (London: SCM Press, 1955), pp. 96–130.
12. Antony Flew, *New Essays in Philosophical Theology*, p. 96.
13. Antony Flew, *New Essays in Philosophical Theology*, pp. 98–99.
14. For "God loves his creatures" Flew would be prepared to substitute any of a large number of theological claims, so his argument is meant to be a quite general attack on theology.
15. Antony Flew, *New Essays in Philosophical Theology*, pp. 99–100.
16. Antony Flew, *New Essays in Philosophical Theology*, p. 100.
17. D. R. Duff-Forbes, "Theology and Falsification Again," *Australasian Journal of Philosophy*, XXXIX, No. 2(1961), p. 145.
18. Antony Flew, *New Essays in Philosophical Theology*, pp. 107–108.
19. Antony Flew, *New Essays in Philosophical Theology*, p. 108.
20. For a penetrating discussion of this and related questions see William P. Alston, "The Elucidation of Religious Statements," in *The Hartshorne Festschrift: Process and Divinity*,

eds. William L. Reese and Eugene Freeman (La Salle, Illinois: Open Court Publishing Co., 1964), pp. 429–443.

21. See *Summa Theologica*, pt. I, Question 12, Articles 1–12. Also see Thomas De Vio, Cardinal Cajetan, *The Analogy of Names*, 2nd ed. (Pittsburg, Pa.: Duquesne University Press, 1959).

22. See E. L. Mascall, *Existence and Analogy* (New York: Longman Group Limited, 1949), pp. 101–115.

Topics for Review

1. What is the Verifiability Principle of Meaning and what implication was it thought to have for theological statements?
2. Explain the three objections that were raised against the Verifiability Principle of Meaning.
3. Explain Flew's argument against the meaningfulness of religious assertions. How did Hare try to answer Flew? Is his answer successful?
4. For what reasons might we reject Flew's argument against the meaningfulness of religious assertions?
5. What features of the theistic God give rise to the problem of explaining how religious statements are meaningful? What is the theory of analogy and how is it supposed to deal with this problem? Is it successful?

Topics for Further Study

6. Compare the statements "There is a gardener who tends this plot" and "There is a God who cares for his creatures." What sort of evidence might be used to support or reject each statement? Do you think the claim that God cares for his creatures is a hypothesis that can be supported or rejected by evidence based on human experience in this life? Explain.
7. Do you think that terms like *love* and *power* change their meaning when applied to God? If so, what do you think they do mean when applied to God? Explain.

8

FREUD AND
RELIGIOUS BELIEF

Among the major figures of the nineteenth and twentieth centuries, perhaps only Darwin (1809–1882) and Marx (1818–1883) come close to matching the impact of Sigmund Freud (1856–1939) on humanity's understanding of itself and its place within nature and society. In this chapter we shall examine Freud's theory of religion. In particular, we shall study the account he gives both for the emergence of religious ideas within civilization and for their being so readily accepted by continuing generations. We shall then consider Freud's view of the psychological status and role of religion in society, as well as his hope that civilization will one day outgrow its need for religion. And finally, we shall consider the extent to which Freud's account of religious beliefs, if it should be true, tends to show that the basic claims of theism are false.

THE EMERGENCE OF RELIGIOUS IDEAS

Although Freud wrote several books about religion, the simplest and clearest account of his ideas is contained in *The Future of an Illusion*.[1] In this book Freud gives an account of why religious ideas emerged in human civilization and why they have remained so attractive to continuing generations. His explanation has three parts to it, only one of which is the direct result of his own original psychological theory concerning what takes place in a person's unconscious life. The first part begins with the obvious truth that people were born into an unfriendly world where at every turn the forces of nature threaten to destroy them—earthquake, flood, famine, storm, disease, and inevitable death. "With these forces nature rises up against us, majestic, cruel and inexorable."[2] Out of fear, then, of the hostile forces of nature, the first development of religious ideas takes place: people *personify* the inimical forces of nature in the hope of gaining some measure of control over them.

Impersonal forces and destinies cannot be approached; they remain eternally remote. But if the elements have passions that rage as they do in our own souls, if death itself is not something spontaneous but the violent act of an evil Will, if everywhere in nature there are Beings around us of a kind that we know in our own society, then we can breathe freely, can feel at home in the uncanny and can deal by psychical means with our senseless anxiety. We are still defenceless, perhaps, but we are no longer helplessly paralysed; we can at least react. Perhaps, indeed, we are not even defenceless. We can apply the same methods against these violent supermen outside that we employ in our own society; we can try to adjure them, to appease them, to bribe them, and, by so influencing them, we may rob them of a part of their power.[3]

The birth of humanity's belief in gods is due in large part to its fear of the untamed forces of nature. And a major purpose of the store of religious ideas that came to be formed about the gods is to allay our fears and anxieties caused by the powers of nature. However, not only nature threatens humankind, human civilization itself is felt by us as a great burden. And the second part of Freud's explanation of the emergence and attractiveness of religious ideas concerns the way in which they serve to bring relief from the suffering, privations, and frustrations imposed on human life by the very social structures that enable us to survive at all.

Apparently, Freud sees human beings as by nature aggressive, seeking their own personal ends without regard to the wants and needs of others. Civilization with its rules and institutions, while essential for human survival, brings with it *coercion* and *suppression* of some of our deepest natural urges and instincts. And, whether aware of it or not, people feel an enormous hostility toward society for the sacrifices it forces upon them. Thus, for Freud, the defense of civilization against human hostility toward it is a matter of great concern. And one of the major functions of religion is to defend civilization by compensating people for the sufferings and privations which a civilized life in common has imposed upon them. Why should it matter, for example, if the rules of society prevent us from simply taking what we want, if in the life hereafter we will be rewarded for living in accordance with the rules of society? Thus, religious beliefs serve not only to allay our fears of untamed nature, they also serve to reconcile us to the sacrifices society imposes upon us. Religious ideas perform these tasks by (1) enabling us to see all of nature under the ultimate control of a powerful, benevolent being whom we might influence in our favor, and (2) by sanctioning the basic rules of society and promising in the life to come to make up for the injustices and sacrifices we must bear in this life.

Thus far we have considered two of the three parts that are woven together by Freud into an explanation both of the emergence of religious beliefs within civilization and the continuing power of religious ideas on succeeding generations. He speaks of these two parts as "motives." "I have tried to show that religious ideas have arisen from the same need as have all the other achievements of civilization: from the necessity of defending oneself against the crushingly superior force of nature. To this a second *motive* was added—the urge to rectify the shortcomings of civilization which made themselves painfully felt."[4] The third part of his explanation, the distinctly Freudian part, is the longing for the *father-figure.* By means of this last part Freud endeavors to account for the emergence of the idea of a supreme being who is all-powerful, wise, loving, just, and mysterious. For these are the very features that make up the small child's picture of father. In childhood, Freud reminds us, one also felt helpless, threatened, in need of protection. The child turned to the father (whom he or she feared as well as loved) for help and protection. As children become adults, however, they realize that they remain in a state of helplessness, in need of relief and protection. Now, however, it is nature itself and the privations and sufferings imposed by society that are responsible for this state of helplessness. Reverting to the solution of childhood, people are led to believe in gods or a supreme being, beings who take on features like those attributed to a father. As Freud expresses it,

> When the growing individual finds that he is destined to remain a child for ever, that he can never do without protection against strange superior powers, he lends those powers the features belonging to the figure of his father; he creates for himself the gods whom he dreads, whom he seeks to propitiate, and whom he nevertheless entrusts with his own protection. Thus his longing for a father is a motive identical with his need for protection against the consequences of his human weakness. The defence against childish helplessness is what lends its characteristic features to the adult's reaction to the helplessness which *he* has to acknowledge—a reaction which is precisely the formation of religion.[5]

Freud's explanation of the emergence of religious ideas, particularly the theistic idea of God, blends together what he calls the *hidden motive,* the longing for the father-figure, with what he calls the *manifest motives;* human helplessness and the need for protection brought about by untamed nature and the privations and sufferings imposed by society. The manifest motives were well known before Freud; he merely took them over. The hidden motive, however, Freud viewed as "the particular contribution which psycho-analytic discussion can make to the solution of the problem of religion."[6] In any case, it's clear that on Freud's explanation, human beliefs about the gods not only help people to feel protected against the dangers of untamed nature and the injuries that threaten them from society itself, they also satisfy one of the deepest and most pervasive of human wants, the longing for the father-figure.

RELIGION AS ILLUSION

Having explained the emergence of religion in civilization and the human needs it serves, both manifest and hidden, Freud turns to the task of evaluating religious ideas in the light of psychology. The conclusion he reaches is that religious ideas, although presented as profound teachings about the world and human destiny, are really no more than *illusions.* "These, which are given out as teachings, are not precipitates of experience or end-results of thinking: they are illusions, fulfilments of the oldest, strongest and most urgent wishes of mankind. The secret of their strength lies in the strength of those wishes."[7]

But what does Freud mean by *illusion?* And what are his reasons for classifying religious beliefs as illusions? Freud distinguishes (i) an error (a false belief), (ii) an illusion, and (iii) a delusion. Aristotle believed that vermin are developed out of dung. Aristotle's belief was an error, but, according to Freud, not an illusion. For what is characteristic of illusions is "that they are derived from human wishes."[8] (Presumably, Aristotle had no strong wishes about the origin of vermin.) "One may describe as an illusion the assertion made by certain nationalists that the Indo-Germanic race is the only one capable of civilization; or the belief, which was only destroyed by psychoanalysis, that children are creatures without sexuality."[9] The crucial difference between these two "errors" and Aristotle's error is that the belief about the Germanic race and the belief about the sexual innocence of children both satisfy deep wishes in those who believe them.

Is it, then, that by an *illusion* Freud means an erroneous belief that satisfies some deep wish? No. For Freud insists that an illusion may be *true*. It is a mark of a *delusion* that it be a false belief; an *illusion*, however, may be true. "In the case of delusions, we emphasize as essential their being in contradiction with reality. Illusions need not necessarily be false—that is to say, unrealizable or in contradiction to reality."[10] If we call religious beliefs delusions, we are committed, given Freud's meaning of *delusion*, to the view that religious beliefs are false. If we call religious beliefs illusions, given Freud's meaning of *illusion*, we are not committed to the view that religious beliefs are false. "Thus we call a belief an illusion when a wish-fulfillment is a prominent factor in its motivation, and in doing so we disregard its relations to reality, just as the illusion itself sets no store by verification."[11]

Suppose a certain woman is running for a seat in the United States Senate, a position she has longed to obtain for some years. To win the election would satisfy some of her deepest wishes. She believes fervently that she will be successful. Is her belief an illusion? Well, it can't be denied that the belief satisfies some very deep wish and may well be motivated by that wish. Suppose, however, that it is very close to the election, no surprising reversals in public opinion are expected, and the most sophisticated polling techniques have shown that she has a quite substantial lead over her opponent. It's true that her belief expresses her very strong wish. But it is also true that she has good rational grounds for her belief. Is, then, her belief an illusion or not? I suspect that Freud would say that the belief would be an illusion only if the candidate would cling to it were there to be no evidence in its favor or even evidence against it. That is, the mere fact that a belief satisfies some wish or need is not sufficient for the belief to be an illusion. It must also be true that the belief (a) *is held* in the absence of any good rational grounds in its behalf, or (b) *would be held* in the absence of any good rational grounds in its behalf. Perhaps, had the evidence been in favor of her opponent, the candidate would have given up her belief that she would win—in which case her belief would not be an illusion. Of course, if someone holds to a belief that satisfies some deep wish and has nothing in the way of good evidence in support of the belief, it will be highly likely that this belief is an illusion.

Freud's reasons for judging religious beliefs to be illusions are (1) that they satisfy one of humanity's deepest wishes; the longing for the father-figure, and (2) that they are held in the absence of any good rational grounds in their behalf.

We've already considered reason 1, that the belief in God is causally related to the childhood longing for the father-figure. Concerning 2, Freud argues that when the question of evidence is raised, religious people appeal to the authority of their ancestors, to ancient writings such as the Bible, or maintain that it is wrong to even inquire into the evidence for religious doctrines. The last point, Freud notes, is bound to arouse our suspicions, for it can only mean that society is aware that religious beliefs lack adequate rational support. And appealing to our ignorant ancestors and to ancient writings cannot yield rational grounds for religious beliefs.

> But these ancestors of ours were far more ignorant than we are. They believed in things we could not possibly accept to-day; and the possibility occurs to us that the doctrines of religion may belong to that class too. The proofs they have left us are set down in writings which themselves bear every mark of untrustworthiness. They are full of contradictions, revisions and falsifications, and where they speak of factual confirmations they are themselves unconfirmed. It does not help much to have it asserted that their wording, or even their content only, originates from divine revelation; for this assertion is itself one of the doctrines whose authenticity is under examination, and no proposition can be a proof of itself.[12]

It's perhaps fair to say that Freud has pointed out the inadequacy of appealing to one's ancestors and ancient writings in order to provide rational justification for religious beliefs. It's a pity, however, that he did not take into account the sorts of reasons an Anselm or an Aquinas would cite as the rational foundation for religious beliefs. Anselm and Aquinas would appeal to their philosophical proofs of God's existence as justification for the belief in God. And in *The Future of an Illusion* there is not even a hint that Freud is aware of these other sources as possible rational grounds for religious beliefs. Perhaps, however, this failure on Freud's part does not seriously damage his claim to have shown that religious ideas are *illusions*. For it is with the masses of religious believers that he is concerned, and not with highly trained philosophical theologians like Augustine, Anselm, and Aquinas. And it may well be that for the masses of religious believers, the sort of reasons they would give in support of their beliefs would resemble rather closely the three points Freud shows to be inadequate as rational support for religious doctrines. If he is right about this, and if we accept his view that religious beliefs have their hidden motivation in the childhood longing for the father-figure, then we must agree with him that, so far as the masses of people are concerned, religious beliefs are illusions. For they satisfy, and are motivated by, some of mankind's deepest wishes and they are held in the absence of any good rational grounds in their behalf.

We have considered Freud's explanation of the formation of religious ideas, what he means by the psychological term *illusion,* and his argument for the view that religious beliefs are illusions. Two questions remain to be considered: What view does Freud take concerning the *worth* for society of its grandest illusion, religion? What does Freud's view of religious beliefs imply concerning the basic issue of whether religious beliefs are *true* or *false*?

THE WORTH OF THE ILLUSION

It is something of a paradox to discover that the very person whose research into the human psyche has disclosed the enormous influence of unconscious forces in human affairs, and the weakness of human reason in the face of these powerful forces, should, when faced with the question of the future of an illusion (religion), not only *advocate* that civilization give up religion, but actually *predict* that humanity will soon outgrow its need for religion. But this is precisely what Freud does in the last chapters of *The Future of an Illusion*. When Freud's view that reason is on its way to replacing civilization's fondest illusion (religion) became known among some of his disciples in the psychoanalytic movement, a few of his followers began to joke about Freud's own "illusion" concerning the future. Putting aside his prediction, we will try to see why Freud thought civilization *should* give up religion.

Freud conducts his argument in the form of a debate with an imaginary opponent who stresses the human need for illusions in general and the religious illusion in particular. The opponent makes two major points. First, he notes that our civilization is built on the doctrines of religion and the maintenance of human society is based on the masses believing those doctrines.

> If men are taught that there is no almighty and all-just God, no divine world-order and no future life, they will feel exempt from all obligation to obey the precepts of civilization. Everyone will, without inhibition or fear, follow asocial, egoistic instincts and seek to exercise his power; Chaos, which we have banished through many thousands of years of the work of civilization will come again.[13]

The opponent's second point is that the effort to deprive people of religious beliefs would be a purposeless cruelty.

> Countless people find their one consolation in religious doctrines, and can only bear life with their help. You would rob them of their support, without having anything better to give them in exchange. It is admitted that so far science has not achieved much, but even if it had advanced much further it would not suffice for man. Man has imperative needs of another sort, which can never be satisfied by cold science; and it is very strange—indeed, it is the height of inconsistency—that a psychologist who has always insisted on what a minor part is played in human affairs by the intelligence as compared with the life of the instincts—that such a psychologist should now try to rob mankind of a precious wish-fulfillment and should propose to compensate them for it with intellectual nourishment.[14]

In response to these two points Freud concedes that religion has performed great services for civilization and brought mankind some measure of comfort. Indeed, he confesses that if religion had been fully successful in reconciling people to civilization and making them happy, he would not wish to see it replaced.[15] But in fact, Freud argues, religion has not succeeded very well, and what success it has achieved has been at the expense of suppressing the growth of reason. Countless violations of the fundamental principles of society have been countenanced by religion. Indeed, the priests have set up institutions to accommodate such violations.

> One sinned, and then one made a sacrifice or did penance and then one was free to sin once more. . . . It is no secret that the priests could only keep the masses submissive to religion by making such large concessions as these to the instinctual nature of man. Thus it was agreed: God alone is strong and good, man is weak and sinful. In every age immorality has found no less support in religion than morality has. If the achievements of religion in respect to man's happiness, susceptibility to culture and moral control are no better than this, the question cannot but arise whether we are not overrating its necessity for mankind, and whether we do wisely in basing our cultural demands upon it.[16]

In the place of a religious foundation for obedience to societal rules, Freud proposes a rational foundation, that children be educated to understand why human survival depends on a general obedience to the rules, practices, and institutions of human civilization. For, as he himself had discovered through years of research, people are not very accessible to reasonable arguments and are governed largely by their instinctual wishes. But he expresses the belief that although people *are* like this, there is nothing in human nature that *forces* them to be this way. He allows that this belief may be an illusion, but he thinks his experiment to see if the masses will respond to a rational foundation for society is worth a try.

To the charge of cruelty, Freud acknowledges that relinquishing religion will probably make life more of a hardship.

> They will have to admit to themselves the full extent of their helplessness and their insignificance in the machinery of the universe; they can no longer be the centre of creation, no longer the object of tender care on the part of a beneficent Providence. They will be in the same position as a child who has left the parental house where he was so warm and comfortable. But surely infantilism is destined to be surmounted. Men cannot remain children for ever; they must in the end go out into "hostile life". We may call this *"education to reality"*.[17]

Although life may in some respects be harder without religion, Freud argues that by giving up expectations about another world, people may well concentrate their liberated energies into their life on earth, bringing about a civilization tolerable to everyone and oppressive to no one.

Freud's final comment on the place of religion in civilization is expressed in terms of an analogy between the development of the child into a responsible adult and the development of the human race from its infancy to maturity. According to Freudian theory the child cannot complete its development into a responsible adult without passing through a phase of neurosis. This is because so many instincts must be tamed at a stage when the child's reason is insufficiently developed and too weak to do the taming. Consequently, these instinctual wishes are tamed by acts of repression, resulting in infantile neuroses that are usually overcome spontaneously in the course of growing up. In a similar way, Freud suggests, in the infancy of the human race, when the intellect was too weak to bring about the instinctual renunciations necessary for communal life, humanity passed through a period of neurosis. Religion, Freud suggests, is the chief neurosis to emerge in the period of humanity's infancy and, like the neuroses of childhood, it too will be discarded as humankind reaches maturity.

> Religion would thus be the universal obsessional neurosis of humanity; like the obsessional neurosis of children, it arose out of the Oedipus complex, out of the relation to the father. If this view is right, it is to be supposed that a turning-away from religion is bound to occur with the fatal inevitability of a process of growth, and that we find ourselves at this very juncture in the middle of that phase of development. Our behavior should therefore be modelled on that of a sensible teacher who does not oppose an impending new development but seeks to ease its path and mitigate the violence of its irruption.[18]

THE TRUTH OF THE ILLUSION

Whether Freud's view of the future of religion is correct or merely the expression of his own illusion is a question which only the future can answer for us. What does seem clear, however, is that in judging the *worth* of religious beliefs, Freud is all the while supposing these beliefs to be *false*. For if these beliefs are thought to be true, then the estimate of their worth to us would be quite different. If, for example, we believe that it is true that the theistic God exists and true that all those and only those who believe in him will receive eternal life, then surely we would judge these beliefs to be a major asset to humanity and would not be inclined to advocate that civilization should abandon them. It is time, therefore, to turn to our final question: Does Freud's account of the emergence of religious beliefs provide him or us with rational grounds for thinking that the basic beliefs of theistic religion are false?

Let's suppose that Freud has made a good case for the view that religious beliefs are illusions, that they owe their origin and continuing appeal to the fact that they satisfy people's deepest wishes. Let's also suppose that not only would religious people cling to these beliefs in the absence of rational grounds for them, but that most people do not in fact have good rational grounds for their religious beliefs. Does Freud think that in showing that religious beliefs are illusions he has succeeded in showing that they are *false*? This question must be answered in the negative for two reasons. First, as we noted earlier, Freud is careful to explain that an illusion need not be false. Thus the mere fact that religious beliefs are illusions is insufficient to establish that they are false. Second, Freud is careful to point out that the question of the truth or falsity of religious ideas is not a question that his investigations are able to answer. Thus he remarks:

> Of the reality value of most of them we cannot judge; just as they cannot be proved, so they cannot be refuted. We still know too little to make a critical approach to them.[19]

And again he says:

> To assess the truth-value of religious doctrines does not lie within the scope of the present enquiry. It is enough for us that we have recognized them as being, in their psychological nature, illusions.[20]

Thus it seems clear that Freud did not take himself to have shown that religious beliefs are false.

Of course, if Freud's explanation of the emergence of the idea of God is correct, then what causes the appearance of this idea, as well as its acceptance by continuing generations, has nothing to do with any immediate divine activity or force; the causes lie within the natural world. But this would show that the belief in God is false only if we had some conclusive reason for thinking that if God exists, then the cause of someone's coming to believe in his existence would have to be supranatural. And there does not seem to be any good reason for thinking that God's existence rules out natural causes for the belief that he exists.

Still, someone might object, if the causes of the belief in God are purely natural, due to a longing for the father-figure, doesn't that somehow throw doubt on the issue of God's existence? To the extent that we think that it does, we are probably falling into a way of thinking that logicians have called "the genetic fallacy." We commit the genetic fallacy whenever we fallaciously infer that a belief is true or false from a premise stating the causal origin of that belief. Sometimes what causes us to hold a belief is highly relevant to the truth or falsehood of the belief. "What caused me to believe that Purdue defeated Michigan is the fact that I saw the game and the final score." Here the cause of my belief has a direct bearing on its truth. But often, what causes someone to take up a belief has little or nothing to do with what justifies one in holding that belief. Perhaps what caused me to believe that the earth is not flat was my mother's telling me so. But I would hardly try to justify that belief by appealing to what caused me to accept it. There is, then, an important distinction between the *causation of belief* and the *justification of belief*. To ignore this distinction, to suppose that from whatever is the *cause* of someone's holding a belief we can determine whether the belief is true or false, is to commit the genetic fallacy. Although he does not discuss this fallacy, it's clear that Freud has not committed it.

Although Freud's causal explanation of religious ideas does not, by itself, show these ideas to be false, there are, I believe, some special features about his account that perhaps render it somewhat unlikely that religious ideas are true. Indeed, there is, I think, an interesting argument against the truth of religion that can be developed out of Freud's view that religious beliefs are wish-fulfillments. Although he does not explicitly develop the argument Freud alludes to it. Directly after pointing out that assessing the truth-value of religious doctrines lies beyond the scope of his work, that it is enough to have shown them to be illusions, Freud remarks:

But we do not have to conceal the fact that this discovery also strongly influences our attitude to the question which must appear to many to be the most important of all. We know approximately at what periods and by what kind of men religious doctrines were created. If in addition we discover the motives which led to this, our attitude to the problem of religion will undergo a marked displacement. We shall tell ourselves that it would be very nice if there were a God who created the world and was a benevolent Providence, and if there were a moral order in the universe and an after-life; but it is a very striking fact that all this is exactly as we are bound to wish it to be. And it would be more remarkable still if our wretched, ignorant and downtrodden ancestors had succeeded in solving all these difficult riddles of the universe.[21]

The question which "must appear to many to be the most important of all" is, of course, the question of whether religious beliefs are true or false, whether God exists or does not exist. And in the passage quoted there is, I think, an unexpressed argument for the view that religious beliefs are false. Let's state it as follows:

1. Among those beliefs which we come to accept, not on the basis of rational proof, but because they satisfy certain profound wishes, the majority turn out to be false.
2. Religious beliefs are beliefs which we come to accept, not on the basis of rational proof, but because they satisfy certain profound wishes.

Therefore,

3. Probably, religious beliefs are false.

Insofar as Freudian psychology provides any reason for thinking that religious ideas are false, its reason, I think, is expressed in the above argument. The second premise merely expresses Freud's view that religious beliefs are illusions. The first premise is based on the conviction that reality does not often conform to our wishes. It would be nice if reality were exactly as we are bound to wish it to be, but if experience has taught us anything about our wishes it is that only infrequently does reality satisfy them. Freud adds that the beliefs in question are even more doubtful since they were formulated by our ignorant ancestors.

The argument I've attributed to Freud is not especially compelling. Aside from the question of whether Freud has succeeded in establishing that religious beliefs are illusions, his argument, at best, shows only that it is unlikely, strange, or odd that religious beliefs should be true. Perhaps it is, but it is doubtful that any religious believer would find this in itself surprising. One of the features of religion is that it is out of the ordinary, strange, and wonderful. Consequently, many religious thinkers would allow that Freud's reasoning shows that it is somewhat "striking" or unlikely that religious beliefs are true, but contend that this is not a sufficient reason for rejecting those beliefs. Futhermore, we must not forget that Freud has not considered the reasons that sophisticated religious thinkers such as Anselm or Aquinas give for their religious beliefs. Hence, he has not shown that no one has good grounds for these beliefs, only that many who accept them do not. If a belief is a wish-fulfilment, and if we show that *no one* has good reasons for accepting it, we will perhaps have some reason for thinking that it will likely turn out to be a false belief. But Freud has not shown that no one has good reasons for religious beliefs, only that many do not. Thus his argument is not as compelling as, at first glance, it may appear to be.

Notes

1. The best edition of *The Future of an Illusion* is in *The Complete Psychological Works of Sigmund Freud*, trans. and ed. James Strachey (London: The Hogarth Press Ltd., 1961), XXI. This edition of *The Future of an Illusion* is available in a paperback Anchor Books edition, 1964. For ease of reference, quotes will be taken from the Anchor Books edition.
2. *The Future of an Illusion*, p. 21.
3. *Ibid.*, pp. 22–23.
4. *Ibid.*, p. 30. Emphasis mine.
5. *Ibid.*, p. 35.
6. *Ibid.*, p. 33.
7. *Ibid.*, p. 47.
8. *Ibid.*, p. 48.
9. *Ibid.*
10. *Ibid.*, p. 49.
11. *Ibid.*
12. *Ibid.*, pp. 40–41.
13. *Ibid.*, p. 56.
14. *Ibid.*, p. 57.
15. *Ibid.*, pp. 60–61.
16. *Ibid.*, pp. 61–62.
17. *Ibid.*, p. 81.
18. *Ibid.*, pp. 70–71.
19. *Ibid.*, p. 50.
20. *Ibid.*, p. 52.
21. *Ibid.*, pp. 52–53.

Topics for Review

1. Explain the three parts of Freud's explanation of the emergence of religious ideas within civilization and the continuing power of these ideas.
2. Explain what Freud means by an illusion. If he is right in classifying religious beliefs as illusions, would religious beliefs have to be false?
3. For what reasons does Freud claim that religious beliefs are illusions?
4. Explain Freud's view concerning the future of religion. Does he justify his belief that culture would be better off without religion? Explain.
5. Explain the bearing of Freud's view of religion as an illusion on the question of the truth or falsity of these beliefs. Can we accept Freud's account and still reasonably accept religious beliefs as true? Explain.

Topics for Further Study

6. Explain the distinction between the *causation* of belief and the *justification* of a belief. Think up an example where it would be important to make this distinction. If God caused us to believe that he exists, would our belief that God exists be justified? Explain.

7. Discuss the following argument.

The importance of Freud's work for religion is that he has uncovered the mechanism by which God creates an idea of himself in the human mind. Religion has long taught that the relation of the good father to his children is like the relation of God to his creatures. Instead of rejecting Freud's view, the theologian can embrace it as providing an explanation of how God works through natural means to enable us to form a correct idea of our creator.

9

MIRACLES AND THE MODERN WORLD VIEW

Theistic religions generally stress the occurrence of miracles. The major figures in Judaism (Moses), Christianity (Jesus), and Islam (Mohammad) have all "worked miracles" in the course of establishing their divine missions. Stories of miraculous events are frequent in both the Old and New Testaments. Indeed, Christianity was founded on the claim that Jesus was miraculously raised from the dead. Miracles in Christianity are also associated with saints' bodies and relics and with shrines. Millions of people, for example, make their way each year to Lourdes, a small town in France, where miraculous cures are attributed to the waters of a shrine raised at a place where the Blessed Virgin is believed to have repeatedly appeared in 1858 to Saint Bernadette. Clearly, then, miracles are a rather basic element in theistic religions. Our concern in this chapter is whether it is any longer possible to believe in miracles, and, if possible, whether it is ever reasonable to believe that a miracle has occurred.

MIRACLES: INCOMPATIBLE WITH A SCIENTIFIC WORLD VIEW?

The foremost exponent of the view that it is no longer *possible* to believe in miracles is the German biblical historian and theologian Rudolf Bultmann (1884–1976). Miracles, Bultmann argues, belong to a prescientific picture of the world in which supernatural beings invade the natural world and bring about extraordinary events: people raised from the dead, or the turning of water into wine. Science and technology, however, have given rise to the modern world view; a view of nature as a closed, autonomous realm in which one event in nature is accounted for by another event in nature. This world view, so Bultmann believes, has shaped the mind of modern people to such an extent that they can no longer believe in stories of miraculous events like those recorded in the Bible. Saint Augustine believed that sickness, at least in a Christian, was due to demons. But modern people can scarcely hold such a belief. Sickness and the cure of disease are now attributed to causes within nature such as germs, and drugs. As Bultmann remarks: "It is *impossible* to use electric light and the wireless and to avail ourselves of modern medical and surgical discoveries, and at the same time to believe in the New Testament world of spirits and miracles."[1]

Surely Bultmann's claim is too strong. People now still believe in miracles, so clearly it is *possible* to do so. And as some of the unfortunate consequences of the technology spawned by modern science become apparent, there seems to be, if anything, a reaction against the scientific world view and a growing willingness to embrace prescientific modes of thought. In response to these points, Bultmann argues that while there are exceptions to his thesis, they are relatively unimportant.

> It may of course be argued that there are people alive to-day whose confidence in the traditional scientific view of the world has been shaken, and others who are primitive enough to qualify for an age of mythical thought. And there are also many varieties of superstition. But when belief in spirits and miracles has degenerated into superstition, it has become something entirely different from what it was when it was genuine faith. The various impressions and speculations which influence credulous people here and there are of little importance, nor does it matter to what extent cheap slogans have spread an atmosphere inimical to science. What matters is the world view which men imbibe from their environment, and it is science which determines that view of the world through the school, the press, the wireless, the cinema, and all the other fruits of technical progress.[2]

What matters, according to Bultmann, is not that people still exist who believe in miracles—people who either live in primitive areas relatively untouched by science and technology or live in the civilized world but somehow manage to reject modern science or maintain a kind of schizophrenic existence, accepting both modern science and a superstitious belief in the miraculous. What matters is that the modern world view leaves little or no room for spirits and miracles. Modern people, conditioned by science and technology into adopting the scientific world view, are naturally inclined to accept an explanation of events in nature only if it is given in terms of other events in nature. When the television breaks down or the automobile stalls, moderns cannot seriously entertain the idea that a demon caused it. The explanation is given in terms of some mechanical or electrical failure. Consequently, there is less room in the world of nature for God to intrude, less room, therefore, for miracles to occur.

I think we must concede to Bultmann that it is more difficult to believe in miracles than it once was. To accept modern science is to expect to find natural causes for *most* of the events occurring in nature. Consequently, fewer events will be referred to supernatural forces intervening in the natural world. This much seems undeniable. Bultmann, however, claims much more. He argues that to accept modern science is somehow to be committed to rejecting *any* explanation of events in the natural world in terms of the activities of supernatural beings or powers (angels, gods, demons, or others). But there seems to be little or no justification for this stronger claim, and the facts about what civilized people do believe fail to prove Bultmann's stronger claim.

AN UNREASONABLE BELIEF
Hume's Definition of Miracles

The second and by far more serious attack against miracles holds that although it is possible to believe in miracles, it is never reasonable to do so. The classic statement of this view occurs in a famous essay by David Hume.[3] In this essay Hume rests his major argument on a certain understanding of what a miracle is. A miracle, says Hume, is an event which satisfies two conditions: (1) it is a violation of a law of nature, and (2) it is due to the direct activity of God.[4] We can best begin our study of Hume's argument against miracles by reflecting on his statement of the conditions an event must satisfy if it is to qualify as a miracle.

Why is a miracle defined, in part, as "a violation of a law of nature" and not as "an extraordinary, astounding, unusual event"? Suppose that someone has just returned from a trip to the Near East. While hiking around the Sea of Galilee, he happened upon an ancient, abandoned salt mine, found the salt to taste slightly different from ordinary salt, and so collected some in order to have it chemically analyzed. Suppose, furthermore, that while walking near the region where the biblical town of Cana once stood, he found an old well, drank some of its water, found it also to have a somewhat peculiar taste, and acquired several barrels of it. Later, while showing slides of his trip to some friends, and offering them a taste of his acquisitions—the strange salt and the water with the peculiar taste—he accidentally dropped a bit of the salt into the water. To the amazement of all, the water very quickly changed color and, when tasted, was discovered to be wine, indeed, a very nice sherry. After drinking the sherry, he experimented with the salt and water and found that by mixing the proper proportions he could produce an excellent sherry within a moment or two.

Surely the turning of the water, when mixed with the salt, into wine is a rather extraordinary happening. But suppose that under chemical analysis the water and salt are both found to have certain properties not normally present in water and salt, properties, furthermore, that are found in wine, and particularly in sherry. That is, suppose that the chemist is able to give a reasonably good explanation of why this strange salt and peculiar water, when mixed together, turn into a very pleasant wine. While nonetheless unusual and extraordinary, would the turning of this water into wine be thought to be a *miracle*? The answer seems to be no. For although we may use the word "miracle" in a loose sense to mean no more than an extraordinary or surprising event, in its strict sense, an event is a miracle only if it cannot be accounted for in terms of natural laws and natural causes. Since the chemist was able to discover in the properties of the water and salt a *natural* process by which the mixture of the two substances would result in wine, it is no miracle that the water turned into wine. Indeed, having made this remarkable discovery, I suppose we might begin to wonder whether the biblical story (John 2:1-11) of the wedding feast at Cana, where Jesus turned water into wine, is really the story of a miracle after all. Perhaps Jesus had somehow discovered the "trick" of turning water into wine.

What we have just seen is that an event is a genuine miracle only if it is not due to any *natural process* or *natural cause*. Once we have discovered what we believe to be the natural process or the natural cause which brought the event about, we will no longer believe the event to be a genuine miracle. And if, by following that process we can bring about an event just like the original one, we will thereby strengthen our belief that the original event was due to such a process or natural cause and, therefore, was not a genuine miracle.

We will understand an event to be "a violation of a law of nature" only if the event was not due to any natural process, force, or cause. The laws of nature enable us to explain events in the physical world in terms of other events, things, or processes in the physical world. Thus we explain why the water froze in terms of a natural process that takes place when the temperature lowers beyond a certain point. Or we explain why a stone, when released from a height of ten feet, falls to the earth in terms of the principle of gravitation according to which bodies are attracted toward one another. Suppose a stone does not fall to the ground when released from a height of ten feet. This event will either be due to some natural force, process, or cause, or it will not. If the stone's being suspended in air is *not* due to any natural force, process, or cause then some law of nature— presumably, the law stated by the principle of gravitation—has been violated. If, however, the stone's remaining in the air is due to some natural force, then either that force is accounted for by the principle of gravitation or the principle of gravitation is false and not really a law of nature. If, for example, some violent wind or natural force equal to the gravitational pull of the earth is acting on the stone, we don't have an exception to the law of gravitation. On the other hand, if there is a natural force keeping the stone in the air, but that natural force is *less than* what, *according to the principle of gravitation,* is required to prevent the stone from being drawn to the earth, then the principle of gravitation is false as stated and, therefore, not a true law of nature. The important point to note here is that if an event is not due to any natural force, process, or cause, it "violates" a law of nature but does not show that the statement of the law is incorrect. Only if an event is due to a natural force, process, or cause could it show that a statement of a law is not really a law after all. The miraculous event is contrary to the laws of nature not in the sense of showing that something we thought to be a law is not in fact a law. It is contrary in the sense of being an event that is different from what would have taken place in the normal situation had everything that happened been due to some natural cause or force. If the stone's remaining in air is not due to any natural force or cause then it is contrary to the law of gravitation in the sense of being different from what would have occurred—the stone's falling to the ground—had the situation been normal and had everything that happened been due to some natural force or cause.

We have been considering the first of the two conditions an event must satisfy if it is to be, in Hume's definition, a genuine miracle. We have interpreted the first condition to mean that the event is not due to any natural force, process, or cause. The second condition tells us that the event is due to a supernatural cause, God. These conditions are not two different ways of saying the same thing. Denying a natural cause is not the same thing as affirming a supernatural cause. If a stone's being suspended in air is not due to any natural cause, it may or may not be due to some supernatural cause. If it is an event that is due to no cause or force whatever, natural or supernatural, then although the event will be a violation of a law of nature, it will not be a miracle. For an event is a miracle only if it is due to the direct activity of God or some other supernatural agent.

Objections to Hume's Definition

Is Hume's characterization of a miracle adequate? Objections to it fall into two classes: those which claim that Hume's two conditions are not *sufficient* conditions for something being a miracle, and those which claim that one or the other of his two conditions is not *necessary* for something being a miracle. It will be instructive to consider an example or two of each sort of objection.

Two features often associated with the idea of a miracle, features in addition to Hume's two, are (3) that a miracle is a surprising, astounding event, and (4) that a miracle serves some important, beneficial purpose. The miracle stories in the bible generally exhibit features 3 and 4. Lazarus' being raised from the dead (John, 11) is clearly an astounding event and beneficial—at least to Lazarus and his sisters. The healing of the two blind men (Matt, 9:27–31) and the feeding of the five thousand from five loaves and two fishes (Mark, 6:35–44) also exhibit these two features. Perhaps, then, Hume's two basic features are inadequate. For an event to be a genuine miracle it must also be astounding and beneficial. If a person rushing to rescue a child from an approaching train suddenly falls dead, with the result that the child is struck by the train, we would certainly not call the person's death a miracle, for it serves, so far as we can see, no beneficial purpose whatever. And if a leaf stirs ever so gently on the ground, no one would call that event a miracle, for it is not in the least an astounding or surprising event.

To the objection that a miracle must be astounding or surprising, Hume has a reply:

> A miracle may either be discoverable by men or not. This alters not its nature and essence. The raising of a house or ship into the air is a visible miracle. The raising of a feather, when the wind wants ever so little of a force requisite for that purpose, is as real a miracle, though not so sensible with regard to us."[5]

Suppose the breeze is sufficient to move a leaf no more than half an inch along the ground, that no other natural force is causing the leaf to move, but that God directly intervenes so that the leaf actually moves a distance of one full inch. This event, the leaf's moving one full inch, would hardly be deemed surprising or astounding. Actually, if we *knew* that no natural force was sufficient to bring about the event, we might find it rather astounding. But if we understand an astounding or surprising event to be one which a normal observer would *readily* recognize as such, then the slight movement of the leaf would not be in the least astounding or surprising. Similarly with Hume's example of the raising of the feather. A building rising by other than natural means, however, would be an astounding, surprising event.

Hume's reply can be understood as follows. Something may be a miracle even though we are unable to *recognize* it as such. Being astounding or surprising may be a condition that an event must satisfy if we are to *believe* that it is a miracle, but it is not a condition that an event must satisfy in order for it *to be* a miracle. We shouldn't confuse conditions which must be present in order for us to *determine* that a miracle has taken place with conditions that must be present in order for it to be true that a miracle has taken place. Conditions 3 and 4, Hume would argue, are perhaps necessary for us to be in a position to determine that a miracle has occurred, but unlike 1 and 2, they are not conditions that need be present for a miracle to occur. To put his point in different terms, we might distinguish between *visible* and *invisible* miracles. Hume is giving the conditions that are sufficient for a miracle to take place. Conditions 3 and 4 are perhaps necessary for a *visible* miracle to take place, something that ordinary people might be in a position to judge to be a miracle, but 3 and 4 are not necessary for an event to be a miracle, since thay are not present in an event which is an *invisible* miracle.

We have considered an example of the objection that Hume has not given conditions that are *sufficient* for something being a miracle. The second sort of objection claims that Hume's condition that an event be a violation of a law of nature is not a *necessary* condition for something being a miracle. R. F. Holland, for example, suggests the example of a child who has wandered onto a railroad track not knowing that a train is rapidly approaching. The train is coming around a curve, obscuring the child from the engineer. Just at the right moment the engineer faints, due to some natural cause that has nothing to do with the presence of the child on the track. As he faints his hand ceases to exert pressure on the control lever, bringing the train to a halt a few feet from the child. The child's mother, watching from a distance and unable to help, "thanks God for the miracle; which she never ceases to think of as such although, as she in due course learns, there was nothing supernatural about the manner in which the brakes of the train came to be applied."[6]

We are to suppose in this example that the extraordinary event—the train's coming to a halt just a few feet from the child—is entirely due to natural causes. Had the child not been on the track, the train would have come to a stop at exactly the same spot. Had the child been on the track just a few feet more in the direction of the train then, short of divine intervention, he would have been killed. Where then is the miracle? Where is the hand of God in this spectacular event? Let's grant that some natural cause brought about the engineer's fainting. Perhaps what the mother believes is that although the fainting was due to a natural cause, the *timing* of the fainting, that it did not occur a few moments *later*, was in some way due to God's intervention. Some distinction, it seems, must be made between a *fortunate coincidence* and a *genuine miracle*. And once we try to make this distinction, it is likely that we will be drawn into Hume's two conditions. Consequently, although there may be doubts about the adequacy of Hume's characterization of a miracle, it is less than clear that any other characterization is more adequate.

The Argument Against Miracles

It is now time to consider Hume's central argument against miracles. As we noted earlier, Hume thinks that it is never reasonable to believe that a miracle has occurred. His argument is derived from the first of the two conditions an event must satisfy to be a miracle: the condition of being a violation of a law of nature.

> A miracle is a violation of the laws of nature; and as a firm and unalterable experience has established these laws, the proof against a miracle, from the very nature of the fact, is as entire as any argument from experience can possibly be imagined. Why is it more

than probable, that all men must die; that lead cannot, of itself, remain suspended in the air; that fire consumes wood, and is extinguished by water; unless it be, that these events are found agreeable to the laws of nature, and there is required a violation of these laws, or in other words, a miracle to prevent them. . . . But it is a miracle, that a dead man should come to life; because that has never been observed, in any age or country. There must, therefore, be a uniform experience against every miraculous event, otherwise the event would not merit that appellation.[7]

The above passage contains Hume's major argument for the view that it is never in fact reasonable to believe that a miracle has occurred. The argument, simply put, proceeds as follows:

1. The evidence from experience in support of a law of nature is extremely strong.
2. A miracle is a violation of a law of nature.

Therefore,

3. The evidence from experience against the occurrence of a miracle is extremely strong.

Why is the evidence from experience in support of a law of nature always extremely strong? For the simple reason that we would never believe a principle to be a law of nature unless certain events in nature had been constantly observed to occur when other conditions in nature were observed to be present. The principle of gravitation tells us, to use one of Hume's examples, that lead (or any heavy body) cannot of itself remain suspended in mid-air. Over and over again bodies of considerable weight have been observed to fall toward the earth when left in the air without support. Observations of this sort have helped confirm our belief that the principle of gravitation is a law of nature. When some heavy object *appears* to be suspended *by itself* in mid-air (as in some magician's stage performance), we generally believe that there is some natural force, undetected by us, that is acting on the body with a force equal to the force exerted by the gravitational pull of the earth. To believe otherwise is to go against the constant experience that has led us to believe the principle of gravitation. For our past experience is that heavy objects fall unless there is some natural object or force that is counteracting the pull of gravity on the heavy object.

A miracle, Hume tells us in his second premise, is a violation of a law of nature. And we have taken this to mean that a miracle is an event that is due to no natural cause or force whatever. Now when would we ever be tempted to think that such an event has occurred? Only when the event is one which appears to conflict with the common course of nature; only when there appears to be no natural cause that could account for it—an event like someone being raised from the dead, or a piece of lead remaining in mid-air without there being any natural force equal to the pull of gravity acting upon it. If the event appears to conform to what we believe to be the laws of nature, then we will not be tempted to believe it to be a miracle.

The conclusion Hume draws is that the evidence which went into establishing a certain principle as a law of nature will be *against* the hypothesis that a miraculous event occurred. And surely he is right about this. If someone tells us that he threw a piece of lead into the air and it fell to the ground, we will have no difficulty in believing that it fell to the ground because of our constant experience of heavy objects falling to the ground when they are thrown into the air. Constant experiences like this lead us to believe that events in nature have natural causes, and lead us to formulate principles like the principle of gravitation that specify those connections in nature. But if he tells us that the piece of lead simply remained in the air and that no violent wind or natural force was counteracting the pull of gravity, we will be very hard put to believe that his story is true. For to do so would be to believe either that the principle of gravitation is false or that the piece of lead was somehow not subject to natural forces at all. But since our experience is strongly in favor of the principle of gravitation being true and in favor of the behavior of pieces of lead and other material bodies being due to natural causes and forces, we will have considerable evidence against his story right from the start.

Is it, then, never reasonable to believe that an event has occurred which violates a law of nature? Hume appears to believe that this is so. For the only evidence we have in support of a miracle is the testimony of witnesses. And Hume thinks it is always more reasonable to believe that the witnesses were in error than to believe that the miracle occurred. For against the testimony of the witnesses stands all of our experience that supports the law of nature the alleged miracle violates. In addition, Hume notes that the witnesses to so-called miracles are often ignorant, primitive people who have a natural tendency to believe in extraordinary happenings.

Hume does allow that human testimony might be so extensive and trustworthy as to make it more than reasonable to believe that some absolutely extraordinary event has occurred, something that runs counter to "the usual course of nature."

> Thus, suppose all authors in all languages agree that, from the first of January 1600, there was a total darkness over the whole earth for eight days: suppose that the tradition of this extraordinary event is still strong and lively among the people: that all travellers, who return from foreign countries, bring us accounts of the same tradition, without the least variation or contradiction: it is evident, that our present philosophers, instead of doubting the fact, ought to receive it as certain, and ought to search for the causes whence it might be derived.[8]

But we can see from this passage that he thinks the amount of the testimony in support of the event must be incredibly large before it can possibly offset the weight of the evidence against the event drawn from our past experience. Only if the falsehood of the testimony would be more miraculous than the event to which it testifies is Hume prepared to believe that the event occurred rather than that the witnesses were in error. And so far as the miracle stories in Christianity and other religions are concerned, it's clear that Hume's judgment is that the weight of the evidence is on the side of the witnesses being in error.

A Violation of Nature

Before we try to evaluate Hume's argument against miracles, we need to review the question of just what it is we must be prepared to believe if we are to believe that an event violates a law of nature. Suppose we throw a piece of lead up into the air and watch, bewildered, as it remains suspended in mid-air for several minutes before slowly falling to the ground. There are basically three alternatives among which to choose. First, there is the possibility that some natural force, perhaps a violent wind, is acting upon the lead with a force equal to that which, according to the principle of gravity, is pulling the lead toward the earth. Second, there is the possibility that the principle of gravity is false as stated, that some natural force does account for what is happening to the lead, but it is a force which, if the principle of gravity were true, would be insufficient to maintain the lead in mid-air for that period of time. We might then revise the principle of gravity in the light of this new knowledge. Finally, there is the possibility that no natural force or cause whatever accounts for what is happening to the piece of lead. In the first alternative what happens is in *accordance* with the principle of gravity. In the second case what happens *refutes* the principle of gravity and shows that it is not, as stated, a law of nature. And in the third case what happens *violates* a law of nature—assuming that the principle of gravity is indeed a law of nature. The third case does not show that the principle of gravity is not a law of nature because the laws of nature tell us what must happen only if what happens is due entirely to natural forces.

The problem is to determine which of these three alternatives is the correct account of the lead's remaining in mid-air. Presumably, it is not too difficult to rule out the first alternative. But how do we decide whether this amazing event is a genuine counter-example to the principle of gravity (alternative 2), or is a genuine violation of a law of nature (alternative 3)? Well, if we could pin down the natural forces involved, revise the principle of gravity to take account of them, and then bring about similar events in circumstances where these forces obtain, we would have grounds for thinking that alternative (2) is the correct account. But if we are unsuccessful in revising the principle of gravity to take account of this strange event, if we cannot find a revision in terms of which we can predict future occurrences of events like the one in question, then it may well be reasonable to conclude that the lead's remaining in mid-air for those few minutes was a genuine violation of a law of nature, something not due to any natural force whatever.[9]

The difficulty in choosing between alternatives 2 and 3 will be greater or less depending on how unusual and striking the event happens to be. If a person's body is dismembered, the parts allowed to decay over a period of weeks, and then, when the various parts are placed on a table, they suddenly reunite and the person comes back to life in full health, no one would think it at all likely that some slight revision of what we take to be the laws of nature would account for such an event. Thus it seems that there are imaginable events which, should they occur, would be held, with good reason, to be violations of the laws of nature.

Hume argues, as we saw, not that a miracle is impossible, but that it is never reasonable for a wise man to believe that a miracle has occurred. For a miracle is a violation of a law of nature, and since the evidence from experience in support of a law of nature is evidence for the view that the events covered by the law are due to natural causes, the evidence against any miracle will likely be very strong. On the other side, the only evidence that supports a miracle is the testimony of those who claim to have witnessed it. But it is always more reasonable to believe that the witnesses were in error than to believe that the miracle occurred, particularly when we take into account the character, lack of education, and number of witnesses to a miracle.

The Weaknesses in Hume's Argument

There are, I think, at least two major weaknesses in Hume's argument. The first of these is that Hume is wrong in suggesting that the only evidence in favor of a miracle is the testimony of those who claim to have witnessed it. We need to distinguish between *direct* and *indirect* evidence for the claim that a certain event took place. If I come back to my campsite and discover that the ice chest is damaged, food gone, and the camp in general disarray, a fellow camper may tell me that she saw a bear going through my camp. Her testimony is direct evidence that a bear was in my camp. But the damaged ice chest, missing food, and general disturbance may also be evidence that a bear was in my camp. For they are facts which may be explained best (and perhaps even only) by the hypothesis that a bear did indeed go through my camp. Evidence of this latter sort is *indirect* evidence. And Hume has failed to take into account that our evidence for a miracle may include not only the testimony of witnesses (direct evidence) but also many facts that are best explained by the hypothesis that the miracle occurred. Indeed, it may well be the case that the indirect evidence for a miracle is stronger than the direct evidence.

> An example is provided by the story of the Resurrection in the Christian religion. The direct testimony for this event appears to me to be very feeble. . . . But the indirect evidence is much stronger. We have testimony to the effect that the disciples were exceedingly depressed at the time of the Crucifixion; that they had extremely little faith in the future; and that, after a certain time, this depression disappeared, and they believed that they had evidence that their Master had risen from the dead. Now none of these alleged facts is in the least odd or improbable, and we have therefore little ground for not accepting them on the testimony offered us. But having done this, we are faced with the problem of accounting for the facts which we have accepted. What caused the disciples to believe, contrary to their previous conviction, and in spite of their feeling of depression, that Christ had risen from the dead? Clearly, one explanation is that he actually had arisen. And this explanation accounts for the facts so well that we may at least say that the indirect evidence for the miracle is far and away stronger than the direct evidence.[10]

The second objection is that Hume has certainly overestimated the weight that should be given to the past experience in support of some principle thought to be a law of nature. The experience of an *exception* to some principle strongly supported by past experience has often led to the revision of the principle so as to account for the exception. But following Hume's argument, it would seem to be more reasonable to conclude that the exception really didn't occur, for it conflicts with the wealth of past experience supporting the principle. As C. D. Broad remarks:

> Clearly many propositions have been accounted laws of nature because of an invariable experience in their favor, then exceptions have been observed, and finally these propositions have ceased to be regarded as laws of nature. But the first reported exception was, to anyone who had not himself observed it, in precisely the same position as a story of a miracle, if Hume be right.[11]

The general point here is that on Hume's weighing of the evidence, it is difficult to understand how anyone could reasonably believe that an exception to a supposed law of nature had occurred, since the supposed law will have an invariable experience in its favor. It is clear, however, that exceptions do occur to supposed laws and also clear that reasonable people revise their scientific principles accordingly. Clearly, then, in his efforts to attack miracles Hume has weighted the scale so heavily in favor of the invariable experience in support of a supposed law of nature that a reasonable practice of scientists—rejecting and revising supposed laws in the light of exceptions—has been made to appear unreasonable.

Putting together these two objections to Hume's argument, it is fair to say that he has both left out of his account an important kind of evidence for miracles (indirect evidence) and grossly overestimated the weight that should be given to the past experience in support of some principle thought to be a law of nature. It remains true, however, that a reasonable person will require quite strong evidence before believing that a law of nature has been violated. It is easy to believe the person who claimed to see water run downhill, but quite difficult to believe that someone saw water run uphill.

TO BELIEVE IN DIVINE INTERVENTION

We have been preoccupied with Hume's argument that it is always more reasonable to believe that the witnesses were in error than to believe that a miraculous event actually occurred. His argument, as we saw, concerns only the first part of the definition of a miracle—that it is an event which violates a law of nature. It must be remembered, however, that to be a miracle an event must not only be a violation of a law of nature, it must also be due to the activity of God. As we noted earlier, it is one thing for an event to be due to no natural cause or force and quite another thing for it to be due to a supernatural cause.[12] In reply to Hume, we have argued that in certain circumstances it would be reasonable to believe that an event has occurred that is not due to any natural force or cause. But it must be recognized that this does not mean that it is reasonable to believe that a *miracle* has occurred. For there is still the question of whether the event was due to the activity of God. And, one might wonder, what reasons could we have or discover for thinking that the event in question is due to God's intervention?

If we already have good reason to believe that God exists and that he exercises providential care over his creation, then we might have good reasons for thinking that a particular violation of a law of nature is due to God. For the event itself and the circumstances in which it occurs might be just what one would expect given that God exists and exercises providential care over his creation. Indeed, insofar as we have reasons to believe that God exists and exercises providential care over his creation, the occurrence of miracles now and then might be what one would reasonably expect.

If we have no reason to believe that God exists, then it will be a good deal more difficult to discover reasons for thinking that a particular violation of a law of nature is due to the activity of God. For we would then have to have reasons for thinking that the violation is itself *evidence* for the existence of God. And if it is the *theistic* God that concerns us, it hardly seems possible that this should be so.[13]

In this chapter we have been concerned with three questions: (1) What are the conditions an event must satisfy if it is to be a genuine miracle? (2) Does the world-view due to the growth of science and technology render modern people incapable of believing in miracles? (3) Is it ever reasonable for us to believe that a genuine miracle has occurred? So far as the first question is concerned, we followed Hume's definition in terms of (i) being a violation of a law of nature, and (ii) being due to the direct activity of God. In response to question 2, although admitting that it is now more difficult to ascribe some happening in nature to a supernatural cause, I argued that the modern world view does not make it impossible to believe in miracles. Concerning 3, we concerned ourselves largely with Hume's classic argument against the reasonableness of believing that any event has occurred that violates a law of nature. His argument, we concluded, is not entirely successful since it ignores the possibility of strong indirect evidence for the occurrence of an event, and places too much weight on the side of the uniform past experience as evidence against the occurrence of a miraculous event. I concluded that there may well be circumstances in which it would be reasonable to believe that a violation of a law of nature has occurred. We noted, however, that it is reasonable to believe that a genuine miracle has occurred only if it is reasonable to believe both that a violation of a law of nature has occurred and that the violation is due to the direct intervention of God. If we have good reasons for believing that God exists, then in certain circumstances it might well be reasonable to believe that a violation is due to God's activity. But in the absence of good reasons for God's existence, it is highly unlikely that a violation of the laws of nature and the circumstances in which it occurs would justify us in inferring that the theistic God exists and brought about the violation.

Notes

1. Rudolf Bultmann, *Kerygma and Myth* (New York: Harper & Row Publishers, 1961), p. 5. Emphasis mine.
2. Bultmann, *Kerygma and Myth*, p. 5.
3. The essay "Of Miracles" appears as Section X of Hume's *Enquiry Concerning Human Understanding*, and is on pp. 109–31 in the Selby-Bigge edition of Hume's *Enquiries*, 2d ed. (London: Oxford University Press, 1902). The account I shall give, although derived from Hume's essay, is not intended to cover the troublesome issues that have arisen in the various interpretations of his essay. For an account of some of these issues

see Antony Flew, *Hume's Philosophy of Belief* (London: Routledge & Kegan Paul Ltd., 1961), Chapter VIII.

4. Hume's own words are: "A miracle may be accurately defined, a transgression of a law of nature by a particular volition of the Deity, or by the Interposition of some invisible agent." *Enquiries*, p. 115.

5. Hume, *Enquiries*, p. 115.

6. R. F. Holland, "The Miraculous," *American Philosophy Quarterly* (1965), 43–51.

7. Hume, *Enquiries*, pp. 114–15.

8. Hume, *Enquiries*, pp. 127–28.

9. For a more detailed account along these lines see R. G. Swinburne, "Miracles," *The Philosophical Quarterly*, XVIII, No. 73 (1968), pp. 320–28.

10. C. D. Broad, "Hume's Theory of the Credibility of Miracles," reprinted in Alexander Sesonske and Noel Fleming, eds., *Human Understanding* (Belmont, Calif.: Wadsworth, 1965), pp. 91–92. Broad's essay was originally published in *Proceedings of the Aristotelian Society*, XVII (London, 1916–1917), pp. 77–94.

11. Broad, "Hume's Theory," p. 93.

12. An event may violate a law of nature by having no natural cause and still not be a miracle by virtue of not having a divine cause. But if an event is due solely to the direct activity of God then, if it is an event that is covered by a natural law, it will also violate that law and thus be a miracle.

13. R. G. Swinburne has argued that it might be reasonable to infer the existence of some sort of deity if the violation occurred in ways and circumstances "strongly analogous" to those in which events occur due to human agents. See his "Miracles," *The Philosophical Quarterly*, XVIII, No. 73 (1968), pp. 320–28.

Topics for Review

1. For what reasons does Bultmann think that modern people cannot believe in miracles? Are his reasons convincing?
2. Explain Hume's notion of a miracle, and indicate some of the objections that may be raised against it.
3. What is Hume's central argument for the view that it is never reasonable to believe that a miracle has occurred?
4. What weaknesses can be found in Hume's argument?
5. If it can be shown that a violation of a law of nature has occurred, what more must we have reason to believe before we can call that violation a miracle? Does it make a difference whether we already have good reason to believe that God exists?

Topics for Further Study

6. Some theologians hold that miracles should not be understood as violations of the laws of nature. Rather they should be understood as events in which someone experiences the work of God. Discuss this view of miracles and compare it with the view elaborated in the chapter.
7. Suppose Hume is right in thinking it is never reasonable in practice to believe that a miracle has occurred. What implication would this view have for traditional theism? Would we be justified in rejecting theism or only justified in modifying it slightly? Explain.

Chapter

10

LIFE AFTER DEATH

VARIETIES OF IMMORTALITY

Since ancient times people have thought and wondered about the possibility of life after death. From the various major religions and civilizations there have emerged several distinct conceptions of the afterlife. Before we can think clearly about the question of life after death, therefore, we need to distinguish some of the different ways in which that life has been envisaged, for it is a mistake to think that all those who believe in human immortality believe in precisely the same thing.

In the civilization of ancient Greece there appear two distinct ideas of life after death, which, for ease of reference, I shall call the *Homeric* and the *Platonic* conceptions of immortality. In early Greek religion with its belief in the many gods of Olympus—Zeus, Hera, Poseidon, Hades and many others—the general conviction was that both human beings and gods had come into existence, but the gods, unlike people, never die; they alone are the *immortals*. No human being, properly speaking, can be immortal; for to be so he or she would have to be a god and not human. But in spite of the conviction that only the gods are immortal, the early Greeks did hold to some form of human life after death. They believed that some semblance of the living person survives bodily death, that, to quote Homer, "there is still something in the house of Hades, a soul and a phantom but no real life in it at all."[1] That which survives is but a shadow of the person who once lived on earth. At death a human being's spirit takes up some form of continued existence in Hades, the land of the dead. Compared to life before death, however, the life that survives death is seen as a poorer form of existence. Thus Homer has the mighty Achilles say: "Let me hear no smooth talk of death from you, Odysseus, light of councils. Better, I say, to break sod as a farm hand for some poor country man, on iron rations, than lord it over all the exhausted dead."[2] The *Homeric* belief in immortality, then, is a belief in some sort of survival of bodily death. But that which survives is apparently but a shadow of the mind and soul that inhabit the earthly body.

The *Platonic* conception of immortality involves the abandonment of the Homeric idea that only the gods are immortal. Human beings, too, on Plato's view, are truly immortal. Their bodies, of course, perish at death. But the person is not properly identified with his or her body; the person is the human soul, and the soul is that spiritual thing in us which reasons, imagines, and remembers. For the duration of its life on earth the soul is connected to, or imprisoned in, a particular body. But with physical death the soul escapes the prison house of the body and achieves its true state of endless life. In his dialogue *Phaedo*, Plato dramatically develops these ideas. Socrates, who has been condemned to drink the poison hemlock, meets for the last time with his followers and argues for the view that *he* is not his body but is really a spiritual soul in his body, that the soul is indestructible and, therefore, immortal, and that the life of the soul after bodily death is superior to its life in the body. At the end of the argument, Socrates' friend Crito asks, "But how shall we bury you?"

> "Any way you like," replied Socrates, "that is, if you can catch me and I don't slip through your fingers." He laughed gently as he spoke, and turning to us went on: "I can't persuade Crito that I am this Socrates here who is talking to you now and marshalling all the arguments; he thinks that I am the one whom he will see presently lying dead; and he asks how he is to bury me! As for my long and elaborate explanation that when I have drunk the poison I shall remain with you no longer, but depart to a state of heavenly happiness, this attempt to console both you and myself seems to be wasted on him."[3]

The Homeric and Platonic conceptions of immortality differ in at least three ways. First, unlike the Homeric person, the Platonic person is a true immortal. Second, Plato *identifies* the real person with the soul that occupies a physical, human body. There is no such clear separation of the person from the body in the Homeric conception. And, finally, in Plato, unlike in Homer, the life after death is viewed not as an inferior existence, but as actually superior to life on earth.

The common element in the two Greek conceptions of immortality we've considered is a belief in *individual* immortality. There are, however, nonindividual forms of the belief in immortality. The religions arising in India (Hinduism, Buddhism, and Jainism) generally consider individual immortality undesirable. In Hinduism, as expressed in its sacred writings, the *Upanishads*, there is developed a doctrine of the transmigration of souls, the passage of a soul at bodily death to another body. This "cycle of rebirth" continues until, by strenuous moral and spiritual effort, the soul gains its release and achieves its ultimate goal, its absorption into God, the Universal Soul. In this absorption the soul loses all individuality and consciousness.

One final form of the belief in life after death is associated with the idea of the *resurrection of the body*. According to this idea, as opposed to the Platonic view, the body is not simply the prison house of the real person, the soul.

Instead, the person is generally viewed as some sort of *unity* of soul and body, so that the continued existence of the soul after the destruction of the body would mean the survival of something less than the full person. On this view, a belief in a future life of the full person requires the reuniting of the soul with a resurrected body. Although strongly associated with Christianity, the doctrine of the resurrection of the body is also a tenet of the religion of Islam and, among the Jews at the time of Christ, was a distinguishing feature of the powerful group, the Pharisees. According to traditional Christian doctrine, at the day of judgment, when the world ends, the souls of all people will be reunited with their risen bodies. It is less than clear, however, just what the resurrected body will be like. According to Saint Paul it differs remarkably from the bodies with which we go through life. For unlike our earthly body, the resurrected body is neither corporeal (physical) nor perishable (mortal). The resurrected body is spiritual and immortal.[4]

We have been looking at some different conceptions of life after death. If we focus on those which emphasize the continued existence of the *individual,* we can distinguish at least three views: (i) disembodied existence of the soul after the death of the body; (ii) reincarnation of a soul after bodily death, and (iii) the reuniting of the soul with its resurrected body. And among these, the two ideas that have been dominant in western culture are the Platonic version in which the person is essentially the soul which survives bodily death, and the Christian version in which the person is a unity of soul and body and survives death by means of the reuniting of its soul with its resurrected body. Underlying these two major forms of the idea of life after death is a common conviction: *the human person exists and has experiences after the death of his or her body.* In the Platonic version the person is identified with a soul; in the Christian version the human person is viewed as a composite of body and soul. What we are concerned with, however, is the fundamental conviction that the person survives the death of his or her body.

There are two questions we need to raise concerning the basic conviction that the human person survives the death of his or her body. There is the *conceptual question:* Is the conviction *meaningful?* And there is the *factual question:* is the conviction *true?* Of course we can sensibly raise the factual question only if we assume an affirmative answer to the conceptual question. So we had best begin with it. Is the idea that the human person survives bodily death a meaningful idea?

THE MEANINGFULNESS
OF IMMORTALITY

What is the problem about the meaningfulness of personal immortality? Actually, philosophers have raised two problems. The first concerns *what it is for something to be a person.* The second concerns *what it is for something to be the same person.* If we think about what it is to be a person, what features or characteristics persons possess, we might form a list of some of the more important ones. Persons have or perform:

1. actions and intentions,
2. sensations and emotions,
3. thoughts and memories,
4. perceptions,
5. physical characteristics (height, coloring, shape, weight).

But if we think of something surviving bodily death, if we think of something having disembodied existence, can we reasonably think that that something has or performs any of characteristics 1–5? A soul, since it is incorporeal, has neither height, coloring, shape, nor weight. So we must rule out physical characteristics. What about perceptions: seeing, hearing, tasting, touching, smelling? It's difficult to understand how something that is purely spiritual could have any of these. Could it act or do things?

The problem is that our idea of human action seems closely bound up with that of physical movement, just as the idea of human emotion seems closely connected to the way people talk and behave. The general problem, then, is that many of the very basic things that human persons have and do either directly involve or in some way presuppose the human *body*. So, some philosophers have genuine doubts that the idea of a human person in the absence of a human body makes any sense at all. If their doubts are well founded, there is something basically wrong with the Platonic idea that the human person is to be identified with an immaterial substance, the soul. The idea that the person survives the death of the body is also thrown into question. The Christian version in which the person is a unity of soul and body, however, is not so clearly affected by these doubts. For in this version, the person is believed to be reconstituted after death by the uniting of soul and resurrected body. Here too, however, a difficulty will remain if the resurrected "body" is not really a body (that is, a *physical* thing) after all, as, we saw earlier, Saint Paul seemed to have held. One problem, then, about the meaningfulness of life after death concerns the question of whether it makes sense to think of a human person existing apart from a human body.

The second problem concerns what it is for something to be the *same person*. Let's suppose that in some way or another it is possible that a disembodied soul exists and is a person. The belief in life after death, however, is not just the belief that after bodily death something continues in existence and is a person. It is also the belief that the person that exists after bodily death is the *same* person that exists before bodily death. And this raises profoundly difficult questions about what it is that constitutes the *identity* of a person through time. On the Platonic view of human immortality, one would have to hold that there is some wholly mental or spiritual feature which constitutes the identity of the person. On the Christian version of life after death, there is the possibility of appealing to the sameness of body as a basis for the sameness of person. The general question raised by this second problem may be put as follows. What is the difference between the *same* person existing after bodily death and a *new* person existing after bodily death that resembles very closely the person that existed before death? A number of philosophers have thought that until we can give a clear, cogent answer to this question, we have no grounds for thinking it possible that the person who exists after bodily death is the *same* person that existed before bodily death.

We've noted the two major difficulties that give rise to the conceptual question concerning human immortality, the question of whether it is *meaningful* to believe in life after death. The solution to these difficulties involves some of the most complicated and controversial issues in philosophy, issues which we cannot pursue adequately here.[5] Having familiarized ourselves with the conceptual question concerning life after death, we shall here assume that the two problems giving rise to that question can be solved, and proceed to the factual question: Is the belief in life after death true?

THE CASE FOR IMMORTALITY

There are three main arguments in support of the view that human persons survive bodily death. For ease of reference we shall speak of these three arguments as the *philosophical* argument, the *scientific* argument, and the *theological* argument. Of these three, the philosophical is the oldest, dating back to Plato, and, as we shall see, the weakest. Let's begin our study of the case for immortality by examining it.

The Philosophical Argument

The *philosophical* argument rests on the Platonic view that the person is essentially a soul and that a soul is an immaterial, purely spiritual substance. Given this view as a starting point, philosophers, since Plato, have often employed the following argument in support of the view that the person (soul) is immortal.

1. A thing can be destroyed only by separating its parts.
2. The soul has no parts.

Therefore,

3. The soul cannot be destroyed.

This is an interesting argument and it has a good deal of persuasive force. Its persuasiveness, I think, derives from the fact that the destruction of a material thing always seems to involve, to a lesser or greater degree, the separation of its parts. But, it is argued, being immaterial the soul is not composed of parts; it is an indivisible unity. Therefore, the soul cannot be destroyed.

There are, I think, two forceful objections to this argument; one concerns the argument itself, and the second concerns the argument's assumption that the soul or mind is an *immaterial* substance. The objection to the argument itself rejects its first premise, the claim that the *only* way in which a thing can be destroyed is by separating its parts. This claim, so the objection goes, might well be true if it were restricted to *material* things. Perhaps all destruction of material things amounts to a separation of their parts. But then, of course, if the first premise were restricted to material things, all that we could conclude from the first and second premises is that the soul is not a material thing. So in order for the argument to yield its conclusion that the soul cannot be destroyed, the first premise must apply both to material and immaterial things. And it must say that the *only* mode of destruction that there is is destruction by separation of parts. But the question has been raised as to whether there is not a mode of destruction different from destruction by separation of parts, a mode of destruction appropriate to an immaterial substance. The German philosopher Immanuel Kant (1724–1804) thought that there was such a mode of destruction.

> Even if we admit the simple nature of the soul, namely, that it contains no manifold of constituents external to one another, and therefore no *extensive quantity*, we yet cannot deny to it, anymore than to any other existent, *intensive quantity*, that is, a degree of reality in respect of all its faculties, nay, in respect of all that constitutes its existence, and that this degree of reality may diminish through all the infinitely many smaller degrees. In this manner the supposed substance . . . may be changed into nothing, not by dissolution, but by gradual loss of its powers, . . .[6]

The point Kant is making is that although an immaterial substance has no extensive quantity and, therefore, cannot be destroyed by dissolution (separation of its parts), it may well have intensive quantity and, therefore, may be subject to destruction through the reduction of that intensive quantity to zero. Since the soul is conscious, for example, it may be more or less conscious. That is, the soul may be conscious to a greater or lesser *degree* (intensive quantity). If its degree of consciousness diminishes to zero, and a similar reduction occurs in its other functions, then we may say that the soul, although an immaterial substance, has been destroyed.

The second main objection to the argument for immortality based on the indestructibility of the soul challenges the underlying assumption that the human soul or mind is an *enduring, immaterial substance*. One line of attack is represented by *materialism*, the view that only physical things are real. On this view, as expressed, for example, in the writings of the Roman poet and philosopher Lucretius, the soul, like any other thing, is material in nature, closely associated with the body, and doomed to lose consciousness with the death of the body.[7]

Another line of attack rejects the idea that the soul or mind is a *substance* at all. Instead of viewing the soul or mind as an enduring thing which has experiences from time to time, many thinkers in the modern period have held that the mind is nothing more than a *series of mental events or experiences* that are related together by ties of succession, memory, and in other ways. On this view, sometimes called "the bundle theory of the self" the soul is a particular series of mental events and not an enduring substance. There is no underlying *mental substance* which endures through time and to which experiences like seeing and remembering occur. Rather there is just a series of *mental events*, events like seeing a cat, thinking about a friend, remembering an earlier experience. The soul is nothing more than a series of these mental events, events that are related to a particular human body. We can still raise the question of personal survival on this view. But the question will now be whether after bodily death the series of mental events associated with that body will cease or continue to have new members. On this conception of the soul or mind, therefore, the argument for immortality that we've been considering rests on a false assumption, the assumption that the soul is an enduring substance. For those thinkers in the modern period who reject this assumption, the philosophical argument for immortality gives no grounds whatever for believing in life after death.

The Scientific Argument

The *scientific* argument for the view that human persons survive bodily death consists almost entirely of the results of the scientific investigation of the strange phenomena of *mental mediumship*. Mediumistic phenomena are divided into physical and mental. The physical variety involves the apparition of a face or a hand or some quasi-physical representation of a person now dead. This material is very hard to study scientifically due to the restrictions imposed by the medium. The Society for Psychical Research (S.P.R.), founded in the eighties of the last century, and dedicated to the scientific study of paranormal phenomena, has endeavored to submit all mediumistic phenomena to careful study. It is the opinion of the society that most mediums that produce apparitions of hands and faces or other representations do so by trickery and fraud. Mental mediumship, however, is more easily studied scientifically and does yield results of such a startling nature that the hypothesis of communication with departed spirits is perhaps the most plausible hypothesis by which we can account for them. It is important, therefore, to consider carefully the phenomena of mental mediumship.

A medium is a living person who professes to be able to contact and receive messages from departed spirits, the spirits or minds of persons who have survived bodily death. The mechanics by which these messages are received and transmitted to living persons other than the medium are roughly as follows. Some living person who wishes to contact a departed spirit will contact a medium (directly or indirectly) and arrange a sitting. The *sitter* (the living person who wishes to contact a departed spirit) will either make the arrangements and appear in person at the sitting or have someone else, a *proxy sitter,* make the arrangements and meet with the medium. The proxy sitter will not have known the person now departed and may not even know the actual sitter. The proxy sitter will be given only a few scraps of information about the departed spirit and may communicate very little of this to the medium. When the actual sitter attends the sitting, he or she will usually conceal his or her identity from the medium in order to prevent the medium from using normal means to discover information about the person now dead. Considerable precautions, therefore, are taken to rule out the possibility that the medium could obtain by normal means the information she (most mediums are women) transmits.

At the sitting itself the medium generally enters a trancelike state. What happens then is that the medium's *control* takes over and speaks with the sitter. It is important to distinguish between the *control* and the *communicator*. The control purports to be a departed spirit that is somehow closely associated with a particular medium. The communicator is the departed spirit that the sitter wishes to contact. In the trancelike state the voice and personality of the medium may change considerably, taking on the characteristics of the control. The control may then establish a contact with the communicator and relay messages to the sitter from the departed spirit. The mediumistic evidence for survival, whatever weight we may attach to it, is provided by the messages from the communicator. The control generally runs the seance, looks after the medium, and brings the seance to a close when the medium is exhausted. Some investigators believe that the control is a secondary personality of the medium herself, or some subconscious level of the medium's personality that is repressed in ordinary conscious life.

Perhaps the best way to get a sense of the sort of evidence provided by mental mediumship is to consider a particular case. Among the many cases reported, there is the case of Edgar Vandy.[8] Vandy, an inventor, died under somewhat mysterious circumstances on August 6, 1933. His two brothers, George and Harold, unsatisfied by the results of the inquest, contacted several mediums on the chance that they might be able to shed some light on the last moment of their brother's life. George, although not a believer in survival after bodily death, had been a member of the S.P.R. for some years. He wrote to a Mr. Drayton Thomas, a well-known member of the Society, and asked him to make arrangements with a medium and to act as a proxy sitter. The only information given to Thomas was that information was being sought about a brother who had died recently, particularly about the cause of death. No names or details were given to Thomas, although he was told that there was a sister and a brother still living. Thomas agreed to arrange a proxy sitting. In addition, George and Harold each had sittings with several mediums, being careful to conceal their identities on each occasion and to give no actual information about Edgar Vandy. All the remarks made by the mediums were taken down verbatim by accomplished stenographers. In all, including the proxy sitting by Thomas, there were six sittings using four different mediums: Mrs. Leonard, Miss Campbell, Mrs. Mason, and Miss Bacon.

On the day of his death Edgar Vandy drove with a friend, N. J., to a private estate where N. J.'s sister was employed. The owner of the estate was away at the time and Edgar and N. J. decided to swim in the outdoor swimming pool. The pool was small, four feet deep at one end and seven feet deep at the other. They changed into swim trunks at some distance from the pool. When N. J. arrived at the pool, according to his testimony at the inquest, Edgar was lying on the surface of the water, face downwards, with his arms stretched out and fluttering his hands. Realizing something was wrong, N. J. jumped in and tried to pull Edgar out, lost his grip, and was unable to prevent Edgar from sinking in the cloudy water. N. J. went for help. Edgar's body was recovered by the police some time later. According to the medical evidence death was due to drowning. There were bruises under the chin and the tongue had been bitten through. The doctor suggested that Edgar had dived in (there was a diving board), struck his jaw and lost consciousness, and had then drowned. According to his brothers, however,

Edgar could not dive and could barely swim at all. Thus the mystery of his death prompted them to seek the help of mediums.

Although the messages received from the mediums did not satisfactorily clear up the matter, information was given by the mediums both about Edgar's death and about the nature of his work that is quite impossible to account for by any normal means. It must be remembered that the mediums had been given no information about these matters at all, nor were they told the identity of the departed person. Despite this, however, the mediums received messages to the effect that the person in question had died by some sort of strange accident, that he had drowned in an outdoor pool, that some sort of stunning blow had been received just prior to the drowning, and that someone else was present, tried to help, but for some reason was unable to do so. A typical example runs as follows:

> (The sitter interpolated the question: "Can he tell us exactly what happened?" and the medium continued as follows) . . . He passed out through *water.* I don't think it was a *swimming-bath.* I am in a *private kind of pool,* and I am getting *diving* and things like that. Yes, I am *out of doors,* I am not enclosed—it is like a private swimming-pool . . . You know he had a *blow on the head* before he passed over. . . . There was a *diving-board,* and whether someone knocked him or not, I don't know . . . He remembers going under and feeling a distinct blow on the head. He could not come up, as he apparently *lost consciousness under the water.* . . . It is an open-air pool, and he says he must have *fallen forward,* and *crashed in,* and *knocked his head* . . . I will try to re-enact his passing, which he is trying to show me: "I was sliding to the bottom of the pool in this very fainting condition, owing to pitching forward in some way and knocking my head just before" . . .[9]

At the time of his death Edgar Vandy had just invented a rather elaborate machine which he called the "Electroline" Drawing Machine. The machine was designed to accomplish by mechanical means results which had before been achieved only by skilled hand-work. The machine was not yet patented, and had been put together with considerable secrecy by Edgar in a room in the house of a cousin. Other rooms in the house contained some business machines, but in this room only the newly constructed Drawing Machine was kept. In the sitting with Miss Bacon, Harold Vandy asked: "Can he" (Edgar) "describe the nature of his principle work?" She responded as follows:

> He was extremely clever at something he was doing, and it has upset him terribly because all his work on earth has stopped. That is his greatest grief . . . He shows me a room, and I don't know if it has to do with wireless or radio, but it is like machinery and machines going very rapidly, as though they were producing something. All this machinery seems to go up and down. I don't say that it is electrical, the machines are actually producing something . . . He seems to have something to do in tending them. I don't get it quite accurately. There is a terrific noise . . .[10]

Harold then asked: "Were there several machines?"

> . . . Not in the room he was in. There are in *other parts,* but there seems to be *only one with him* . . . There were more machines, but he did a particular thing . . . Would

lithography or something of that sort come into it? He says *"lithography* or something to do with *printing"* . . . I don't know whether *photography* comes into it as well, but he is trying to show me *plates* or something . . . It seems to be *very fine work*, but in the room he is in I do not get many machines, but *one special machine*. In other parts of the building there are more, but he had a special thing. He was very accurate in it and took a great pride in it.[11]

What are we to make of these rather extraordinary revelations by the several mediums contacted in the Edgar Vandy case? We can certainly agree with C. D. Broad that "It is quite incredible that the amount and kind of concordance actually found between the statements made by the various mediums at the various sittings should be *purely a matter of chance-coincidence."*[12] It is also simply incredible that the degree of correspondence between what the mediums revealed and the known facts about Edgar Vandy should be due to chance-coincidence. It seems clear that we must either suppose an elaborate fraud perpetrated by both the sitters and the mediums or admit the occurrence of modes of perception beyond those we are familiar with in everyday life. If we reject the supposition of fraud, it would seem that by far the simplest explanation of the facts of the case is the hypothesis that Edgar Vandy's personality survived bodily death and somehow communicated various messages through the mediums. The only other hypothesis that is in the least plausible is what has been called "the Super Extra-Sensory Perception Hypothesis." According to this hypothesis all the relevant information conveyed at the sittings came from the minds of people still living, presumably from N. J. and the surviving brothers. By some paranormal process the mediums gathered the information from these various sources and, while in a trance-like state, presented it in the form of communication from the surviving spirit of Edgar Vandy.

Between the survival hypothesis and the Super ESP hypothesis it is difficult to choose. When we think of proxy sittings when the proxy does not personally know either the deceased or the surviving relatives, it stretches the mind almost beyond limits to believe that during the sitting the medium, or her unconscious, manages somehow to get in touch with various documents or with the minds of the surviving relatives. Does the medium somehow follow a telepathic link from the sitter, who is just a proxy, to the absent friends and relatives of the deceased, and then tap their memories of the deceased?[13] On the other hand, as we shall see, the survival hypothesis has against it not only the philosophical difficulties noted earlier, but a formidable scientific argument as well.

The Theological Argument

The *theological* argument for life after death rests on the belief that the theistic God exists. If we begin with this belief as a foundation, a quite formidable argument for human survival can be built. For according to theism, God has created finite persons to exist in fellowship with himself. But if this is true then it seems to contradict his own purpose and his love for his creatures if he allows them to perish completely when his purpose for them remains unfulfilled. Consequently, if it is reasonable to believe that the theistic God exists it is certainly reasonable to believe in life after death.

THE CASE AGAINST IMMORTALITY

We have been looking at the three major lines of argument making up the case for the view that the human person survives the death of its body. Before we make some final assessment of the case for human immortality, it will be instructive to consider the major line of argument constituting the case against life after death. Like the argument from mental mediumship, this argument is scientific in nature, rather than strictly philosophical or theological. Unlike the argument from mental mediumship, however, this argument is based on facts familiar to all of us.

The general theme of the scientific argument against immortality has been set forth by Bertrand Russell.

> Persons are part of the everyday world with which science is concerned, and the conditions which determine their existence are discoverable. A drop of water is not immortal; it can be resolved into oxygen and hydrogen. If, therefore, a drop of water were to maintain that it had a quality of aqueousness which would survive its dissolution we should be inclined to be skeptical. In like manner we know that the brain is not immortal, and that the organized energy of a living body becomes, as it were, demobilized at death and therefore not available for collective action. All the evidence goes to show that what we regard as our mental life is bound up with brain structure and organized bodily energy. Therefore it is rational to suppose that mental life ceases when bodily life ceases. The argument is only one of probability, but it is as strong as those upon which most scientific conclusions are based.[14]

The central point in this argument is that the evidence we have indicates that our mental life is *dependent* on certain bodily processes, particularly those associated with the brain. We know, for example, that damage to various parts of the brain results in the cessation of certain kinds of conscious states—memories, thought processes, and the like. It seems eminently reasonable to infer from this that consciousness is dependent for its existence on the existence and proper function of the human brain. When at death the brain ceases to function, the reasonable inference is that our mental life ceases as well.

The English philosopher J. M. E. McTaggart (1866–1925) has suggested that the strength of the scientific argument against immortality perhaps depends on a *false analogy* of the relation of the mind to the body. If we think of the mind as a person enclosed in a room with only one window, we can readily understand the dependence of mental functions on the body without having to suppose that with the death of the body the life of the mind must cease. For while a person is enclosed in the room, experience of the outside world will *depend* on the condition of the window. Board up the window partly or completely and you will affect tremendously the sorts of experiences the person in the room can have. So too, when the human person is alive in a body, changes to that body (particularly the brain) will have considerable effect on the sorts of mental experiences the person is capable of having. But perhaps bodily death is *analogous* to the person gaining freedom from the enclosed room so that she or he is no longer dependent on the window for experience of the outside world. At death perhaps, so McTaggart suggests, the mind loses its dependency on the bodily organs such as the brain.

The mere fact that the mind is dependent on the functioning of the brain *while it (the mind) is associated with a living body* is no more proof that the mind will cease functioning at bodily death than is the fact that the person is dependent on the window *while she or he is in the room* proof that when the room and window are no more the person will cease having experiences of the outside world.[15]

How are we to assess the evidence for and against immortality? Clearly, the strongest argument for immortality rests on the belief that the theistic God exists. Many theists would not quarrel with this conclusion. The grounds for life after death are perhaps no better or worse than the grounds we have for accepting theism. The scientific argument against immortality appears fairly strong. Perhaps, as McTaggart argues, its strength depends on our accepting a certain view of the relation of the mind to the body. But against McTaggart, the evidence seems to show that the relation between our bodies and our mental life is enormously more intimate and complex than that between a human being and a room in which he or she happens to be enclosed. If we discount the argument based on the view that the soul is an immaterial substance, we are left with the argument based on the extraordinary phenomenon of mental mediumship. That phenomenon does seem to provide evidence for some form of personal survival of bodily death.

Perhaps the most reasonable view to accept at this point is (1) that the argument from the nature of the soul is unconvincing, (2) that the scientific argument for and the scientific argument against personal survival both have merit, (3) that the scientific arguments tend to balance one another out, and (4) that the belief in life after death is reasonable provided that it is reasonable to accept theism.

Notes

1. *The Iliad,* Book 23, tr. W. H. D. Rouse (New York: The New American Library, 1950), p. 267.
2. *The Odyssey,* Book 11, tr. Robert Fitzgerald (Garden City, New York: Doubleday & Company, Inc., 1963), p. 201.
3. *Phaedo,* 115 C, D. in *Plato: The Last Days of Socrates,* tr. Hugh Tredennick (Baltimore, Maryland: Penguin Books, 1954), p. 179.
4. I Corinthians, 15: 42–44.
5. For further discussion of these conceptual issues see Anthony Quinton, "The Soul," *The Journal of Philosophy* XLIX (1962), pp. 393–409; Peter Geach, *God and The Soul* (London: Routledge & Kegan Paul Ltd., 1969); and Terrence Penelhum, *Survival and Disembodied Existence* (London: Routledge & Kegan Paul Ltd., 1970).
6. Immanuel Kant, *Critique of Pure Reason,* tr. Norman Kemp Smith (London: Macmillan & Co., 1956), p. 373. Emphasis mine.
7. Lucretius, *De rerum natura.*
8. The report is in the S. P. R. *Journal,* XXXIX (1957). A lengthy analysis of the case is given by C. D. Broad in *Lectures on Psychical Research* (London: Routledge & Kegan Paul Ltd., 1962), Chapter XV, pp. 350-83.
9. Quoted by Broad in *Lectures on Psychical Research,* pp. 364–65.
10. Quoted by Broad in *Lectures on Psychical Research,* p. 374.
11. Quoted by Broad in *Lectures on Psychical Research,* p. 375.
12. Broad, *Lectures on Psychical Research,* p. 380.

13. For a careful discussion of the Super ESP hypothesis to which I am indebted see H. H. Price, "The Problem of Life After Death," *Religious Studies*, III, pp. 447–59.
14. Bertrand Russell, *Why I Am Not a Christian* (New York: Simon and Schuster, 1957), p. 51.
15. See J. M. E. McTaggart, *Some Dogmas of Religion* (London: Edward Arnold, 1906; reprinted, New York: Kraus Reprint Co., 1969), pp. 103–6.

Topics for Review

1. Explain the various conceptions of life after death that have emerged in human civilization. What are the two ideas of personal survival that have been dominant in western culture?
2. Explain the two difficulties philosophers have raised about the meaningfulness of personal survival.
3. Explain the philosophical, scientific, and theological arguments in support of the view that human persons survive bodily death.
4. What are the chief objections to the three arguments in support of the view that human persons survive bodily death?
5. Explain and evaluate the major scientific argument against life after death. What final judgment can we make about the reasons for and against personal survival after bodily death?

Topics for Further Study

6. How important to religion is the belief in personal survival after bodily death? Do you think that religion must stand or fall with this belief? Can you imagine a viable religion which accepts the view that death ends everything? What would such a religion be like? Explain.
7. Of the various arguments for and against personal survival, select what you think is the strongest for and the strongest against. Carefully discuss each of these two arguments, indicating which of the two is, in your judgment, the most plausible.

11

PREDESTINATION, DIVINE FOREKNOWLEDGE, AND HUMAN FREEDOM

HUMAN FREEDOM AND DIVINE PREDESTINATION

As a seventeen-year-old convert to a quite orthodox branch of Protestantism, the first theological problem to concern me was the question of Divine Predestination and Human Freedom. Somewhere I read the following line from the Westminster Confession: "God from all eternity did . . . freely and unchangeably ordain whatsoever comes to pass." In many ways I was attracted to this idea. It seemed to express the majesty and power of God over all that he had created. It also led me to take an optimistic view of events in my own life and the lives of others, events which struck me as bad or unfortunate. For I now viewed them as planned by God before the creation of the world—thus they must serve some good purpose unknown to me. My own conversion, I reasoned, must also have been ordained to happen, just as the failure of others to be converted must have been similarly ordained. But at this point in my reflections, I hit upon a difficulty, a difficulty that made me think harder than I ever had before in my life. For I also believed that I had chosen God out of my own free will, that each of us is responsible for choosing or rejecting God's way. But how could I be responsible for a choice which, from eternity, God had ordained I would make at that particular moment in my life? How can it be that those who reject God's way do so of their own free will, if God, from eternity, destined them to reject his way? The Westminster Confession itself seemed to recognize the difficulty. For its next line read: "Yet . . . thereby is no violence offered to the will of the creatures."

For a time I accepted both Divine Predestination and human freedom and responsibility. I felt that although I could not see how both could be true, they, nevertheless, might both be true, so I accepted them both on faith. But the longer I thought about it the more it seemed to me that they couldn't both be true. That is, I came to the view, rightly or wrongly, that I not only could not see how both could be true, I *could* see that they could not both be true. Slowly I abandoned the belief that before eternity God ordained whatever comes to pass. I took the view, instead, that before eternity God knew whatever comes to pass, including our free choices and acts, but that those choices and acts were not determined in advance.

What I did not know in those early years was that the topics of Predestination, Divine Foreknowledge, and Human Freedom had been the focus of philosophical and theological reflection for centuries. In this chapter we shall acquaint ourselves with the various views that have emerged from those centuries of intellectual endeavor, thus enlarging our understanding of the theistic concept of God and one of the problems that has emerged in connection with it.

Freedom of Will or Choice

Perhaps it's best to begin with the idea of human freedom. For, as we shall see, there are two quite different ways in which this idea has been understood, and which way we follow makes a great deal of difference to the topic under consideration. According to the first idea, *acting freely consists in doing what you want or choose to do.* If you want to leave the room but are forcibly restrained from doing so, we certainly would agree that *staying in the room* is not something you do freely. You do not freely stay in the room because it is not what you choose or want to do, it happens against your will.

Suppose we accept this first idea of human freedom, whereby acting freely consists in doing what you want or choose to do. The problem of divine predestination and human freedom will then turn out to be not much of a problem at all. Why so? Well, to take the example of my youthful conversion, my conversion was free if it was something I wanted to do, chose to do, did not do against my will. Let's suppose, as I believe is true, that my conversion was something I chose to do, wanted to do. Is there any difficulty in believing also that before eternity God ordained that at that particular moment in my life I would be converted? It doesn't seem that there is. For God could simply have ordained also that at that particular moment in my life I would *want* to choose Christ, to follow God's way. If so, then, on our first idea of human freedom, my act of conversion was both a free act on my part and ordained by God from eternity. On our first idea of human freedom, then, there does not seem to be any real conflict between the doctrine of divine predestination and human freedom. Is our first idea of human freedom correct? One reason for thinking that it is not was provided by the English philosopher John Locke (1632–1704). Locke asks us to suppose that a man is brought into a room while asleep. The door, which is the only way out of the room, is then securely bolted from the outside. The man does not know that the door is bolted, does not know, therefore, that he *cannot* leave the room. He awakens, finds himself in the room, looks about and notices that there are friendly people in the room with whom he would like to converse. Accordingly, he decides to stay in the room rather than leave.[1]

What are we to say of this man? Is his act *staying in the room* something he does *freely*? Well, according to our first idea of human freedom, it would seem that it is. For staying in the room is what he wants to do. He considers leaving, not knowing that he cannot leave, but rejects it because he prefers to stay in the room and engage in friendly conversation. But can we really believe that staying in the room is something he does *freely*? After all, it is the only thing that can be done. He stays in the room *of necessity*, for leaving the room is something that is not in his power to do. What is the difference between him and a second man, similarly placed, who wants to leave, but being unable to leave, also stays in the room of necessity? Is the difference that the first man does something freely, whereas, the second man does not? Or is it, rather, that the first man is just more *fortunate* than the second? Each does what he does (stay in the room) of necessity, not freely, but the first man is more fortunate in that what he *must do* turns out to be the very thing that he wants to do. Locke concludes that the first man is not more free than the second, only more fortunate. For freedom, Locke contends, consists in more than simply doing what one wants or chooses, it also must be that *it was in one's power to do otherwise*. And the reason why the first man, no less than the second, did not stay in the room freely is because it was not in his power to do otherwise, to leave the room.

The Power to Do Otherwise

The second idea of human freedom is that we do something freely only if, at the time just before we do it, it is in our power to do otherwise. And I think that on reflection we can see that the second idea is more adequate than the first. Consider, for example, growing old. This is something we do of necessity, not freely. The mere fact that someone prefers to grow old, wants to grow old, is not sufficient for it being true that he or she grows old *freely*—at best we might say that he or she grows old gracefully. Suppose, however, a process is discovered and made available whereby each of us has the power not to grow old in the sense of physical aging. Although time continues to pass, the aging process in our bodies can now be slowed enormously. Under these conditions it could be true that someone grows old freely, for one would not then grow old of necessity, it being in a person's power to do otherwise. The first idea of freedom must be abandoned in favor of the second, more adequate idea.

It is the second idea of freedom that appears to be in conflict with the idea of divine predestination. For if God has determined, from eternity, that I will be converted at a certain moment on a particular day, how can it be in my power just prior to that moment to refrain from being converted? To ascribe such a power to me is to ascribe to me the power to prevent from taking place something that God from eternity has ordained to take place. Surely if from eternity God has determined that something will happen it cannot be in some creature's power to prevent that thing from taking place. Therefore, if from eternity God did ordain whatever comes to pass, then there is nothing that happens which we could have prevented from happening. So, since whatever I do has been ordained by God to take place, it is never in my power to do otherwise. And if it is never in my power to do otherwise, then nothing I do is done freely. Human freedom, it seems, is inconsistent with divine predestination.

If the above argument is correct, as I'm inclined to believe it is, the theist must either abandon the belief in human freedom or the doctrine of divine predestination. And it seems reasonable that between the two, the doctrine of divine predestination should be given its walking papers. That God has *ultimate control* over the destiny of his creation and that he *knows* in advance of its happening everything that will happen are ideas that preserve the majesty of God and provide for some degree of human optimism, without requiring that God has *decreed* to happen whatever does happen. And on the surface at least, it does not appear that the doctrine of divine foreknowledge conflicts with human freedom. So perhaps the reasonable thing to do is to reject the doctrine of divine predestination, while preserving the belief in human freedom and the doctrine of divine foreknowledge.

THE CONFLICT BETWEEN HUMAN FREEDOM AND DIVINE FOREKNOWLEDGE

But if God has not ordained from eternity everything that will happen, how is it possible for him to have known from eternity everything that happens? Doesn't the doctrine of divine foreknowledge presuppose the doctrine of divine predestination? Having decreed that something will happen at a certain time would be a way in which God could know in advance that it will happen. But it is not the only way in which God might have possessed such knowledge. We possess telescopes, for example, that enable us to know what is happening at places some distance away, because by means of the telescope we can see them happening. Imagine that God has something like a *time* telescope, a telescope that enables one to see what is happening at times some distance away. By turning the lens one focuses on a certain time, say a thousand years from now, and sees the events that are occurring at that time. With some such image as this we might account for God's foreknowledge without supposing that his knowledge is derived from his prior decree that the events in question will occur. He knows in advance the events that will take place by *foreseeing* them, not by *foreordaining* them. The doctrine of divine foreknowledge, then, does not presuppose the doctrine of divine predestination. And, as we noted earlier, there does not appear to be any conflict between divine foreknowledge and human freedom. For although God's *foreordaining* something makes that something happen, his *foreknowing* does not make it happen. Things occur not because God foreknows them; rather, he foreknows them because they occur.

Unfortunately, things are not so simple as that. There is a serious problem about divine foreknowledge and human freedom. And although we may not be able to solve this problem, it will be instructive to try to understand the problem and see what the various "solutions" are that have been advanced by important philosophers and theologians. Perhaps the best way to start is by stating the problem in the form of an argument, an argument that begins with the doctrine of divine foreknowledge and ends with the denial of human freedom. Once we understand the major premises of the argument, as well as the reasons given in support of them, we will have come to an understanding of one of the major problems theologians have wrestled with for almost two thousand years: the problem of reconciling the doctrine of divine foreknowledge with the belief in human freedom.

1. God knows before we are born everything we will do.
2. If God knows before we are born everything we will do, then it is never in our power to do otherwise.
3. If it is never in our power to do otherwise, then there is no human freedom.

Therefore,

4. There is no human freedom.

The first premise of the argument expresses an apparent implication of the doctrine of divine foreknowledge. The third premise simply states an implication of the second idea of freedom we considered earlier. According to that idea, we do something freely only if, at the time just before we do it, it is in our power to do otherwise. Thus, we concluded that the act of staying in the room was freely done only if, at the time of the decision to stay in the room, it was in the person's power to do otherwise, that is, to leave the room. Since the door was securely bolted from the outside, we concluded that he did not *freely* stay in the room. Now premise (3) merely draws the logical conclusion from this second idea of freedom: if it is *never* in our (any human being's) power to do otherwise, then there is no human freedom. Since the argument is clearly valid, the remaining question concerns premise (2): if God knows before we are born everything we will do then it is never in our power to do otherwise. Why should we accept this premise? Clearly if we replaced the word *knows* with the word *ordains* the statement would be true. But the whole point of abandoning divine predestination in favor of divine foreknowledge was that although

a) If God *ordains* before we are born everything we will do, then it is never in our power to do otherwise,

seems surely true, it does not seem to be true that

b) If God *knows* before we are born everything we will do then it is never in our power to do otherwise.

Since premise 2 is the same as b why should we now accept it as true? What is the reasoning by which the proponent of this argument hopes to convince us that 2 is true?

The reasoning in support of 2 is complex, so it will be best to develop it by means of an example. Let's suppose it is 2:00 P.M. on a particular Tuesday and that you have a class in philosophy of religion that meets at 2:30. Your friends ask you to go with them to an afternoon movie, but, after considering the proposal, you somehow manage to resist temptation, and elect to attend class instead. It is now 2:45 and your instructor is carrying on about foreknowledge and free will. Somewhat bored, you now wish that you had gone to the movie instead of coming to class. You realize, however, that although you now regret your decision there is nothing that you can do about it. Of course, you could get up from your seat and rush off to see what is left of the movie. But you cannot now, at

2:45, bring it about that you did not go to class at 2:30, you cannot *now* bring it about that you actually went to the movie instead. You can regret what you did, and resolve never to make that mistake again, but, like it or not, you are stuck with the fact that instead of going to the movie you went to class at 2:30. You are stuck with it because it is *a fact about the past* and you cannot *alter the past*. Our inability to alter the past is enshrined in the colloquialism, "There's no use crying over spilt milk." Within limits, however, the future seems open, pliable; we can make it to be one way or another. You believe, for example, that on Thursday, when the class meets again, it will be in your power to go to class and it will be in your power to go to a movie instead. But the past is not open, it is closed, solid like granite, and in no way within your power to alter. As Aristotle observed:

> No one deliberates about the past but only about what is future and capable of being otherwise, while what is past is not capable of not having taken place; hence Agathon is right in saying: "For this alone is lacking, even in God, to make undone things that have once been done."[2]

There are, of course, a large number of facts about the past relative to 2:45 on Tuesday. In addition to the fact that at 2:30 you came to class, there is the fact of your birth, the fact that you became a college student, the fact that Nixon resigned from the Presidency, indeed, all the facts of past history. And what you now know is that at 2:45 it is not in your power to alter *any* of them. There is nothing that is now in your power to do such that were you to do it, any of these facts about the past would not have been facts about the past. Pondering your powerlessness over the past, you notice that your instructor has written on the board another fact about the past:

F. Before you were born God knew that you would come to class at 2:30 this Tuesday.

If God exists and the doctrine of divine foreknowledge is true, F is certainly a fact about the past, and it has been a fact about the past at every moment of your life. It is a fact about the past *now*—at 2:45 on Tuesday—it was a fact about the past *yesterday*, and it will be a fact about the past *tomorrow*. At this point your instructor turns and asks: "Was it in your power at 2:00 to have refrained from coming to class today?" You certainly think that it was—indeed, you now regret that you did not exercise that power—so the instructor writes on the board:

A. It was in your power at 2:00 to do something other than come to class at 2:30 this Tuesday.

But now let's think for a bit about F and A. At 2:00, F was a fact about the past. But according to A, it was in your power at 2:00 to do something (go to a movie, say) such that had you done it, what is a fact about the past (F) would not have been a fact about the past. For, clearly, if you had *exercised* your power to refrain from coming to class at 2:30 what God would have known before you were born is not what he in fact knew, that you would come to class this Tuesday, but something quite different, that you would do something else. And this in turn means that if F is a fact about the past—as it surely is if the doctrine of divine foreknowledge is true—and if A is true, then it was in your power at 2:00 this Tuesday to *alter the past;* it was in your power to do something (go to a movie) such that had you done it, what *is* a fact about the past (F) would not have been a fact about the past. If then, *it is never in our power to alter a fact about the past,* it cannot be both that F was a fact about the past and also that it was in your power at 2:00 to refrain from coming to class at 2:30 this Tuesday.

What we have just seen is that given the doctrine of divine foreknowledge and the claim that it is in our power to have done something we did not do, it follows that it was in our power to have altered the past. For given the doctrine of divine foreknowledge it follows that *before you were born* God knew that you would come to class at 2:30 this Tuesday. And if we now claim that *at 2:00* it was in your power to have done otherwise, we imply that at 2:00 it was in your power to alter a fact about the past, the fact that before you were born God knew that you would come to class at 2:30. But we earlier concluded that we are powerless over the past, that facts about the past are not within our power to alter. If we keep to this conviction—as it seems we must—then we must conclude that if God did know before you were born that you would be in class at 2:30 (this Tuesday) then it was *not* in your power at 2:00 to do otherwise. And generalizing from this particular example, we can conclude that if it is never in our power to alter the past, then if God knows before we are born everything we will do, then it is never in our power to do otherwise.

We have worked our way through the rather complex reasoning that can be used to support premise 2 of the argument designed to show a conflict between divine foreknowledge and human freedom. That premise, as you recall, says that if God knows before we are born everything we will do, then it is never in our power to do otherwise. Reduced to its simplest terms, the reasoning given in support of 2 consists in arguing that if 2 is not true, then it is in our power to alter the past. But it is never in our power to alter the past, so 2 must be true. From

(i) God knows before we are born everything we will do and,
(ii) It is sometimes in our power to do otherwise

it follows, so the reasoning goes, that it is sometimes in our power to alter the past. Since it is never in our power to alter the past, premises (i) and (ii) can't both be true. Hence, if (i) is true then (ii) is false. But to say that (ii) is false is just to say that it is *never* in our power to do otherwise. So if (i) is true then it is *never* in our power to do otherwise—and this is exactly what premise 2 says.

SOME SOLUTIONS TO THE CONFLICT

We've had a look at perhaps the strongest argument for the view that the doctrine of divine foreknowledge, no less than the doctrine of divine predestination, is in fundamental conflict with the belief in human freedom, an argument that has troubled philosophers and theologians for centuries. It is now time to consider the various "solutions" that have been offered and to assess their strengths and weaknesses.

The argument itself limits the number of possible solutions that can be advanced to the following four:

I. *Rejection of premise 3:* denies that we do something freely only if it is in our power to do otherwise

II. *Rejection of premise 2:* denies that divine foreknowledge implies that it is never in our power to do otherwise

III. *Rejection of premise 1:* denies that God has foreknowledge of future events

IV. *Acceptance of the conclusion 4:* denies that we have human freedom

Solutions III and IV are "radical" solutions since they amount to a denial either of the doctrine of divine foreknowledge or of human freedom. No theist seriously proposes IV, so we may safely dismiss it. III, however, as we shall see, is the solution preferred by a number of important theologians, including Boethius and Aquinas. Let's consider, then, the first three solutions to this perplexing problem.

The Definition of Freedom

The first solution rejects premise 3 of the argument, charging that 3 expresses a mistaken idea of human freedom. As we saw earlier, there are two different ideas of freedom. According to the first idea, acting freely consists in no more than doing what you want or choose to do; freedom does not require the power to do otherwise. Those who accept this idea of human freedom rightly see no conflict between it and divine foreknowledge. Indeed, as we noted earlier, there is no conflict between this idea of human freedom and the doctrine of divine predestination. A solution along these lines was developed most fully by the American theologian Jonathan Edwards (1703–58). The adequacy of this solution depends entirely on whether its idea of what human freedom consists in can be defended against the criticisms philosophers have advanced against it.[3] However, having rejected this idea of freedom in favor of the second idea—the idea that we do something freely only if it is in our power to do otherwise—we shall not pursue further this first solution to the problem of divine foreknowledge and human freedom. For given the second idea of human freedom, premise 3 must be accepted as true.

Power to Alter the Past

The second major solution rejects premise 2, thereby denying that divine foreknowledge implies that it is never in our power to do otherwise. Actually, what this solution shows, if successful, is not that 2 is false, but that the reasoning given in support of it is mistaken. What is that reasoning? Well, reduced to its briefest terms, the reasoning is that if 2 is not true then it is in our power to alter facts about the past—facts about what God knew before we were even born. But, so the reasoning goes, it is never in anyone's power to alter the past, therefore 2 must be true. The second solution challenges the claim that it is never in our power to alter the past, arguing that we do have the power to alter certain facts about the past, including certain facts about what God knew before we were even born. This solution was suggested by the most influential philosopher of the fourteenth century, William of Ockham (1285–1349).

The basic point on which the second solution rests involves a distinction between two types of facts about the past: facts which are *simply* about the past, and facts which are *not simply* about the past. To illustrate this distinction, let's consider two facts about the past, facts about the year 1941.

f_1: In 1941 Japan attacks Pearl Harbor.
f_2: In 1941 a war begins between Japan and the United States that lasts five years.

Relative to 1992, f_1 and f_2 are both *simply* about the past. But suppose we consider the year 1943. Relative to 1943, f_1 is a fact that is simply about the past, but f_2 is not simply about the past. It is a fact about the past relative to 1943, for f_2 is, in part, a fact about 1941, and 1941 lies in 1943's past. But f_2, unlike f_1, implies a certain fact about 1944; namely,

f_3: In 1944 Japan and the United States are at war.

Since f_2 implies f_3, a fact about the future relative to 1943, we can say that relative to 1943 f_2 is a fact about the past, but not simply a fact about the past. We have then three facts, f_1, f_2, and f_3, about which we can say that relative to 1992 each is a fact simply about the past. Relative to 1943, however, only f_1 is simply about the past—f_2 is about the past but not simply about the past, and f_3 is not about the past at all.

Having illustrated the distinction between a fact which, relative to a certain time t, is simply about the past and a fact which, relative to t, is not simply about the past, we are now in a position to appreciate its importance. Think of 1943 and the groups of persons then in power in both Japan and the United States. Neither group had it in its power to do anything about f_1. Both groups may have regretted the actions which brought it about that f_1 is a fact about the past. But it is abundantly clear that among all the things which, in 1943, it was in their power to do, none is such that, had they done it, f_1 would not have been a fact about the past. It makes no sense to look back upon 1943 and say that if only one of these groups had *then* done such-and-such, f_1 would never have been a fact about the past. It makes no sense precisely because, relative to 1943, f_1 is a fact *simply* about the past. Nothing that could have been done by anyone in 1943 would have in any way altered the fact that in 1941 Japan attacked Pearl Harbor.

But what about f_2, the fact that in 1941 a war begins between Japan and the United States that lasts five years. We know that in 1943 neither group did anything that altered this fact about 1941. The question, however, is whether there were things that were not done in 1943, things which, nevertheless, were in the power of one or both of the groups to do, and which, had they been done, a certain fact about 1941, f_2, would not have been a fact at all. Perhaps there were not. Perhaps the momentum of the war was such that neither group had the power to bring it to an end in 1943. Most of us, I suppose, think otherwise. We think that there probably were certain actions that were not, but could have been, taken by one or both of the groups in 1943, actions which, had they been taken, would have brought the war to an end in 1943. If what we think to be so is so, then it was in the power of one or both of the groups in 1943 to alter a fact about the past; it was in their power in 1943 to do something such that, had they done it, a certain fact about 1941, f_2, would not have been a fact about 1941. The basic reason why in 1943 f_2 may have been in their power to alter, whereas f_1 certainly was not, is that, unlike f_1, f_2 is not simply about the past relative to 1943, for f_2 implies a certain fact about 1944, that in 1944, Japan and the United States are at war (f_3).

What the above reasoning suggests is that our conviction that the past is beyond our power to affect is certainly true, so far as facts which are simply about the past are concerned. Facts which are about the past, but *not simply* about the past, may not, however, be beyond our power to affect. And what Ockham saw is that the facts about divine foreknowledge which are used as the basis for denying human freedom are facts about the past, but *not simply* about the past. Consider again the fact that before you were born, God knew that you would be in class at 2:30 this Tuesday. We want to believe that at 2:00 it was in your power to do otherwise, to refrain from coming to class at 2:30. To ascribe this power to you implies that it was in your power at 2:00 to alter a fact about the past, the fact that before you were born God knew that you would be in class at 2:30. This fact about the past, however, is not, relative to 2:00, a fact simply about the past. For it implies a fact about the future relative to 2:00, namely, that at 2:30 you are in class. And the solution we are exploring holds that such a fact about the past was in your power to alter if it was in your power at 2:00, as we believe it was, to have gone to a movie instead of coming to class. For it was then in your power to have done something such that, had you done it, what *is* a fact about a time before you were born *would not have been* a fact at all—instead it would have been a fact that before you were born God knew that you would not be in class at 2:30. Of course, there will still be many facts about God's foreknowledge that are not in your power to alter: all those facts, for example, that relative to the time you are at, are facts simply about the past. The very fact which may have been in your power to alter at 2:00—the fact that before you were born God knew you would be in class at 2:30—is, at 2:45 when you are sitting in class regretting that you did not go to a movie, a fact that cannot *then* (at 2:45) be altered, because at 2:45 it is a fact simply about the past. And there are many facts involving divine foreknowledge that are not simply about the past, which, nevertheless, are not in your power to alter, for the facts that they imply about the future do not fall within the scope of your power. For example, God knew before you were born that the sun would rise tomorrow. This fact about the past is not simply about the past because it implies a fact about tomorrow, that the sun will rise. It is nevertheless, a fact which is not in your power to alter.

We have been considering the second solution to the problem of divine foreknowledge and human freedom. As we saw, this solution consists in denying the reasoning supporting the second premise of the argument by means of which the problem was developed, the premise stating that if God knows before we are born everything we will do, it is never in our power to do otherwise. According to the reasoning in support of this premise, given divine foreknowledge, it is in our power to do otherwise only if it is in our power to alter some fact about the past, a fact about what God knew before we were born. The solution we have been considering accepts this point in the reasoning given in support of premise 2, but denies the next point: that it is never in our power to alter the past. The solution argues that some facts about the past are not simply about the past, that some such facts may be within our power to alter, and that the facts about divine foreknowledge used in the reasoning for premise 2 are examples of such facts. So according to the second major solution, we have no good reasons for accepting the second premise of the argument leading from divine foreknowledge to the denial of human freedom. And without such reasons, it has yet to be shown that there is any real difficulty in holding both that God knows before we are born everything we will do and that we sometimes have the power to do otherwise.

The Denial of Foreknowledge

The third and final solution we shall consider rejects premise 1 of the argument, thereby denying that God has foreknowledge of the future events. Earlier I called this a "radical" solution since, unlike the first two solutions, instead of trying to reconcile divine foreknowledge with human freedom, it appears to deny that there is any foreknowledge at all. But, as we shall see, this was the solution preferred by a number of important theologians within the western religious tradition.

There are two different forms of the third solution. According to the first form, statements about certain events in the future, events which might or might not happen, are neither true nor false; they become true (false) when the events they are about actually occur (don't occur). For example, the statement, "You will attend class at a certain hour on a certain day next week" is, on the view we are considering not now true, nor is it false. When next week comes and the hour of that particular day occurs, then the statement will become true if you attend class, and false if you do not. This view concerning statements about the future, a view often ascribed to Aristotle, has the consequence that God does not *now* know whether or not you will attend class at that hour next week, that God does not have foreknowledge of such future events. For knowledge is of what is *true*, and if statements about the future are neither true nor false, they cannot then be known.

The more widely accepted form of the third solution rests upon the idea that God is "eternal" in the second of the two senses introduced in chapter one. There we noted that to be eternal in the first sense is to have infinite duration in both temporal directions. To be eternal in the second sense, however, is to exist outside of time and, therefore, independent of the fundamental law of time according to which every being in time, even an everlasting being, has its life divided into temporal parts. As Boethius wrote:

> For whatever lives in time lives in the present, proceeding from past to future, and nothing is so constituted in time that it can embrace the whole span of its life at once. It has not yet arrived at tomorrow, and it has already lost yesterday; even the life of this day is lived only in each moving, passing moment.[4]

In contrast to things in time, God is viewed as having his infinite, endless life wholly present to himself, all at once. As such, God must be outside of time altogether. For, as we've just seen, whatever is in time has its life divided into temporal parts, only one of which can be present to it at any one time.

The idea that God is eternal in the sense of being outside of time has a direct bearing on the doctrine of divine foreknowledge. For the notion of *fore*knowledge naturally suggests that a being *located* at one point in time knows something that is to take place at some later point in time. Thus we speak of God knowing *at a time before you were born* what you would do at 2:30 this Tuesday. But if God is outside of time then we cannot say that he has a *fore*knowledge of future events, if to do so implies he is located at some point in time and at that point knows what will take place at some *later* point in time. According to Boethius, Aquinas, and a number of other theologians who hold that God is eternal in the second sense, there is nothing that happens in time that is unknown to God. Every moment in time is ever *present* to God in just the way that what is happening at this particular moment within the field of our vision is present to us. God's knowledge of what to us is past and future is just like the knowledge that we may have of something that is happening in the present. Being above time, God takes in *all* time with one glance just as we who are in time may with a glance take in something that is happening in the present. Speaking of God's knowledge of what takes place in time, Boethius tells us:

> It encompasses the infinite sweep of past and future, and regards all things in its simple comprehension as if they were now taking place. Thus, if you will think about the foreknowledge by which God distinguishes all things, you will rightly consider it to be not a foreknowledge of future events, but knowledge of a never changing present. For this reason, divine foreknowledge is called providence, rather than prevision, because it resides above all inferior things and looks out on all things from their summit.[5]

According to Boethius, God does not, strictly speaking, have *fore*knowledge, for he is not in the position of knowing that something will occur *in advance* of its occurring. And yet God knows everything that has occurred, is occurring, and will occur. But he knows them in the way in which we know what occurs in the present. Perhaps we can clarify his position if we distinguish two senses of *foreknowledge*, foreknowledge$_1$ and foreknowledge$_2$. A being foreknows$_1$ some event x, we shall say, provided that the being exists at a certain time *earlier* than when x occurs and knows at that time that x will occur at some later time. This is the sort of foreknowledge which God cannot have if he is eternal in the second sense, for he will not then exist at a certain moment of time, but will be completely outside of time. A being foreknows$_2$ some event x, we shall say, provided that the occurrence of x is *present* to that being but is such that its occurrence is at a moment later than the moment at which we (who are in time) *now* exist. Given that God is eternal in the second sense he cannot have foreknowledge$_1$ of any event, but this does not preclude his having a complete foreknowledge$_2$ of all those events which, from the position of those who exist in time, are yet to come.

We can now see how Boethius and Aquinas solve the problem of divine foreknowledge and human freedom. As we saw, the problem is that to assert both implies that it is sometimes in our power to alter a fact about the past, a fact about what God knew at a time before we were born. If we hold that it is never in our power to alter any fact about the past, it seems we must deny either divine foreknowledge or human freedom. What Boethius and Aquinas point out is that this is a genuine problem only if it is foreknowledge$_1$ that is being ascribed to God. For if God has foreknowledge$_1$, there will be facts about some past time which, if we have human freedom, would have to be within our power to alter. But according to them, we cannot ascribe foreknowledge$_1$ to God, for such ascription implies that God exists in time. God has foreknowledge$_2$ of everything that is yet to come to pass. But foreknowledge$_2$ does not imply that there is some fact about some past time. For God does not exist in time at all. His foreknowledge$_2$ of some event in time is really no different from the knowledge that your instructor had at 2:30 on Tuesday when she saw you entering the classroom. No one thinks that the knowledge obtained by seeing you come into the classroom takes away the power you had earlier to have done something else. Similarly God's foreknowledge$_2$, since it looks down from above time and sees what is future *in time*, but *present* from God's vantage point, imposes no necessity on what it sees. For there is no *past fact* involving God's knowledge which you would have had to alter if you had exercised your power to do otherwise.

In this chapter we have studied one of the ageless problems for theism, the problem of divine foreknowledge and human freedom, and considered in detail the principal solutions which have emerged in the centuries of reflection on the problem. Of the three solutions we've considered, only the last two are tenable if, as I've suggested, the first rests on an inadequate idea of human freedom. The last solution, based as it is on the idea that God exists outside of time, will suffer from any defects associated with that idea. Some philosophers have thought that the idea itself is incoherent, and others have argued that while the idea may be coherent, any being that is eternal in the sense of existing outside of time could never *act within time*, and, therefore, could not create a world or bring about a miracle—activities generally ascribed to the theistic God. We cannot, however, pursue these matters here.[6]

The second solution fits well with the idea that God is eternal in the first sense introduced in chapter one, eternal in the sense of being everlasting, having infinite duration in both temporal directions. On this view, foreknowledge is ascribed to God, but it is argued that insofar as we act freely we do have the power to alter some facts about the past. If both the second and third solutions are successful, then, whether God is held to be eternal in the first or second sense, the problem of divine foreknowledge and human freedom is not an insoluble problem for theism.

Notes

1. John Locke, *An Essay Concerning Human Understanding*, Book II, Chapter XXI, paragraph 10, ed. Peter H. Nidditch (London: Oxford University Press, 1975), p. 238.
2. Aristotle, *Nicomachean Ethics* VII, 2. 1139^b in *The Basic Works of Aristotle*, ed. Richard McKeon (New York: Random House, 1941).
3. For a brilliant defense of the first idea of freedom, as well as a response to the objections raised against it, see Jonathan Edwards, *Freedom of the Will*, eds. A. S. Kaufman and W. K. Frankena (Indianapolis: The Bobbs-Merrill Co., 1969).
4. Boethius, *The Consolation of Philosophy*, Prose VI, tr. Richard Green (New York: The Bobbs-Merrill Company, Inc., 1962).
5. Boethius, *The Consolation of Philosophy*, Prose VI.
6. For an excellent study of these problems see Nelson Pike, *God and Timelessness* (New York: Schocken Books Inc., 1970).

Topics for Review

1. Explain the two different ideas of human freedom. Which idea is more adequate? Why?
2. What is the problem about divine foreknowledge and human freedom?
3. Explain the basic reasoning given in support of the claim that if God knows before we are born everything we will do, then it is never in our power to do otherwise.
4. Explain the various solutions that have been given to the problem of divine foreknowledge and human freedom.
5. How is the idea that God is eternal used by Boethius and Aquinas in the solution they favor?

Topics for Further Study

6. Discuss the following argument:

   If God is eternal in the sense of existing outside of time, then he could never *act*, for all action takes place in time. But if God could never act, he could never create anything, forgive anyone, answer any prayer, or perform any of the acts commonly attributed to him. Therefore, if we think of God as creating, forgiving, and so forth, we cannot consistently believe that he exists outside of time.

7. Of the various solutions to the problem of divine foreknowledge and human freedom, pick the one that you think is the best and explain your reasons for regarding it as better than the other proposed solutions.

Chapter

12

FAITH AND REASON

The central question that has occupied our attention since the first chapter is whether there are rational grounds supporting the basic claims of theistic religions. In the main we have been preoccupied with the study of the reasons that are often given for and against the claim that the theistic God exists. To put it in its most general terms, the central question we've pursued is this: Does reason establish (or show it to be probable) that theism is true? To this end we looked with some care at the evidence for theism as expressed in religious experience and the traditional arguments for the existence of God. So, if we were to characterize the approach we have taken, we might say that we have proceeded on two assumptions: first, we have assumed that religious beliefs, like scientific and historical beliefs, should be judged in the court of reason; second, we have assumed that religious beliefs will find favor in the court of reason only if they are adequately supported by evidence in their favor. It is time now to take a critical look at both of these assumptions.

Against our first assumption it is often said that religious beliefs are to be accepted on *faith*, not on the basis of *reason*. At the very least, then, we need to consider what faith is and whether it is rational or irrational to accept religious beliefs on the basis of faith. Against our second assumption it is noted that not every belief that finds favor in the court of reason can do so by virtue of being supported by some *other belief* that is evidence for it. It is claimed that some of our beliefs are *rational* (find favor in the court of reason) even though we do not hold them on the basis of any other beliefs that might be evidence for them. If this be so (and I think it is so), we need to consider the question of whether religious beliefs might fit into this category and therefore find favor in the court of reason even in the absence of evidence for them provided by our other beliefs.

RELIGIOUS BELIEFS AND FAITH

Some religious thinkers have argued that the very nature of religion requires that its beliefs rest on faith, not reason. For, so the argument goes, religious belief requires *unconditional* acceptance on the part of the believer, an acceptance, moreover, that results from a *free decision* to become a believer. But if religious belief were based on reason, reason would either establish the belief beyond question or it would merely render the belief probable. In the first case, where reason proves the belief, the informed intellect would compel belief and leave no room for the exercise of a free decision. And in the second case, where reason merely shows the belief to be probable, if religious belief rested entirely on reason then the unconditional acceptance of religious belief would be unwarranted and absurd. Perhaps, then, religious belief does rest on faith, rather than reason.

But what is faith? And how is faith related to reason? Does it conflict with reason or supplement it? In trying to answer these questions we shall focus our attention on two views concerning faith and reason: the first, a traditional view developed by Aquinas; the second, a more radical view expressed by William James.

Both Aquinas and James take the objects of faith to be *statements* mainly about the divine. Faith, then, is the acceptance of certain statements concerning God and his activities. Sometimes, however, we think of faith not as the acceptance of certain statements as true, but as trust in certain persons or institutions. Thus we say things like, "Have faith in your friends" or "Let's restore faith in our government." But since trusting some person or institution generally involves accepting or believing certain statements about them, faith in someone or something presupposes beliefs that certain statements about them are true. Where such beliefs do not rest on reason, *faith in* someone or something may presuppose a *faith that* certain statements are true.

AQUINAS: A TRADITIONAL VIEW

Aquinas tells us that faith falls between knowledge and opinion, that in one respect it is like knowledge and unlike opinion, and in another respect it is like opinion and unlike knowledge. When we come to know that something is so, reason is in possession of conclusive evidence that it is so and our *intellectual assent to the proposition we know* is compelled and, therefore, not a free act on our part. Moreover, our assent to the proposition we know is firm and sure. According to Aquinas, faith shares with knowledge the aspect of an intellectual assent that is firm and sure. But in order that the act of faith be a free act, it is necessary that the intellect not be compelled by conclusive evidence that yields knowledge. Unlike knowledge, then, faith lacks conclusive evidence for the proposition that is believed. In the act of faith the intellect is moved to assent by a free act of the will.

Opinion differs from knowledge in lacking conclusive evidence for the proposition assented to, and in being unsure, fearing that the alternative may turn out to be the truth. Faith, like opinion, lacks conclusive evidence, but like knowledge is firm and unwavering in its intellectual assent to the proposition in question.

Aquinas divides truths about the divine into truths that it is possible to demonstrate by human reason and truths that cannot be known by the power of human reason. Truths of the first sort include such statements as "God exists," "God is good," and "God created the world." But there are many truths about the divine that, Aquinas claims, "exceed all the ability of human reason."[1] Many of these truths are important for our salvation. So although reason cannot prove them to be true, it is important that they be believed. They are believed on faith, not on the basis of reason. Since our intellect is not compelled by reason to assent to these truths about the divine, we may accept them *freely* on faith. Moreover, since the acceptance of these beliefs is a free act, the believer's act of faith may be a meritorious deed, deserving God's approval and reward. Faith, then, for Aquinas does not conflict with reason but "perfects the intellect" and can be a free, meritorious act of the mind.

What of the truths about the divine that can be demonstrated by human reason? Are they, nevertheless, proper objects of faith? Aquinas answers that they also are properly proposed to be accepted by faith. For coming to *know* these propositions by way of demonstrating their truth is a difficult task for which few have the time, training, and resources to succeed. Nevertheless, those who do come to know these propositions by demonstration do not also hold them by faith. For it is impossible that one and the same proposition should be (at the same time) both an object of knowledge and an object of faith. In the life to come when the faithful come to see God clearly, they will no longer live by faith.

There are, of course, many statements about the divine which exceed the ability of human reason to grasp. That God is triune, for example, can be neither proved nor disproved by reason. How does Aquinas determine which statements about the divine should be accepted on faith? Should we, for example, believe that God is triune or believe that God is not triune? To learn the answer to this question is to see that although faith is distinct from reason, it cannot exist on its own. For reason guides faith by showing that the statements to be accepted on faith have been revealed by God. As Aquinas tell us: "Faith . . . does not assent to anything, except because it is revealed by God."[2]

We must distinguish, therefore, between a statement S and the statement "God has revealed S." If S is a statement which properly belongs only to faith, reason will be unable to prove or adduce direct evidence for S. But reason serves faith by adducing evidence in support of the statement that God has revealed S. According to Aquinas, reason gives us probable arguments to support the view that God has revealed many truths in the Scriptures. These arguments appeal to such considerations as the fulfillment of prophesies foretold in the Bible, the success achieved by the Church without promise of pleasure or resort to violence, and the working of miracles.[3] By such means Aquinas thinks he can show that it is reasonable to regard the Scriptures as revealed by God. Since the Scriptures, according to Aquinas, teach that God is triune, faith accepts that belief, even though such belief is beyond the ability of reason to prove or disprove directly.

The difficulties with Aquinas' classic treatment of faith and reason reduce basically to two. First, it accords to reason the power of proving certain basic

claims about God—that he exists, is supremely good, is creator of the world—
which many nowadays would think, to use Aquinas' phrase, "exceed all the
ability of human reason." Second, it makes faith somewhat dependent on reason
for determining which statements God has indeed revealed. As the English
philosopher John Locke noted: "Whatever God hath revealed, is certainly true;
no doubt can be made of it. This is the proper object of faith; but whether it be a
divine revelation or no, reason must judge."[4]

JAMES: A RADICAL VIEW

In modern times a more radical view of the scope of faith has been elaborated
by William James in his now classic essay "The Will to Believe,"[5] a view of faith
that is not subject to the two difficulties affecting Aquinas' treatment of faith and
reason.

Clifford's Shipowner: "The Ethics of Belief"

To understand James' view we first need to consider the position reached by
the English mathematician and philosopher William Clifford (1845–1879), to
which James' essay is a reply. In an essay entitled "The Ethics of Belief" Clifford
tells the story of a shipowner:

> A shipowner was about to send to sea an emigrant-ship. He knew that she was old, and
> not over-well built at the first; that she had seen many seas and climes, and often had
> needed repairs. Doubts had been suggested to him that possibly she was not sea-
> worthy. These doubts preyed upon his mind, and made him unhappy; he thought that
> perhaps he ought to have her thoroughly overhauled and refitted, even though this
> should put him to great expense. Before the ship sailed, however, he succeeded in
> overcoming these melancholy reflections. He said to himself that she had gone safely
> through so many voyages and weathered so many storms that it was idle to suppose
> she would not come safely home from this trip also. He would put his trust in Provi-
> dence, which could hardly fail to protect all these unhappy families that were leaving
> their fatherland to seek for better times elsewhere. He would dismiss from his mind all
> ungenerous suspicions about the honesty of builders and contractors. In such ways he
> acquired a sincere and comfortable conviction that his vessel was thoroughly safe and
> seaworthy; he watched her departure with a light heart, and benevolent wishes for the
> success of the exiles in their strange new home that was to be; and he got his insurance-
> money when she went down in mid-ocean and told no tales.[6]

Of this man, Clifford says that he was guilty of the death of those who went
down at sea. The fact that the shipowner sincerely believed in the soundness of
his ship does not diminish his guilt, for, Clifford emphasizes, "he had no right to
believe on such evidence as was before him." Instead of arriving at his belief by
carefully inspecting the ship's condition, the shipowner had arrived at his belief
without any adequate evidence at all. Taking up a belief on insufficient evidence
is, Clifford argues, *completely unjustified*. The shipowner, having failed to assem-
ble any significant evidence concerning the soundness of his ship, was, there-

fore, wrong in believing his ship to be sound. Suppose his ship was actually sound and made her voyage safely. Would this have altered Clifford's judgment of the shipowner? Not at all:

> The man would not have been innocent, he would only have been not found out. The question of right or wrong has to do with the origin of his belief, not the matter of it; not what it was, but how he got it; not whether it turned out to be true or false, but whether he had a right to believe on such evidence as was before him.[7]

Against Clifford's judgment of the shipowner, we might object that he has confused *the shipowner's believing his ship to be sound* with *the shipowner's action of sending the ship to sea without proper inspection*. It is the latter, we might argue, that was wrong. After all, even though the shipowner believed (without good evidence) that his ship was sound, he still could have ordered a proper inspection before sending her to sea. It is actions that are right or wrong, and not the mere taking up of beliefs. Clifford, however, acknowledges the distinction we've made between the shipowner's belief and his action of sending the ship to sea. He agrees, furthermore, that the action was wrong. But he insists that the shipowner's belief also must be condemned. For beliefs naturally lead to action. And a person who habitually believes things on insufficient evidence, or without any evidence at all, will often take up beliefs that naturally lead to actions positively harmful to others, as the shipowner's case illustrates.

Reflecting on the shipowner's case and Clifford's remarks about it, we might go along with him in his judgment of the shipowner. When a belief is such that it naturally leads to actions that might turn out to be harmful to others, it is wrong to allow oneself to take up that belief on insufficient evidence. Such beliefs should not be accepted without adequate evidence for them. For we know that when people give themselves over to such beliefs in the absence of adequate evidence for them, the results for mankind have often been harmful, if not disastrous. But surely there are beliefs, the believing of which would not tend to lead to actions harmful to others. These beliefs might either be insignificant, trivial matters, like believing that the weather was warm a year ago today, or significant beliefs which tend to lead only to actions helpful to others, like believing that human beings are basically good and kind. If I believe that others are basically good and kind I may be more disposed than otherwise to act kindly toward them. With beliefs such as these, it seems unreasonable, on the surface at least, to claim that it is wrong to believe them in the absence of adequate evidence for their truth. Clifford, however, is uncompromising in his view:

> If I let myself believe anything on insufficient evidence, there may be no great harm done by the mere belief; it may be true after all, or I may never have occasion to exhibit it in outward acts. But I cannot help doing this great wrong towards Man, that I make myself credulous. The danger to society is not merely that it should believe wrong things, though that is great enough; but that it should become credulous, and lose the habit of testing things and inquiring into them; for then it must sink back into savagery.[8]

Whether a belief is trivial, significant and likely to lead to actions harmful to others, or significant and likely to lead to actions beneficial to others, Clifford's judgment is the same: we are justified in taking up that belief only if we have sufficient evidence for its truth. For otherwise we shall harm ourselves and society by weakening the habit of requiring evidence for our beliefs, a habit that has slowly raised us out of the age of superstition and savagery. It's clear, then, that Clifford will tolerate no exception to his injunction to believe only in the presence of sufficient evidence. He sums up his view in a remark quoted by James in "The Will to Believe": "It is wrong always, everywhere, and for everyone, to believe anything upon insufficient evidence."[9] Clearly, then, if Clifford is right, no one can be justified in believing theism to be true without adequate evidence for the truth of theism. Similarly, no one can be justified in believing atheism to be true without adequate evidence for its truth. If we have adequate evidence neither for theism nor for atheism then, on Clifford's view, our obligation is to suspend judgment, that is, to be agnostic.

The Extent of James' Agreement

Although, as we noted earlier, James' "Will to Believe" is an attack against Clifford's view, the extent to which James agrees with Clifford is worth comment. First, he agrees with Clifford's fundamental claim that a person is to be judged (praised or blamed) in terms of beliefs, as well as actions. Second, he agrees with Clifford that it is not the content of a person's belief which determines how he or she is to be judged, but the way in which he or she arrives at the belief. Finally, if we divide Clifford's view into two rules governing beliefs, it is reasonably clear that James is in full agreement with the first of the two.

I. If an individual is aware of evidence against a hypothesis and aware of no good evidence in support of it, and, nevertheless, allows himself to believe it because of some private satisfaction, he has done a wrong.

II. If an individual has no evidence for a belief and no evidence against a belief, it is wrong for him to accept or reject the belief, it is his duty to suspend judgment on the matter and wait for the evidence.

It is over the second of the above two rules that James parts company with Clifford. As we shall see, James' disagreement with rule II is not as extensive as it could be. But before we enter into the details of his disagreement with II, it is useful to express I and II in slightly different terms, terms that James uses in his essay. There are, according to James, two, and only two, determinants of our beliefs: *reason* and the *passions*. Reason weighs a belief in terms of the evidence for or against it, and directs us to believe in accordance with the evidence. The passions are all the factors, other than intellectual, that lead us to accept or reject a hypothesis. Since the time of Plato, philosophers have generally taken the view that our duty is to suppress the passions so far as belief is concerned, to let reason and reason alone be the determining force in shaping our beliefs. It is clear that Clifford stands in this tradition, and that James also has at least one foot planted squarely in it. Clifford's rule I covers the case where reason says no to a belief, but we allow our passions to overrule our reason. Rule II covers the case where reason is neutral, but we, instead of suspending judgment, allow our passions to direct our belief. In both cases reason has been sacrificed to the passions, and such sacrifice, according to Clifford, is *wrong*. James agrees with Clifford on the first case, but disagrees profoundly on the second. James does not hold that whenever reason is neutral it is not wrong for us to believe as our passions direct. Rather he holds that there are special cases, cases where reason is neutral and yet it is not wrong to follow the direction of the passions. We must now try to see what these special cases are and why James thinks that religious belief is such a case.

RELIGIOUS BELIEF: A SPECIAL CASE
Essential Definitions
James' basic point, as it touches on Clifford's second rule, may be expressed as follows:

> When and only when a hypothesis is (i) *intellectually undecidable* and (ii) such that it presents us with a *genuine option*, it is not wrong to believe as we wish concerning the hypothesis, to let our passional nature decide.

In requiring that the hypothesis be intellectually undecidable, James makes it clear that it is Clifford's rule II that is in question: where reason is neutral concerning a hypothesis. And in requiring that the hypothesis express a genuine option before we can claim the right to believe as we wish, James makes it clear that we do not have the right to follow our passions whenever reason is neutral, but only when, in addition to the neutrality of reason, we are confronted with something else, a genuine option.

By a "genuine option" James explains that he means a decision between two hypotheses that is *living, momentous,* and *forced.* An option (a decision between two hypotheses) may be living or dead for us. An option is *living* when both hypotheses are live for us, when both make some appeal to us and strike us as real possibilities for our lives. James illustrates: "If I say to you: 'Be a theosophist or be a Mohammedan,' it is probably a dead option, because for you neither hypothesis is likely to be alive. But if I say: 'Be an agnostic or be a Christian,' it is otherwise: trained as you are, each hypothesis makes some appeal, however small, to your belief."[10] An option may be momentous or trivial. An option is *momentous* when you may not have another chance to decide between the two hypotheses, the choice you make cannot easily be reversed, and something of considerable importance hangs on your making the right choice. During the Vietnam war many young men had to choose between serving their country in a cause they felt to be unjust or refusing to serve. Clearly the choice was a momentous one: making the wrong choice could lead to considerable personal loss; the decision, once made, could not easily be reversed; and the choice could not be put off until some later time.

An option may be forced or avoidable. An option is *forced* when the consequences of refusing to decide for one or the other of the two hypotheses are the same as actually deciding for a certain one of the hypotheses.[11] If I am offered an important job and am given a deadline for accepting it or rejecting it, a deadline that is absolutely firm in the sense that after that time the offer will be withdrawn and given to someone else who is eager to accept it, then I have been presented with a decision between calling by the deadline and accepting the offer or calling by the deadline and rejecting the offer, a decision that is forced. It is forced because the consequences of refusing to decide to accept or to reject are the same as deciding to reject. The two acts of calling to reject the offer and not calling at all are different acts, but their consequences are pretty much the same. To refuse to decide is practically the same as deciding to reject the offer. An option is avoidable when there is some real difference between refusing to decide and deciding for either of the two hypotheses. If you are taking a true-false examination in which you receive five points for a correct answer, lose five points for a wrong answer, and neither gain nor lose points for no answer at all, then your decision between answering "true" and answering "false" is avoidable, not forced. For the consequences of not answering at all are different from the consequences of each of the two ways of answering.

It is important to recognize that, with respect to any given hypothesis, there are always three different ways of responding to it. We can believe it to be true, believe it to be false, or suspend judgment concerning it. It is also important to recognize that the opinion between believing a hypothesis true and believing it false is never forced *so far as truth and error are concerned*. For the person who refuses to believe, who suspends judgment, does not have the truth nor does he or she have an error; only by believing can we have the truth or an error. So if the decision between two hypotheses that cannot both be true—for example, "God exists" and "God does not exist"—is to be *forced then the consequences in question must be something other than truth and error*.

Suppose, for example, that I have decided to give you a million dollars if you believe my proclamation that the world will end by A.D. 2000, and to give you nothing if you disbelieve it or neither believe it nor disbelieve it. The option you have is between believing "The world will end by A.D. 2000" and believing "The world will not end by A.D. 2000." Clearly one of these hypotheses is true and the other is false. So the believer in either hypothesis will have the truth (a true belief) or an error (a false belief). The person who suspends judgment, however, will not have the truth and will not have an error. So the option cannot be forced with respect to truth and error. But it is forced with respect to receiving my gift of a million dollars. For you lose the million by suspending judgment just as you do by believing that the world will not end by A.D. 2000. There is a clear sense, then, in which the consequences (at least one major consequence) of suspending judgment are the same as believing one of the two hypotheses.

JAMES' RELIGIOUS HYPOTHESIS

With these preliminaries out of the way we can turn to James' contention that religion falls under his basic thesis, that the basic claim of religion is both intellectually undecidable and presents us with a genuine option. James characterizes the religious hypothesis as having two parts: (1) what is best or supreme is eternal, and (2) we are better off if we believe that what is best is eternal. The idea that what is best is eternal may be interpreted differently depending on which religious tradition concerns us. Within the Judeo-Christian tradition we can understand the first part of the religious hypothesis to be the claim that the theistic God exists. And its second part affirms that we are better off even now if we believe in the theistic God. Why are we better off? Well, if the God of theism exists and we believe in him, we are the immediate recipients of eternal life, divine grace, and other spiritual blessings. So, for our purposes, we will take the first part of the religious hypothesis to affirm the existence of the theistic God, and we will take the second part to affirm that we are better off even now if we believe in the theistic God. (In nontheistic religions, the sentence "Perfection is eternal" will be interpreted in some way other than by the claim that the theistic God exists.)

Intellectually Undecidable

Is James' implied claim that the religious hypothesis is intellectually undecidable correct? Some, including Aquinas, would argue that it is not. Many theists hold that the arguments for the existence of God and the facts of religious experience provide sufficient rational grounds for believing that God exists. Some atheists, however, think that the facts of evil provide adequate rational grounds for the belief that the theistic God does not exist. Insofar as there is adequate rational evidence either for theism or for atheism, James is, along with Clifford, committed to the view that we should believe in accordance with the evidence, no matter what our passional nature directs us to do. Nevertheless, James' position is not implausible. The truth of the matter may well be that our rational intellects are incapable of deciding the question of the existence of the theistic God, either because there is no good evidence on either side of the question or because what evidence there is on one side is balanced out by equally good evidence on the other side. Perhaps, then, the claim that the theistic God exists is such that its truth or falsehood cannot be determined by rational inquiry. If so, then, according to Clifford, it is our duty to be agnostics. James, however, disagrees because he thinks that the religious question comes to us as a living, momentous, and forced question.

A Genuine Option

For those of us who have been raised within the basic western religious tradition, the option between believing that God exists and believing that he does not may well be living. And the decision between believing that God exists or believing that he does not seems to be a momentous decision, in at least one sense of being momentous. For if God exists and we believe in him, we receive upon believing a certain vital good—eternal life, divine grace, and other blessings. If God exists and we do not believe, then all this is lost. Is the decision unique and irreversible if it should prove unwise? It's less clear that the religious question is momentous in either of these senses. I might take up the belief next year rather than this year, or, taking up one belief now, may later alter my belief on the religious question. But, still, we can agree with James that the religious question is momentous in the most important sense of possibly providing us with a good of infinite dimensions if we choose correctly.

Is the option between believing that the theistic God exists and believing that no such being exists a *forced* option? As we noted earlier, this option is not forced with respects to truth and error. For if God does exist, then the atheist has an error, but the agnostic does not, for one can have an error (a false belief) only if one has a belief. But, as James points out, if the religious hypothesis is *true* then the agnostic and the atheist are in the same boat, they both lose the vital good which religion has to offer. So if theism is true, the option between believing that God exists and believing that God does not exist is a *forced* option so far as that vital good is concerned. Speaking of the religious hypothesis, he says that

> by remaining skeptical and waiting for more light . . . we lose the good, *if it be true,* just as certainly as if we positively chose to disbelieve. It is as if a man should hesitate indefinitely to ask a certain woman to marry him because he was not perfectly sure that she would prove an angel after he brought her home. Would he not cut himself off from that particular angel-possibility as decisively as if he went and married some one else?[12]

It is perhaps worth noting that James does not prove that the option between believing that God exists and believing that he does not is either momentous or forced. All that he succeeds in proving is that it is momentous and forced *if* it is true that God does exist. For it is only if God exists that there is some vital good (eternal life) that is at stake in the decision. If God does not exist, then the decision between the two hypotheses is not momentous. Nor is it forced. For, as we saw, the option is not forced with respect to truth and error, it is forced only with respect to the vital good of eternal life, divine grace, and the other blessings of belief. But if atheism is true, there will be no such vital good in virtue of which the option can be forced. In response to this point, the best that we can say is that James has shown that the religious option *may be* momentous and forced, we can't know that it is not. This means, however, that if the religious question is to exemplify his basic thesis, that thesis must be revised in something like the following way.

> When a hypothesis is intellectually undecidable and the option between believing it and believing its denial is living, then if either (i) simply believing the hypothesis or (ii) believing the hypothesis *and* its being true will result in some vital good for the believer, a good not available to anyone who doesn't believe the hypothesis, then it is not wrong to believe as we wish concerning the hypothesis, to let our passional nature decide.

If case (i) holds, then the option is momentous and forced. If case (ii) holds, then the option *may* be momentous and forced, depending on whether the hypothesis is true. The option between believing that God exists and believing that God does not exist falls under case (ii), it *may* be momentous and forced.

JAMES' DEFENSE OF PASSIONAL BELIEF

We have described James' basic thesis, both in its original and revised form, and have seen how the theistic hypothesis exemplifies the revised form of the thesis.[13] It is now time to consider James' defense of the right to believe as we wish concerning the theistic hypothesis.

Following James' lead we can think of the theist, agnostic, and atheist as adopting different policies. The theist adopts the policy of *risking error for a chance at truth and a vital good*. The theist risks error because he or she believes something (that God exists) for which he or she has no adequate evidence. So, for all the theist knows, the belief is false. But he or she risks this for the chance at having the truth (a true belief, if God does exist) and a chance at being a recipient of a vital good (eternal life and other blessings, which the theist receives if God exists). The agnostic adopts the policy of *risking a loss of truth and a loss of a vital good for the certainty of avoiding error*. By not believing one way or the other concerning the theistic hypothesis, the agnostic can take comfort in the certainty that he or she has avoided error, a certainty that neither the theist nor the atheist can enjoy. But, just as clearly, the agnostic risks missing out on having a true belief and on receiving a vital good, a good that the agnostic, just as much as the atheist, will surely lose. The atheist adopts the policy of *risking error and the loss of a vital good for a chance at truth*.

According to Clifford, given that we lack adequate evidence either for or against the theistic hypothesis, it is *wrong* to adopt the policy of either the theist or the atheist; instead, it is our *duty* to adopt the agnostic's policy. But Clifford's position, James argues, amounts to no more than a passional decision to avoid error at all cost. Better risk loss of truth and a vital good than chance an error. That's the decision that Clifford has made. James finds nothing appealing or compelling in that decision.

> It is like a general informing his soldiers that it is better to keep out of battle forever than to risk a single wound. Not so are victories either over enemies or over nature gained. Our errors are surely not such awfully solemn things. In a world where we are so certain to incur them in spite of all our caution, a certain lightness of heart seems healthier than this excessive nervousness on their behalf.[14]

James' own view is that no rule binds us to choose any particular one of the three policies outlined above. He defends our *right* to follow the theist's policy, but does not think anyone has a *duty* to adopt that policy. Each person has a right to adopt that policy among the three which fits best with his or her own passional nature. Clifford has the right to adopt the agnostic's policy. He goes wrong only in trying to impose that policy as a *duty* on everyone else. James concludes with a plea for tolerance:

> If we believe that no bell in us tolls to let us know for certain when truth is in our grasp, then it seems a piece of idle fantasticality to preach so solemnly our duty of waiting for the bell. Indeed we *may* wait if we will—I hope you do not think that I am denying that—but if we do so, we do so at our peril as much as if we believed. In either case we *act*, taking our life in our hands. No one of us ought to issue vetoes to the other, nor should we bandy words of abuse. We ought, on the contrary, delicately and profoundly to respect one another's mental freedom: then only shall we bring about the intellectual republic, then only shall we have that spirit of inner tolerance without which all our outer tolerance is soulless, . . . then only shall we live and let live, in speculative as well as in practical things.[15]

James has given a forceful defense of the *right* to believe as we wish concerning the theistic hypothesis. He is, however, mistaken, I think, in representing the choice among the three policies as a choice that cannot be made on rational grounds. Indeed, his own view seems to be that the policy of the theist—risk error for a chance at truth and a great good—is a *rational* policy to follow, that the theist is not unreasonable in adopting that policy. And James is perhaps unfair to Clifford in suggesting that Clifford adopts the agnostic's policy—risk a loss of truth and a loss of a vital good for the certainty of avoiding error—simply out of passionate fear of having a false belief. Clifford, after all, has given *reasons* for following the agnostic's policy. His reasons may not be very good reasons, but James should respond to his reasons rather than belittle his motives. It is not that Clifford is personally afraid of making a mistake (believing something that is false), for he knows perfectly well that the man who believes in accordance with the weight of the evidence will sometimes have a false belief—we seldom are in possession of the *total* evidence bearing on a belief. It is that Clifford thinks that when we allow ourselves to believe something on insufficient evidence we weaken an important habit in ourselves and in others, "the habit of testing things and inquiring into them," a habit that has slowly raised us out of the age of superstition and savagery. This is Clifford's basic reason for urging the adoption of the agnostic point of view whenever our intellect cannot decide between two rival hypotheses. And what James must argue in response is that either the habit won't be weakened by adopting the theist's policy or that the possible good to come from adopting the theist's policy outweighs the danger of weakening this habit in ourselves and others. This is the real issue between James and Clifford, and it is unfortunate that James did not address himself to it.

We've had a look at two views of faith presented by Aquinas and James. Both take religious faith to be the acceptance of certain statements about the divine and both are concerned to show that religious faith is not irrational or unreasonable. Aquinas argues that some truths about the divine can be demonstrated by human reason and contends that faith is not unreasonable because reason shows that the statements accepted on faith are probably revealed to us by God. James takes a more radical view. He holds that none of the statements about the divine that are basic to religion can be shown by reason to be true or probably true because probably revealed to us by God. Nevertheless, he argues that adopting the policy of faith is intellectually defensible and not a violation of any genuine intellectual obligation.

RELIGIOUS BELIEFS AND EVIDENCE

Earlier we noted our assumption that religious beliefs, like all other beliefs, will find favor in the court of reason only if they are adequately supported by evidence. We also said that we should subject this assumption to critical scrutiny. For we noted that not all of our rationally held beliefs can be rational solely by virtue of being supported by other beliefs we hold that are evidence for them. In addition, we went on to consider the view of William James who holds that it is not wrong to accept certain beliefs *without evidence* provided those beliefs present us with a genuine option. So let us now turn our attention directly on this assumption we have made. In the course of examining our assumption, we shall consider an important recent view, developed by Alvin Plantinga, that "it is entirely right, rational, reasonable, and proper to believe in God without any evidence or argument at all."[16]

Recall Clifford's judgment to the effect that it is a violation of our intellectual duty to believe anything on insufficient evidence. Such a view is called *evidentialism*. We may characterize evidentialism as the view that *a belief is rationally justified only if there is sufficient evidence for it.*[17] For one of your beliefs to be rational (rationally justified) is for you to be rationally justified in holding it. And, according to evidentialism, for you to be rationally justified in holding a belief is for you to have adequate evidence for it. Since one person may have evidence another person lacks, the same belief may be rational for the one to hold but not rational for the other to hold. A physicist, for example, will be rationally justified in holding some beliefs that would not be rational for someone who knows little about physics.

The assumption we are engaged in examining is what we have identified as evidentialism. Many theists and nontheists (atheists and agnostics) who discuss religious beliefs are evidentialists. They hold, therefore, that belief in God (believing that God exists) is rational only if there is adequate evidence for the existence of God. What they disagree about is whether there is adequate evidence for the existence of God. For example, Thomas Aquinas and Bertrand Russell tend to agree that religious beliefs are rational only if they are or can be sufficiently supported by evidence or reasons. Russell doesn't think there is good evidence for religious beliefs; whereas Aquinas does think that.

Why should someone think that it is or may be rational to believe in God *without any evidence at all?* As a first step in answering this question we need to convince ourselves of the point mentioned earlier: not all of our rationally held beliefs can be rational solely by virtue of being supported by other beliefs we hold that are evidence for them. For suppose this were not so. Then, if we have a rational belief, it would be rational solely because of some other belief we have that is good evidence for it. But that other belief couldn't be good evidence for it in the sense of making it rational unless it also is a belief that we are rational in holding. It too, then, would be made rational for us by virtue of some other rational belief we hold that is evidence for it. You can see that this would be an unending process. Indeed, to have any rational belief at all we would have to hold an infinite number of beliefs each of which we are rational in holding. So, the process of one belief being made rational solely by some other rational belief we hold must have an end. There must be some beliefs we are rational in holding without basing them on other beliefs we have that are evidence for them. Following Alvin Plantinga, let's call such beliefs "properly basic beliefs." A properly basic belief is a belief that is rational for us to hold even though we have no evidence for it in the sense of other rational beliefs that adequately support it.

To understand Plantinga's view we need to distinguish *properly* basic beliefs from beliefs that are basic but not properly basic. A compulsive gambler may suddenly come to believe that the next hand dealt to him will be the winning hand. He may have no other beliefs that he takes to be significant evidence for this belief. Perhaps some deep psychological need has brought about this belief. His belief is basic, but not properly basic. For there is nothing about him or the situation he is in that would render the belief rational. Contrast this with someone who upon looking out the window and having a visual experience which she takes to be of a cat climbing a tree immediately forms the belief that there is a cat climbing a tree. Her belief that there is a cat climbing a tree is rendered rational by the situation she is in—her looking out the window and seeming to see a cat climbing a tree, etc. It's not that she has some other rational beliefs and infers her present belief from them—she doesn't say to herself: "I'm looking out the window and seem to see a cat climbing a tree. Let's see. What can I infer from that belief? Oh yes, I can infer that I see a cat climbing a tree." She has no evidence for her belief in the sense of other beliefs on the basis of which she holds her belief that there is a cat climbing a tree. Her belief is thus basic and rational (a properly basic belief). We might say of her belief that it is grounded in a situation that renders her rationally justified in holding that belief. The gambler's belief is either groundless or grounded in some situation that fails to render his belief rational.

If we accept what has just been said we may still view the person's properly basic belief that there is a cat climbing a tree as a belief for which she has adequate or sufficient evidence. For she has the evidence of her senses, her *experience* of seeming to see a cat climbing the tree, in support of her basic belief that there is a cat climbing a tree. So we may conclude that this example of a properly basic belief is not an exception to our assumption of evidentialism: a belief is rational only if supported by adequate evidence. Nevertheless, although we may be within our rights to view Plantinga's properly basic beliefs as beliefs supported by adequate evidence, we need to understand that according to his conception of evidence a properly basic belief is a belief that is not based on any evidence at all. For Plantinga thinks of evidence solely in terms of *believed propositions*. On such a view, a properly basic belief is not held on the basis of evidence at all. For a basic belief is not based on other beliefs we hold. Thus, if we accept his understanding of good evidence as consisting of other rational beliefs that generate the belief in question and render it rational, a properly basic belief is a rational belief that is not held on the basis of any evidence at all.

Given his understanding of evidence, we can now see how it is that Plantinga can hold the apparently astonishing thesis that it is rational to believe in God *without any evidence at all*. What this comes down to is the claim that persons are sometimes in situations that generate and make rational the belief that there is a God, even though these situations do not include rational beliefs on the basis of which they come to the belief that there is a God. What sort of situations are like this? What comes first to mind are the religious experiences we considered in an earlier chapter. Someone may have an experience which seems to be a *direct encounter of God,* immediately form the belief that he is experiencing God, and thereby conclude that there is a God. In this situation his belief that he is experiencing God is basic and, if rendered rational by his experience and situation, properly basic. His belief that there is a God may be immediately inferred from this basic belief and thus, strictly speaking, not itself basic. (Plantinga notes that typically the belief that there is a God will be inferred from basic beliefs that directly imply it.) Plantinga, however, suggests a fairly wide range of situations that he thinks generate some properly basic belief that directly implies that there is a God.

> Upon reading the Bible, one may be impressed with a deep sense that God is speaking to him. Upon having done what I know is cheap, or wrong, or wicked I may feel guilty in God's sight and form the belief *God disapproves of what I've done*. Upon confession and repentance, I may feel forgiven, forming the belief *God forgives me for what I've done*.[18]

Of course, feeling that one is guilty in God's sight is not itself sufficient to rationally justify the basic belief that God disapproves of what you've done. For suppose you also have very good reason to believe that given your severe religious upbringing you cannot avoid having a sense of religious guilt when you do something wicked. That is, you have good reason to believe that given your religious upbringing you would have a sense of religious guilt when you do something wicked whether or not there is a God. In this situation you may not be rational in holding the belief that God disapproves of what you've done. For you know that even if there is no God at all you still would feel religiously guilty upon doing something wicked.

The point just made reminds us of a general point about the extent to which an experience which seems to be of X can be said to rationally justify a belief in X. I may have an experience that I take to be a perception of a red wall. But that experience won't render the claim that I am seeing a red wall rational if I know that there are red lights shining on the wall. For I then know that even if the wall is white (not red) it will still look red to me. So, in order for a situation to render rational my belief that there is a red wall or my belief that God disapproves of what I've done, the situation must include not only an appropriate experience but also some condition roughly like my not having any good reason to think that the belief is false or that the experience is not sufficiently indicative of its truth.

Once we've seen what the situation must contain in order for a belief that is formed in that situation to be properly basic (basic and rendered rational by the situation), we may be a bit hesitant to agree with Plantinga that situations abound in which belief in God (or some belief that directly implies it) is in fact properly basic. But if we do accept Plantinga's restriction of evidence to other *beliefs* one holds on the basis of which one has inferred the belief in question, I do think we have to agree with him that situations do exist in which belief in God is properly basic. Plantinga provides an example of a 14-year-old theist brought up to believe theism in a community where everyone so believes.

> This 14-year-old theist, we may suppose, doesn't believe in God on the basis of evidence. He has never heard of the cosmological, teleological, or ontological arguments; in fact no one has ever presented him with any evidence at all. And although he has often been told about God, he doesn't take that testimony as evidence; he doesn't reason thus: everyone around here says that God loves us and cares for us; most of what everyone around here says is true; so probably *that's* true. Instead, he simply believes what he's taught.[19]

Clearly, in the situation described our 14-year-old has a basic belief in God and is rationally justified in holding that belief. For part of the stipulation of the case is that he has no good reasons (and couldn't be expected to have any) to think that God doesn't exist or that his community might not be rationally justified in its religious beliefs. And we are told that he doesn't infer his belief from any *other* *beliefs* he holds, thus securing his belief in God as basic. This, then, is a fairly clear case in which belief in God is properly basic. It's clear, moreover, that properly basic beliefs are really not that hard to come by, particularly when we place the believer at a tender age in a community of believers. Had our 14-year-old been raised with similar stipulations in a community of atheists, his belief that there is no God would have been properly basic. And if very young children can have rationally justified beliefs, many of us—at least for a short time—have had a properly basic belief in the existence of Santa Claus. For we have been told by our parents that there is such a being and have immediately believed in the existence of Santa Claus without inferring this belief from other beliefs we hold. Of course, unlike belief in God, after a relatively short period of time our peers manage to disabuse us of this belief so that it ceases to be properly basic.

The interesting question that emerges from our examination of Plantinga's view is whether belief in God (or beliefs that directly imply the existence of God) can be or are properly basic for relatively sophisticated, modern adults who have been exposed to (1) the reasons for disbelief that are prevalent in our culture, and (2) the disparity among the religions of the world in terms of what religious beliefs are rationally supported by religious experiences. Our 14-year-old theist has not only not heard of the ontological argument, he also, we may assume, has never reflected on the profusion of intense pain and suffering that occurs daily in our world and never seriously thought about the question of whether all this suffering that appears so utterly pointless would have been permitted by an omnipotent, omniscient, perfectly loving being. Nor has our 14-year-old read and assessed the psychological and sociological theories that endeavor to explain the emergence of religious beliefs and experience within the framework of a naturalistic (rather than supernaturalistic) account of things. The question is whether an intelligent adult who has investigated these matters will be rationally justified in believing in God in the complete absence of any serious arguments in behalf of theism.[20] In addition, what if our 14-year-old Christian theist comes in contact with other religious traditions—Judaism, Islam, Hinduism, Jainism, Buddhism—and rightly concludes that 14-year-olds in those traditions also hold properly basic religious beliefs on grounds very much like his own? Suppose he comes to see that had he been born a Hindu he would believe in Brahman, and not God, in a properly basic manner. If he then reasons that the Divine cannot be both God and Brahman, won't he then feel the need of something in the way of argument or reasons in behalf of Christian theism over against the religious claims of Buddhism?[21] Thus, while Plantinga has established that belief in God may be properly basic in situations like that of the 14-year-old, it is an open question whether belief in God can be properly basic for intellectually sophisticated modern adults who are aware of quite different religious traditions and the major reasons for disbelief that are prevalent in our culture.

Notes

1. *Summa Contra Gentiles*, Bk. One, Ch. 3, tr. Vernon J. Bourke (New York: Doubleday & Company, Inc., 1956).
2. *Summa Theologica*, II, II, Q1, A1, in *The Basic Writings of Saint Thomas Aquinas*, ed. Anton C. Pegis (New York: Random House, 1945).
3. *Summa Contra Gentiles*, Bk. One, Ch. 7.
4. John Locke, *An Essay Concerning Human Understanding*, Book IV, Ch. 28, Section 10.
5. In William James, *Essays in Pragmatism*, ed. A. Castell (New York: Hafner Publishing Co., 1948), pp. 88–109.
6. William Clifford, *Lectures and Essays*, Vol. II, ed. F. Pollock (London, Macmillan and Co., 1879), pp. 177–78.
7. Clifford, *Lectures*, p. 178.
8. Clifford, *Lectures*, pp. 185–86.
9. James, *Essays in Pragmatism*, p. 93.
10. James, *Essays in Pragmatism*, p. 89.
11. I am guided in this account of a forced option by George Nakhnikian's excellent study of James' "Will to Believe." See George Nakhnikian, *An Introduction to Philosophy* (New York: Alfred A. Knopf, 1967), pp. 273–86.
12. James, *Essays in Pragmatism*, p. 106.
13. If the vital good is understood as certain psychological states (such as peace of mind) that the believer may enjoy whether or not God actually exists, then the theistic hypothesis may exemplify the original statement of James' thesis. (For such an account of the vital good see Nakhnikian, *An Introduction to Philosophy*, pp. 276–79.) But if we interpret the vital good, as I have done, to be something the believer receives only from God, then the theistic hypothesis exemplifies only the revised form of James' thesis. For the theistic hypothesis will be momentous and forced with respect to that vital good only if theism is true.
14. James, *Essays in Pragmatism*, p. 100.
15. James, *Essays in Pragmatism*, pp. 108–9.
16. Alvin Plantinga, "Reason and Belief in God," in *Faith and Rationality*, edited by Alvin Plantinga and Nicholas Wolterstorff (Notre Dame, Indiana: University of Notre Dame Press, 1983), p. 17.
17. Some philosophers have a more restricted view of evidentialism. They identify it with the view that *religious beliefs* are rational only if they are supported by sufficient evidence.
18. "Is Belief in God Properly Basic," *NOUS* 15 (1981), p. 46.
19. "Reason and Belief in God," *Faith and Rationality*, edited by Alvin Plantinga and Nicholas Wolterstorff (Notre Dame, Indiana, University of Notre Dame Press, 1983), p. 33.
20. This criticism is developed by Philip L. Quinn in "In Search of the Foundations of Theism," *Faith and Philosophy* 2 (1985), pp. 469–86. For a related view see Stephen J. Wykstra, "Toward a Sensible Evidentialism: On the Notion of 'Needing Evidence' " (in W. L. Rowe and W. J. Wainwright, eds., *Philosophy of Religion: Selected Readings*, Second Edition; New York: Harcourt Brace Jovanovich, 1989; pp. 426–37).
21. We will return to this issue in the chapter on Many Religions.

Topics for Review

1. What does Aquinas mean by *faith* and how does he think faith is related to reason?
2. What are Clifford's two rules governing beliefs? Does James accept both, one of the two, or neither? Explain.

3. Explain what James means by a genuine option. Is James correct in thinking that the religious hypothesis comes to us as a genuine option that is intellectually undecidable? Explain.

4. How does James' view of faith compare and contrast with Aquinas'? How does each seek to show that faith is not unreasonable?

5. What is a properly basic belief? In what situations can belief in God be properly basic? Explain.

Topics for Further Study

6. Clifford holds that it is never right to do anything that might weaken "the habit of testing things and inquiring into them." Do you agree with Clifford? If not, why not? If you do agree with Clifford, does James' defense of the believer's policy seem plausible to you? Explain.

7. Critically evaluate the argument, mentioned at the beginning of this chapter, for the view that the nature of religion requires that its beliefs rest on faith, not reason.

Chapter

13

MANY RELIGIONS

Several of the world's major religions have been mentioned in earlier chapters: Judaism, Christianity, Islam, Hinduism, Buddhism. To this list one should add Taoism, Confucianism, Shinto, and perhaps others. Thus far, however, we have not focused our attention on any particular religion, nor have we tried to discuss all of them. Instead, we have considered the basic feature that is common to the major religions of the West: Judaism, Christianity, and Islam. That basic feature is the theistic conception of God as a supremely perfect, personal being who has created the world according to his divine purpose. In studying this idea of God, and in considering reasons for and against the belief that such a being exists, we have ignored the many differences separating Judaism, Christianity, and Islam. Indeed, we have even ignored some differences concerning the theistic God—for example, according to Christianity, but not Judaism or Islam, God is a trinity and has become human in an utterly unique way in Jesus of Nazareth (the incarnation). We have also largely ignored those religious traditions, Hinduism and Buddhism, for example, that significantly depart from the theistic conception of the ultimate. It is time now to consider some of the important differences among these religious traditions and to raise the question of whether all these different religions can be true. And if, as seems likely from the outset, they cannot all be true, we must consider how the person who adheres to one of these religions may or should view the other religions.

Although we have located the theistic concept of God in the major religions of the West (Judaism, Christianity, and Islam), it would be a mistake to think that theism is to be found only in these religions. Those who worship the great God *Vishnu* in Hinduism, for example, also belong within the theistic tradition. The theistic tradition in Hinduism is most fully developed in the *Bhagavad-Gita*, the most popular and well-known religious writings in India. The Bhagavad-Gita (Song of the Lord) is a lengthy poem recording a dialogue between *Krishna* (the incarnation of Vishnu) and a man, *Arjuna,* just before a great battle. In this work the way of devotion is presented as the best means to achieve salvation and eternal life. Thus Krishna says:

Quickly I come
To those who offer me
Every action,
Worship me only,
Their dearest delight,
With devotion undaunted.
Because they love me
These are my bondsmen
And I shall save them
From Mortal sorrow
And all the waves
Of Life's deathly ocean.
Be absorbed in me,
Lodge your mind in me:
Thus you shall dwell in me,
Do not doubt it,
Here and hereafter.[1]

Clearly, these lines express a theistic view in which total devotion to a divine being who has personal attributes is claimed to be the best way to personal salvation.

But earlier sacred writings in Hinduism, the *Upanishads,* as well as Theravada Buddhism, teach the doctrine that ultimate reality, *Brahman,* is impersonal and that our liberation from the cycle of death and rebirth occurs when our individual souls are absorbed fully into it in the state of *Nirvana.* Thus, according to the *advaita vedanta* school of Hindu thought, Brahman is totally one, an absolute unity, and exhaustive of reality. The world of individual things and persons is ultimately an illusion. Liberation consists in coming to know one's absolute unity with Brahman.

Clearly, then, there are deep differences among the great religions of the world. First, there is a profound difference as to whether ultimate reality is a personal god or an impersonal absolute. Second, there are important differences concerning our earthly life and ultimate destiny. Is there a cycle of death and rebirth in which our souls survive bodily death and reappear on earth as an animal or human (reincarnation) as the religions of the East teach, and the religions of the West deny? And is our ultimate destiny to lose our individual consciousness in the great ocean of being? Or do we continue as distinct individuals to have experiences and thoughts in the life of union with the divine? Third, there is a difference as to the locus of revelation. In Judaism, the Torah is the locus of God's revelation. According to Christianity, the Bible contains the sacred revelation. But in Islam it is the Koran. In Hinduism it is the Vedas. Fourth, there are differences concerning the incarnation of the divine. According to Christianity, Jesus is God. This is denied in Judaism and Islam. But according to Hinduism, there are many incarnations of the divine in human life. And, finally, there are differences concerning (a) what is wrong with human life, (b) what is required of us if we are to become free of what is wrong in human life, and (c) what our salvation or liberation consists in. According to Orthodox Christianity, every human being is lost in sin due to the willful act of disobedience of our original parents, Adam and Eve. God himself, in the form of Jesus Christ, paid the penalty for our sin. To obtain salvation, however, we must accept God's offer of grace, an acceptance that establishes a relationship of love and obedience to Jesus Christ. The persons thus saved from sin will at death enter into an eternal life of fellowship with God. According to the advaita vedanta school in Hinduism, however, the plight of the human condition centers more in ignorance than in sinful acts of will. The world of individual things is ultimately an illusion. Our liberation from the cycle of death and rebirth consists not in entering another life involving fellowship with a personal deity, but in coming to realize our total oneness with the Absolute (Brahman) and losing our individual identity by merging completely with that universal consciousness that is devoid of all content and distinctions.

Can all these religions be true in what they declare about Divine reality, human existence, and salvation? Clearly not, for they say incompatible things about these matters. After physical death, either human beings undergo reincarnation in another form of earthly existence or they do not. Since religions differ on this matter, some must hold a false view. According to Islam, Jesus was an important prophet but not identical with God. According to Christianity, Jesus was identical with God. Logic requires that at least one of these claims is false. So, as long as we regard these proclamations as purporting to state literal truths about the way things are, not all religions can be true in their religious claims. Having recognized this point, we can now turn to the question of how the adherent of a particular religion may or should view the other religious traditions.

EXCLUSIVISM

Perhaps the most natural position for a believer in a particular religion to take is that the truth lies with his or her own religion and that any religion holding opposing views is, therefore, false. This is a natural position to hold since to be a believer in a certain religion is to accept its basic claims as true. If one believes that at physical death *every* human being either goes to heaven or hell, one cannot then also agree that the adherents of Hinduism and Buddhism are, as those religions teach, reincarnated in another form of earthly existence after bodily death. One can say that reincarnation is *true* for believers in Hinduism and Buddhism. But this is just to say that the adherents of these religions *believe* that reincarnation is true. It is not to say that at death the adherents of Hinduism and Buddhism do undergo reincarnation. So there seems to be something right about exclusivism. But a problem arises when we note that a religion is not just an

assemblage of doctrines, that it also proclaims to be a way of salvation or liberation from what is wrong in human life. Each religion promises salvation or
liberation to its faithful followers. And the question now must be raised as to how
the adherent of a particular religion should view the prospects for salvation of
those who accept some other religion. To some extent this question may be
answered by the religion to which one adheres. For one's own religious tradition
will either say that it alone is the way of salvation, that other religions also
constitute genuine paths to salvation, or say nothing on the matter. If a particular
religion declares that it alone is the path to salvation, that unless a human being
responds appropriately to the message of that religion that human will forever be
beyond the pale of salvation, we shall say that the religion in question is *exclusivistic*. If one's own religious faith is exclusivistic, then, unless one deviates from
that particular doctrine, one will be an exclusivist on the matter of salvation. That
is, one will adhere to a particular religion, believe the way of salvation taught in
that religion, and, what is crucial here, one will also believe that *apart from that
particular way of salvation there is no salvation for anyone*. It is easy to understand how
a religion becomes exclusivistic. In the first place, when religions were formed
very little was generally known of different cultures, different religious faiths,
and different proclaimed paths of salvation or liberation. And second, with the
emergence of monotheism, the view that there is only one God and that one God
is the creator of everything in the universe, it is natural to expect that salvation
would depend on coming into a correct relationship with this God, and natural to
believe that the way laid down in one's religion is *the way* any human being must
follow to come into this correct relationship. Thus it was, for example, that
Orthodox Christianity developed a strong exclusivistic strain. One can see this
exclusivist strain in both Roman Catholic doctrine and in Protestantism. At the
Council of Florence (1438–45) it was affirmed that

> no one remaining outside the Catholic Church, not just pagans, but also Jews or heretics
> or schismatics, can become partakers of eternal life; but they will go to the "everlasting
> fire which was prepared for the devil and his angels," unless before the end of life they
> are joined to the Church.[2]

The Roman Catholic claim that there is no salvation outside the Church is
matched by the strong missionary thrust of Protestantism in the nineteenth
century. The basic conviction underlying Christian missionary activity around
the globe was to extend the possibility of salvation to those who had not heard of
Christ.

Let's consider two difficulties with exclusivism in religion. First, there is the
practical difficulty that hundreds of thousands of people live and die in other
religions and cultures without ever having heard of the path of salvation taught
by a particular exclusivistic religion. If a Christian holds that being raised as a
Christian or being converted to Christ is essential for the salvation of any human
being, he thereby holds that hundreds of thousands of people are deprived of
salvation by what appears to be an accident of place or time of birth.

Speaking as a Christian, John Hick puts the point this way.

> We say as Christians that God is the God of universal love, that he is the creator and Father of all mankind, that he wills the ultimate good and salvation of all men. But we also say, traditionally, that the only way to salvation is the Christian way. And yet we know, when we stop to think about it, that the large majority of the human race who have lived and died up to the present moment have lived either before Christ or outside the borders of Christendom. Can we then accept the conclusion that the God of love who seeks to save all mankind has nevertheless ordained that men must be saved in such a way that only a small minority can in fact receive this salvation?[3]

The second difficulty for an exclusivistic religion arises as soon as we become seriously acquainted with other religions and the lives of their founders and chief saints. Just as in one's own religious tradition, one finds saintly figures in other religions, individuals whose lives exhibit profound ethical commitment and religious devotion. That Mahatma Ghandi, for example, is destined for hell because he did not convert to Christianity or some other exclusivistic religion is bound to seem a dubious, if not absurd, idea to anyone who becomes acquainted with Hinduism and the life of Ghandi.

INCLUSIVISM

The student of religion soon learns that a religious tradition is something living and vibrant, constantly changing even while reaffirming its basic ideas and practices. Although a religion may originally develop a strong exclusivist strain, it is likely over time to moderate its exclusivism to deal with the two difficulties we have just noted. To illustrate how a religious tradition may moderate its exclusivism over time, we will look at how Roman Catholicism has modified or reinterpreted its position that outside the Church there is no salvation.[4] During the Second Vatican Council of 1963–65, the Council said:

> Those also can attain to everlasting salvation who through no fault of their own do not know the gospel of Christ or His Church, yet sincerely seek God and, moved by grace, strive by their deeds to do His will as it is known to them through the dictates of conscience. Nor does divine Providence deny the help necessary for salvation to those who, without blame on their part, have not yet arrived at an explicit knowledge of God, but who strive to live a good life, thanks to His grace. Whatever goodness or truth is found among them is looked upon by the Church as a preparation for the Gospel.[5]

I think one can see an attempt in this passage to address the practical difficulties that confront exclusivism. The basic idea seems to be this. It is still true, according to Roman Catholicism, that there is no salvation outside the Church. But what counts as *being in the Church?* Must one have actually been baptized in the Church or heard the gospel of Christ and responded with an explicit act of faith? The early exclusivistic strain in Christianity tended to give an affirmative answer to this question, resulting in the difficulties we noted. The Second Vatican Council seeks to broaden the idea of what is required for salvation. One need not have been baptized or heard the gospel of Christ or, apparently, have come to a knowledge of (or perhaps even a belief in) God. It is sufficient that one does the best one can to live a good life. Perhaps one must also have an implicit desire to do the will of God. But the chief point seems to be that one can be born, live, and die without having ever heard of God or Christ and still attain salvation within the Church.

An inclusivistic Christian is free to insist that Christianity is the only way of salvation, that apart from the activity of the divine in that particular religion, there would be no salvation for anyone. But an inclusivistic Christian escapes the difficulties of exclusivism by allowing that the Christian path of salvation includes a means of salvation for those who through no fault of their own are deprived of the normal means of salvation because they live at places where or times when the gospel of Christ is not available to them. Thus, while denying the *ultimate validity* of other religions, the inclusivistic Christian may still allow that the adherents of these other religions may attain salvation by following the paths to salvation laid down by those religions. They may attain salvation because they do their best by the light they have and may have an implicit desire to do the will of the God of Christianity. An alternative would be to say that those who through no fault of their own have not had the chance to respond to the gospel of Christ in this life will have the opportunity to do so in the world to come. By such amendments as these the exclusivistic strain in a religion may be set aside in favor of inclusivism.

PLURALISM

We've looked at two more or less traditional approaches to the problem of how an adherent of one religion should view other religions and their adherents. The final view we will consider is advocated by John Hick, a prominent contemporary philosopher of religion. When faced with the many different religious traditions that populate our world, Hick thinks a person can respond in any of three different ways. First, in view of the bewildering variety of divine beings that at one time or another have been the foci of devotion in the various religious traditions in the world, one might take a *skeptical* stance toward all of them. One might, for example, regard the gods and belief-systems of all these religions as illusions, as creations of the human mind resulting from deep personal wishes and an attempt to influence the forces of nature by imagining powerful beings in control of them. For reasons we need not consider here, Hick rejects universal skepticism concerning religion. Second, a person might adopt the *dogmatic* view that with the exception of one's own religion and its divine being(s), all religions are illusions. Hick thinks such a view is dogmatic because he believes that the sorts of experiences that make it rational for a person to accept the basic beliefs of one religious tradition also occur to persons in other religious traditions and make it equally rational for them to accept the basic beliefs of those religious traditions. Thus, as he sees it, " . . . the only reason for treating one's tradition differently from others is the very human, but not very cogent, reason that it is one's own!"[6] And in his view, both exclusivism and inclusivism are dogmatic views of religious traditions. Although he is himself a Christian, Hick thinks that it is incorrect to view other religious traditions as inferior to one's own. Each major religious tradition, in his view, is a genuine response to the presence of the divine in human life, each presents a way of salvation or liberation that is equally valid for the transformation of human beings from self-centered to divine-centered persons. In contrast to exclusivism and inclusivism, this view is pluralistic. It recommends that the adherent of a particular religion view the other great religious traditions and their paths of salvation as *equally valid* as one's own. So, in Hick's scheme of things, the major human responses to the multitude of religious traditions in our world are as follows:

SKEPTICISM   DOGMATISM   PLURALISM
                        Exclusivism Inclusivism

Let's begin our examination of Hick's religious pluralism by asking how anyone can believe that all religions are equally true or valid. For, as we noted earlier in this chapter, if we regard the proclamations of the various religions as purporting to state literal truths about the way things are, not all religions can be true in their basic religious claims. And this is so because the basic claims of a given religion conflict with the basic claims of other religions. How then can Hick think that all religions are equally true or valid?

As a start, Hick would ask us to distinguish the question of whether the theological doctrines of a given religion are true from the question of whether the path of salvation presented in that religion actually enables people to undergo a transformation in their lives from self-centeredness to divine-centeredness. When he says that all the major religions are equally valid he means to be asserting principally that their paths of salvation or liberation work equally well. Suppose we grant this to Hick. What, though, of the basic theological claims that are made in the various religious traditions? Is the divine reality the trinitarian God of Christianity, the purely unitary God of Judaism, or the God Krishna in Hinduism—to name but three of the many gods to be found in the world's religious traditions? It won't do to say that all of these are divine beings, that polytheism is true and the reason why different religions worshiping different gods can all be true. For, as Hick notes, each religious tradition tends to claim that its deity is the "sole creator or source of all finite existence."[7] So, simple polytheism won't work as a defense of religious pluralism.

Hick's view is that the divine reality is beyond all the distinct gods of the various religions. But we cannot experience the ultimate divine reality directly. Rather, divine reality is experienced in and through the god or gods we worship. It is the same divine reality that is experienced in Allah, the God of Judaism, the Christian God, Krishna, Shiva, and all the other personal deities through which human beings in various cultures and religious traditions have encountered the ultimate. The various deities that populate the world's great religions are the manifestations of the divine reality in human experience. It is because all these deities and the religions in which they function manifest the same ultimate divine reality that those who respond in faith to these various deities can undergo transformation from self-centered to divine-centered beings. Moreover, not only do the personal gods of the world's religions manifest the ultimate divine reality to the faithful in these religions, the impersonal absolute Brahman also functions in the same way; it too manifests the ultimate divine reality to those who experience Brahman. What makes all these religions valid and true, then, is that in all of them ultimate divine reality is encountered in the various personal gods and impersonal absolutes that are the foci of religious devotion and experience.

We need to raise two questions about Hick's theory of religious pluralism. First, what can Hick tell us about the ultimate divine reality that is experienced in and through the personal gods and impersonal absolutes of the great religious traditions? Second, given that there is such a reality beyond the numerous personal gods, what is the status of the gods themselves? Do they all exist? And if so, aren't we back with polytheism again, perhaps with the addition of a divine reality in which the many gods participate and manifest to their followers? But before we pursue these questions, we might want to ask why Hick thinks the picture he has drawn of the world's religious traditions is correct. Here is how he asks this question.

> But how can such a view be arrived at? Are we not proposing a picture reminiscent of the ancient allegory of the blind men and the elephant, in which each runs his hands over a different part of the animal, and identifies it differently, a leg as a tree, the trunk as a snake, the tail as a rope, and so on? Clearly, in the story the situation is being described from the point of view of someone who can observe both elephant and blind men. But where is the vantage-point from which one can observe both the divine Reality and the different limited human standpoints from which that Reality is being variously perceived? The advocate of the pluralist understanding cannot pretend to any such cosmic vision. How then does he profess to know that the situation is indeed as he depicts?[8]

Before we consider Hick's answer to this question, it will be helpful to consider the elephant analogy. Suppose one blind man reports experiencing a tree (the elephant's leg), a second reports experiencing a snake (the elephant's trunk), and a third reports experiencing a rope (the elephant's tail). In the analogy the elephant and its parts stand for the ultimate divine reality. The experiences of the elephant (its leg) *as* a tree, (its trunk) *as* a snake, and (its tail) *as* a rope stand for the religious experiences of the divine reality *as* Shiva, *as* Krishna, *as* the God of the Torah, *as* Allah, *as* the Heavenly Father of Christ, *as* Brahman, etc. Now, as Hick notes, he is not in the position of the sighted person who can see that the blind men are all experiencing the *same reality* (the elephant) differently (*as* a tree, *as* a snake, *as* a rope). How then does Hick know that those who claim to experience Brahman (an impersonal absolute) and those who claim to experience Allah (a personal God who created the world) are actually experiencing the same reality (ultimate divine reality) differently (*as* Brahman, *as* Allah)?

Hick's candid answer is that he does not know. Religious pluralism is, for Hick, an *hypothesis*, a theory he is developing to account for the fact that the transformation from self-centeredness to divine-centeredness occurs in all the great religious traditions of the world. Given this point as what needs to be explained, Hick proposes religious pluralism as the hypothesis that provides the most satisfying explanation.

Hick is not the first to develop a theory of religious pluralism. As we shall see in the next chapter, the eminent twentieth-century theologian Paul Tillich presents a somewhat similar view. Tillich calls the ultimate divine reality *Being-itself;* while in his latest writings Hick chooses to call it *the Real in itself.* Hick's idea is that we need to distinguish the Real in itself (ultimate divine reality) from *the Real as it is experienced by us.* The personal gods and impersonal absolutes that form the foci of worship in different religious traditions are the Real as it is experienced by us. What, then, of the ultimate divine reality that is beyond the various gods and impersonal absolutes? What can be said of this ultimate divine reality, the Real in itself? Hick's answer is that nothing significant whatever can be said of the Real in itself. For the distinction between the Real as it is in itself and the Real as it is thought and experienced by us implies that the characteristics that are applied to the various deities and impersonal absolutes belong not to the Real as it is in itself but to the Real as it is thought and experienced by us.

> Thus it [the Real as it is in itself] cannot be said to be one or many, person or thing, conscious or unconscious, purposive or non-purposive, substance or process, good or evil, loving or hating. None of the descriptive terms that apply within the realm of human experience can apply literally to the unexperienceable reality that underlies that realm.[9]

In talking of the Real in itself as ultimate *divine* reality we may have said more than Hick thinks we can say, at least literally. For we have attributed the property of *being divine* to the Real in itself. But *divine* is a descriptive term applicable to the gods which manifest the Real, to the Real as it is experienced, not to the Real as it is in itself. Hick's view is that the Real in itself has no substantive attributes at all. But if ultimate reality (the Real in itself) is not good, not loving, and not divine, why is it manifested in experience *as* good, *as* loving, and *as* divine? Can Hick's hypothesis of the Real in itself really *explain* the religious phenomena of human encounters with gods that are claimed to be good, loving, and divine? We may grant that experiences with the ultimates in different religions, whether personal gods or impersonal absolutes, seem equally valid in transforming human lives. But it is hard to see how postulating some ultimate reality that in itself *has no substantive attributes at all* can help explain why the Real as experienced should have any transforming effect on human beings.

Our second question concerned the various gods that are the foci of worship in the various great religions. Does Hick think that all these divine beings exist independent of our experiences of them? This would be to adopt polytheism with the addition of the Real as what humans experience in their encounters with the gods of the various religions. But, as we've seen, Hick doesn't think polytheism can do justice to the sorts of properties ascribed to the gods—for example, being the sole creator of all finite things. Should we then say that there is in reality only one divine being that is called by different names: "Adonai" by Jews, "the Heavenly Father" by Christians, "Allah" by Muslims, "Shiva" and "Krishna" by Hindus, etc.? This view, while initially attractive, overlooks the fact that the various divine names express different understandings of deity which are integral to different traditions and are embedded in different histories. "Adonai" as used by Jews signifies specifically the God whose covenant relationship with the children of Israel is documented in the Torah. The title "God" as used by Christians refers to the heavenly Father of Jesus Christ, whose incarnation was the uniquely full and final divine self-revelation. The equivalent title "Allah," as used by Muslims, refers to the Qur'anic Revealer whose message, delivered through the prophet Muhammad, completes and fulfils the earlier revelations contained in the Torah and the New Testament. And so on.[10]

If neither many gods nor a single god called by different names or titles in the different religions exist, what then is left for Hick to adopt as the proper view of the many different gods of the world's great religions? Without explicitly endorsing the view, Hick suggests that the gods are "projections of the religious imagination."[11] They are human creations in response to encounters with what is truly ultimate reality. Thus, although no such beings actually exist, they are not simply the mental products of inner psychological needs, as Freud and some religious skeptics would say. They are mental products that are appropriate in view of human encounters with what is truly ultimate and beyond all literal description, the Real itself.

In this chapter we have had a look at some of the intellectual difficulties posed by the existence of the diverse religious traditions in our world. In particular we have considered the question of how the believer in a particular religious tradition may or should view the claims of other religious traditions. We noted that exclusivism is a natural first response but that it faces two practical difficulties. Inclusivism, on the other hand, avoids these difficulties while crediting other religions with some degree of validity. A more radical view, pluralism, was considered at some length. In the final chapter we will consider two thinkers who have proposed religious alternatives to the traditional theism that has been the central focus of our study.

Notes

1. *The Song of God: Bhagavad-Gita*, tr. Swami Prabhavananda and Christopher Isherwood, (New York: Mentor Books, 1954), pp. 97f.
2. Denzinger, 714. *The Church Teaches: Documents of the Church in English Translation* (London: B. Herder Book Co, 1955), p. 165.
3. John Hick, *God and the Universe of Faiths* (New York: St. Martin's Press, 1973), p. 122.
4. For this account I am indebted to John Hick's work. See particularly *God and the Universe of Faiths*, Chapter 9.
5. Denzinger, *The Church Teaches*, Chapter ii, paragraph 16.
6. John Hick, *An Interpretation of Religion* (London: The Macmillan Press, 1989), p. 235.
7. *An Interpretation of Religion*, p. 269.
8. John Hick, *Problems of Religious Pluralism* (New York: St. Martin's Press, 1985), p. 37.
9. *An Interpretation of Religion*, p. 350.
10. *An Interpretation of Religion*, p. 270.
11. *Ibid.*, p. 273.

Topics for Review

1. What are some of the significant differences among the world's major religions?
2. Explain exclusivism and indicate two difficulties for this position.

3. How does inclusivism differ from exclusivism? Explain.
4. What is religious pluralism? Why does this view distinguish the ultimate divine reality in itself from this reality as thought and experienced?
5. Does Hick's hypothesis of the Real in itself really *explain* why transforming religious experiences occur in the world's major religion? Explain.

Topics for Further Study
6. Instead of postulating the Real itself, why not postulate an infinite personal being who appears to people in different religions and is called by different names? What reasons can you give for and against this idea?
7. Suppose we accept something like Hick's religious pluralism. Does this mean that there is no way of evaluating various religions? Could there still be criteria for ranking religions into better and worse? Explain.

14

A GLIMPSE
BEYOND THEISM

We began our study of the philosophy of religion by mentioning Bishop Robinson's *Honest to God*, a book in which he argued that the theistic idea of God is an idea of a being that is becoming more and more irrelevant to human life in the modern world. The modern world view, shaped by the growth of science and the staggering impact of technology, has conditioned us to seek explanations of what occurs in the world of nature in terms of other occurrences in the world of nature. The result of this process, so Robinson thinks, is to make any being that exists in a supernatural realm, a realm beyond the natural world, remote from the life of modern people. What is required in this modern period is the abandonment of this traditional theistic idea of God in favor of an alternative conception of God to which modern people can relate. In this final chapter we will take a look at the religious philosophies of two twentieth-century theologians—Paul Tillich and Henry Nelson Wieman—as representative of the various attempts to develop religious alternatives to theism.

PAUL TILLICH: ULTIMATE CONCERN

Perhaps the best way to approach a philosopher or theologian is to try to discover the problem that perplexes him or her. If we can find the central problem with which a theologian is concerned, if we can understand that problem, then much of his or her thought, however vague and abstract it may be, will fall into place around that problem. The problems with which Tillich grappled are many, but one of them can be singled out as central.

This problem contains two facets: the first of these is captured by Tillich's famous expression "ultimate concern." Tillich describes ultimate concern as what is expressed by the great commandment: "You shall love the Lord your God with all your heart, and all your soul, and with all your mind, and with all your strength."[1] To be ultimately concerned about something is to regard that thing as infinitely important, it is to be completely committed and devoted to that thing, to view it as the center of your life, that which gives meaning and significance to everything else. Complete commitment and utter devotion, then, are the central features of ultimate concern— or, as we might call it, the religious attitude. And the first element in the problem with which Tillich struggled is the pervasity, the depth and universality of ultimate concern in human life. If we look at the history of human religious life we will be struck by the tremendous variety of religious beliefs, practices, and institutions, but the thread which binds all these diverse religions together is that in all of them we find the religious attitude, we find ultimate concern. Some people may focus their ultimate concern on the Buddha, others may be completely devoted to Christ. If we think of the objects of their concern, there is a considerable difference, but if we think just of their ultimate concern—apart from what it is concern about—the two groups are the same, they both are in the state of being ultimately concerned.

Ultimate concern, then, is the pervasive fact in human religious life; it is the common element in all the great religions by which people have lived. In fact, once we distinguish between the object of ultimate concern and the ultimate concern itself, it's clear that ultimate concern is not confined to the "religious life," as traditionally conceived. For some individuals are ultimately concerned about success or money; others may be ultimately concerned about some person or cause to which they give themselves totally. And still others may be ultimately concerned about the truth, and have an unlimited passion not to shield themselves from the truth. Indeed, Tillich took the view that each of us, at some time or other, has an ultimate concern—even if we are unaware of it. One element, then, in the problem Tillich struggled with is the pervasiveness of ultimate concern in human life.

The second element in the problem is that there seems to be no limit on what may become or on what has been an object of ultimate concern. In religion, stones, sacred trees, stars, mythical beings, and extraordinary persons have been objects of ultimate concern. Indeed, almost anything under the sun, and the sun itself, has at one time or another been the focus of ultimate concern for some person or group. And the problem with which Tillich struggled is to understand and explain why a concern of infinite dimensions has been focused on almost any finite object under the sun. Human beings appear driven to attach unlimited importance to limited objects, to give themselves with infinite passion to finite things. How are we to explain this puzzling fact? How are we to explain the depth and universality of ultimate concern in human life? And how are we to explain the fact that limited, finite objects become the content of an unlimited, infinite concern? To explain these puzzling facts about human life is the central problem for Tillich, and the major themes of his thought may be seen as strands in the complex explanation he gives for these facts.

Religious Symbols and the Power of Being

Tillich's explanation begins with an assertion about human existence. We are all, Tillich insists, profoundly anxious about our own being. It's not that we're afraid just of death. What we are profoundly anxious about is not necessarily the end of our life. Rather, we are profoundly anxious about the meaning and significance of human life in general and our own lives in particular. Nonbeing forever threatens us—it is experienced as emptiness, meaninglessness, and despair; a sense that human life is absurd, without any real point or significance. Like Sisyphus, who in Homeric legend is condemned forever to roll a rock up a hill, from the top of which it always rolls down again, our lives seem devoid of any genuine significance. Perhaps no one has more clearly stated the grounds for viewing human life as ultimately absurd and meaningless than Bertrand Russell.

> That man is the product of causes which had no prevision of the end they were achieving; that his origin, his growth, his hopes and fears, his loves and his beliefs, are but the outcome of accidental collocations of atoms; that no fire, no heroism, no intensity of thought and feeling, can preserve an individual life beyond the grave; that all the noonday brightness of human genius, are destined to extinction in the vast death of the solar system, and that the whole temple of Man's achievement must inevitably be buried beneath the debris of a universe in ruins—all these things, if not quite beyond dispute, are yet so nearly certain, that no philosophy which rejects them can hope to stand.[2]

This profound anxiety and despair about the emptiness and meaninglessness of human existence is, Tillich argues, not a manifestation of neurosis, but a condition of human existence. And it produces within us an infinite longing or quest for that which can overcome this threat to our being. We seek for that reality, that power which, because it transcends all limitations, is not itself subject to the threat of nothingness. And we feel that only if we come into some vital contact with it, with what is the true ultimate, can we hope to find the courage to be, the power to affirm meaning in a world threatened by the loss of meaning. Each of us, then, whether aware of it or not, is infinitely concerned to establish some vital contact with the power of being, that power which can overcome the threat of nonbeing.

This mysterious power of being, which alone is not subject to the threat of nonbeing, is not a particular being with magical powers located either somewhere in the sky or everywhere at once. For on Tillich's view every being that exists, no matter how great and mighty it might be, is subject to the threat of nonbeing. The power of being, that reality not subject to the limiting conditions of existence, is beyond description and comprehension. It is not a being, even the highest being, but it can be experienced in human life, and it is only as we do experience it that we find the courage to be, the courage to live fully in spite of the threat of emptiness, the courage to affirm meaning in spite of the threat of meaninglessness.

We can now begin to see the explanation Tillich proposes for the fact that everyone is ultimately concerned, and for the fact that almost every object under the sun has at one time or another been the focus of someone's ultimate concern. Ultimate concern is really directed at the true ultimate, the power of being. And everyone is ultimately concerned about the power of being because each of us longs for some vital contact with that reality which alone can overcome the threat of nonbeing. Finally, since everything participates in the power of being, any object may become the means through which we encounter the power of being. Thus, depending on our personal and cultural environment, any object may be the focus of our ultimate concern. The finite, limited object—whether it be success, the Buddha, or the Christ—is the focus of an infinite, unlimited concern because it mediates the power of being, the true ultimate, to us. The finite object becomes a *religious symbol*, it mediates to us the true ultimate, the power of being. And it is because the finite object manifests the true ultimate, so that through it we encounter the power of being, that something finite becomes the focus of infinite concern.

It is important to realize that an object need not actually exist in order for it to be a religious symbol, to be that through which we experience the true ultimate, the mysterious power of being that is beyond description and comprehension. The gods of ancient Greece and Rome, and other mythical beings, are objects which once mediated the power of being to those who took them as the objects of their ultimate concern. But no such beings actually exist. It is very doubtful that Tillich ever believed that among the beings that exist there is one which satisfies our description of the theistic idea of God. But the important point for him is that the idea of the theistic God (the supreme being) has become an extremely power-ful symbol of the ultimate in western civilization. Indeed, among the religious symbols in western society, it's clear that for Tillich the idea of God as the supreme being has become the fundamental symbol of the ultimate. The true ultimate, as we've seen, is not a being at all. So whether the theistic God exists or not, the experience of the ultimate through the symbol of the theistic God is not affected.

> The divine beings and the Supreme Being, God, are representations of that which is ultimately referred to in the religious act. They are representations, for the uncon-ditioned transcendent surpasses every possible conception of a being, including even the conception of a Supreme Being.[3]

The Autonomous Realm of Faith

The final, important point in Tillich's religious philosophy concerns his discus-sion of the *truth* of faith. If a political movement, such as communism or fascism, and a goal, such as success, can, no less than Christ or Buddha, be a religious symbol by virtue of being the focus of ultimate concern, it is clear that some distinction must be made between true religious faith and false faith, between genuine religious symbols and idolatrous symbols. In short, it is clear that Tillich must provide criteria for judging the worth of various religious faiths (ultimate concerns).

One strong and persistent theme in Tillich's discussion of the truth of faith is his claim that faith is an autonomous realm. By this he means that it cannot be judged by any other kind of truth, whether scientific, historical, or philosophical. The methods and results of science cannot be used, so Tillich claims, to either establish or refute any affirmation of faith. Of course, Tillich is well aware of the historical conflict between science and religion, a conflict which began over the nature of things most remote from humankind and, then, gradually shifted to what was nearer. Thus religion and science first collided over the question of whether the earth or the sun was the center of the solar system. Next, the battle was waged over the age of the earth, and then over human history on the earth—the conflict over evolution. Finally, the human being's innermost self has become the subject of dispute between religion and the youthful science, psychology.

Concerning the entire conflict between religion and the sciences (astronomy, geology, biology, and psychology) Tillich has several interesting points to make. His main theme, however, as we noted above, can be put very simply: "Scientific truth and the truth of faith do not belong to the same dimension of meaning."[4] From this central theme it follows that there can be no conflict between science and religious faith. "Science can conflict only with science, and faith only with faith; science which remains science cannot conflict with faith which remains faith."[5] But if this is so, how are we to interpret the historical conflict between science and religious faith? Tillich's answer is that the conflict has resulted from a *distortion*, either of faith or of science, or of both. That is, the conflict is due either (i) to a dispute between science and a faith which has ceased to be faith because it has lapsed into making claims which fall in the dimension of science or (ii) to a dispute between faith and a science which has ceased to be simply science and has lapsed into a faith.

An example of the way in which Tillich understands the conflict between science and faith may serve to make his view clear.

> When the representatives of faith impeded the beginning of modern astronomy they were not aware that the Christian symbols, although using the Aristotelian-Ptolemaic astronomy, were not tied up with this astronomy. Only if the symbols of "God in heaven" and "man on earth" and "demons below the earth" are taken as descriptions of places, populated by divine or demonic beings can modern astronomy conflict with the Christian faith.[6]

When faith takes its symbols—religious statements concerning God, such as his being in heaven or above the earth—to have implications for astronomy, of course a conflict may result, and historically one did result. But this was a conflict in which, on Tillich's view, faith was distorted. The conflict was possible only because the religious statements were misinterpreted and distorted by biblical literalism. The presupposition of Tillich's view here is clear. It is that religious discourse, when properly seen in its symbolic character, has no implications for the statements of science which purport to describe "the structures and relations in the universe, in so far as they can be tested by experiment and calculation in quantitative terms."[7]

Sometimes, Tillich argues, the conflict between religion and science is due, not to a distortion of faith (as in the example from astronomy), but to a distortion of science, to a lapse of science into a rival faith. His most plausible example of the latter is the conflict between religion and depth psychology.

Contemporary analytic or depth psychology has in many instances conflicted with pre-theological and theological expressions of faith. It is, however, not difficult in the statements of depth psychology to distinguish the more or less verified observations and hypotheses from assertions about man's nature and destiny which are clearly expressions of faith. The naturalistic elements which Freud carried from the nineteenth into the twentieth century, his basic puritanism with respect to love, his pessimism about culture, and his reduction of religion to ideological projection are all expressions of faith and not the result of scientific analysis.[8]

I suspect that only the most unrepentant Freudians would deny Tillich's general point in this passage. Freud's works on religion and culture (*The Future of Religion, Totem and Taboo, Moses and Monotheism, Civilization and Its Discontents*) do, I think, result as much from Freud's peculiar presuppositions of faith as from scientific analysis. There is, of course, nothing wrong with this—so long as the expressions of faith do not masquerade as the results of science. Tillich remarks:

> There is no reason to deny to a scholar who deals with man and his predicament the right to introduce elements of faith. But if he attacks other forms of faith in the name of scientific psychology, as Freud and many of his followers do, he is confusing dimensions. In this case those who represent another kind of faith are justified in resisting these attacks.[9]

We have noted that whatever he means by the phrase "the truth of faith" Tillich maintains that it cannot be refuted by the truths of science, and this is because "scientific truth and the truth of faith do not belong to the same dimension of meaning." Having pressed this point, Tillich is careful to draw the corollary that scientific truth cannot establish religious truth. "The Truth of faith cannot be confirmed by the latest physical or biological discoveries—as it cannot be denied by them."[10]

The Truth of Faith

Faith, Tillich suggests, has both a subjective and an objective side. And his answer to the question "What is meant by the truth of faith?" is given for each of these two sides of faith. "From the subjective side one must say that faith is true if it adequately expresses an ultimate concern. From the objective side one must say that faith is true if its content is the really ultimate."[11] Interpreting Tillich, we may say that a faith is *subjectively true* provided that its symbols are the focuses of ultimate concern for some group. In short, a faith is subjectively true only when its symbols are alive, not dying or dead. Many symbols that once mediated the divine have ceased to do so, they have lost their truth from the subjective standpoint. Even if a faith is subjectively true, however, it may not be objectively true. For a faith is *objectively true* only if its symbols are genuine symbols of the divine and not idolatrous. The great problem in faith is to prevent the identification of the symbol, the finite object, with the holy, the true ultimate, which the symbol manifests. When this identification does occur, the symbols become idolatrous, the religion demonic, and the faith ceases to be objectively true. As Tillich writes,

Innumerable things, all things in a way, have the power of becoming holy in a mediate sense. They can point to something beyond themselves. But if their holiness comes to be considered inherent, it becomes demonic. This happens continually in the actual life of most religions. The representatives of man's ultimate concern—holy objects—tend to become his ultimate concern. They are transformed into idols. Holiness provokes idolatry.[12]

Thus, on Tillich's view, whether the symbol of one's faith is Christ, Buddha, the nation, or success, the real possibility of the symbol dying or becoming idolatrous cannot be precluded from the act of faith. This is the inevitable risk involved in faith. Every faith, then, can heal us or destroy us, depending on whether the finite object of ultimate concern remains transparent to the true ultimate, as in a living, genuine faith, or becomes identified in our minds with the true ultimate, as in idolatrous faith, and thereby ends by driving us deeper into emptiness, meaninglessness, and despair.

We have taken a look at the religious philosophy of Paul Tillich in order to acquaint ourselves with one of the modern religious alternatives to traditional theism. Tillich's views are attractive for three reasons. First, he gives an account of religious faith which both renders it immune from conflict with science and yet makes it more than a matter of emotion and feeling. Second, Tillich's account is comprehensive in that it seeks to illuminate not only the major religions by which human beings have lived, but also the "quasi-religions" where ultimate concern is focused on objects or goals normally not thought of as religious, such as success or the nation. And, finally, he seeks to provide criteria for evaluating the variety of religious faiths, criteria in terms of which one religious or quasi-religious faith might be judged superior to another. Attractive as his views may be, however, they have been forcefully criticized by both philosophers and theologians.[13]

Tillich, although rejecting the traditional theistic view of God, nevertheless continued, in his own idea of God as being-itself, one of the basic features of traditional theism: the idea of *transcendence,* that God is beyond the world of nature. A different alternative to traditional theism was developed by Henry Nelson Wieman (1884–1975), a view we may call "religious naturalism"—for, unlike Tillich, Wieman proposed to locate God within the world of nature.

HENRY NELSON WIEMAN: GOD WITHIN NATURE

A guiding principle of Wieman's thought is that human knowledge can only extend to the things and processes that occur in time and space—the world of nature. Whatever might lie beyond the world of nature is unknowable to us and cannot, therefore, be a subject of inquiry for modern persons. Given this guiding principle, any attempt to achieve knowledge about God, any rational inquiry concerning the existence and nature of God, must confine itself to the natural world.

As with Tillich, the best way to approach Wieman's thought is to begin with the fundamental problem that he wished to solve. Summarizing his life's work, Wieman writes:

My intellectual life has been focussed on a single problem. Every significant influence which has played upon me has been directed to this inquiry. The problem which has engaged me for the past fifty years can be put in the form of a question: What operates in human life with such character and power that it will transform man as he cannot transform himself, saving him from evil and leading him to the best that human life can ever reach, provided he meet the required conditions?[14]

His lifelong effort to answer this question constitutes, Wieman believes, an intellectual and religious investigation of the activity of *God*. For although the word *God* has long been associated in western culture with the concept of a supernatural being endowed with quite spectacular qualities (omnipotence, omniscience, perfect goodness), its most important meaning, Wieman argues, is *evaluative*, not *descriptive*. The descriptive meaning of the word *God*—the sort of being the word has been used to describe—has varied from one age and culture to another. Thus *God* (or its equivalent in another language) has been used *descriptively* to refer to a number of beings with different characteristics (the gods of ancient Greece and Rome), to refer to a good, but finitely powerful deity (for example, Ahura Mazdah, the god of primitive Zoroastrianism), and to refer to the supernatural being of traditional theism. But the word *God*, although changing its descriptive meaning over time, has maintained, Wieman argues, a single *evaluative* meaning. It has always been used to refer to what evokes such human responses as awe, reverence, supreme devotion, and ultimate commitment. Wieman observes:

The word "God" has been associated with these reactions far more than with any clearly defined concept. Therefore, I hold, whatever should *rightfully* engender these reactions in men, is *rightly* called God. It is these fundamental reactions, basic trends and needs of life, which should determine what is called God, far more than the particular concept of God which some group or age may happen to cherish.[15]

What is it then that operates in the natural world so as to transform human beings as they cannot transform themselves, saving them from evil and leading them to the greatest good human life can ever reach, provided they meet the required conditions? As we've just seen, whatever it is that does this is, on Wieman's view, *God*. For whatever does this for and to us is worthy of our loyalty, devotion, and commitment. And, as we've seen, it is human reactions such as these that Wieman thinks constitute the *evaluative* aspect of the word *God*,—God being that which is felt worthy of such human responses.

There are several parts to the fundamental question Wieman tried to answer. First, and perhaps most difficult, is this question: What is human good or the greatest good possible for humans to achieve? Until we answer this question we cannot successfully answer this question: What is God? We can know that God is that within the natural world which, under proper conditions, leads people to the greatest good. But unless we determine what that greatest good is, we cannot hope to learn anything more about God. Second, there is implied in Wieman's problem the view that people are unable by their own efforts to achieve their greatest good. Human beings must be *transformed* by something other than themselves if they are to experience their greatest good. This point gives rise to the question: What is it about people that prevents their realization of great human good, unless they be transformed? And, finally, we must note that in formulating the fundamental problem, Wieman speaks of "required conditions," conditions, presumably, that people must meet if they are to undergo radical transformation so as to achieve the greatest good. We have then the question: What conditions must humans satisfy if they are to undergo transformation so as to be saved from evil and led to the greatest good?

The Greatest Possible Good

To our first question—What is human good or the greatest good possible for humans to achieve? —Wieman's most persistent answer is that human good is the fulfilment or satisfaction of some human interest. The greatest good for an individual, then, would be the most complete satisfaction of that individual's interests that is possible. As Wieman puts it: "It is the most complete satisfaction of the individual that is possible when the individual is viewed in the wholeness of his being. Any good less than the greatest is some approximation to this most complete satisfaction of the individual."[16]

The main difficulty with Wieman's answer to the first question is that it seems to conflict with the plain fact that people sometimes are interested in obtaining things that are positively harmful to themselves and to others. Can the satisfaction of such interests really be *good?* The solution to this difficulty rests on a distinction between two sorts of human good: *instrumental good* and *intrinsic good.* Satisfaction of a human interest is good in and of itself; it is intrinsically good. Sometimes, however, the satisfaction of an interest will have destructive consequences, preventing the realization of deeper and more important interests. When this happens, the satisfaction does not cease to be good, considered in and of itself, but it is bad in terms of what it leads to; it is not instrumentally good. The achievement of the greatest good for an individual, therefore, may require the sacrificing of certain interests, those whose satisfaction would be destructive of the individual's deepest needs and interests. To hold that what is intrinsically good is the satisfaction of interest does not mean that it is a good thing for just any human interest to be satisfied.

The Transformation of Humankind

Having come to this view about the nature of human good, one might expect Wieman to believe that human beings naturally would seek to increase good; naturally would lend their strongest efforts to achieving the greatest good possible. It is at this point, however, that we come upon Wieman's conviction that humans themselves are the great barrier to the achievement of their greatest good, that people must be transformed by something other than themselves if they are to be saved from evil and led to their greatest good. It's true, Wieman would admit, that someone may be naturally inclined to satisfy a desire or interest. But there are at least three reasons why humans are doomed to failure if they think that by their own effort they can achieve their greatest good. First, we must acknowledge that our deepest wishes and longings may be unknown to us.

We may believe that our deepest interests lie in obtaining certain ends, but be mistaken owing to the presence of unconscious longings and desires of which we know little to nothing. Second, there is the fact that humans are capable of radical transformation, including our interests, so that we cannot know in advance what our future interests will be. Finally, there is a natural human tendency to resist transformation, to pursue only those interests which our group finds acceptable, and thereby fail to pursue what would genuinely satisfy us in the wholeness of our being. For these and other reasons Wieman holds that people will not achieve their greatest good if they simply focus their attention upon the pursuit of what they believe their interests to be. Although satisfaction of an interest is intrinsically good, human beings are not likely to achieve their good by simply cataloging their conscious desires and then pursuing their satisfaction. Some guide other than satisfaction of interest must be found if human beings are to achieve their greatest good.

Wieman's deepest conviction, one which he never seriously questioned, is that there is at work in the universe a process which is creative of human good, a process which, if people surrender themselves to it, will lead to the development and fulfilment of the deepest and most important interests possible for human existence. This natural process must be discovered by human reason and people must somehow give themselves over to its transforming power if they are to be saved from evil and led to their greatest good. It is this process, and only this process, that can serve as a reliable guide in humankind's quest for its greatness.

> Not the greatest good he can appreciate but the process which creates him and all the good of life is what he must serve. Not the goal but the source, not the highest but the deepest, not the total unity but the creator of unity, not the universe as known to him but the generator and recreator of every universe he can ever know, must be his guide and master when he reaches the peak of his power.[17]

Wieman distinguishes between *created good*—the satisfaction of human interests—and *creative good*—that process at work in the natural world which, if we give ourselves over to it, will save us from evil and lead us to the best. God is creative good. In his earlier work, Wieman tended to identify God with whatever process there is that sustains the universe as a whole, as well as human life. In his later work, however, he sought to discover that process at work within the community of humans that leads to their greatest good. Increasingly, he became less concerned with discovering some cosmic process which creates and sustains the existence of human life, and more concerned with identifying the particular process at work within human communities that enriches human life, giving it meaning and significance. Eventually, he came to describe this process as *creative interchange*. God, then, is not some being beyond the natural world, nor is God to be identified with any cosmic process that creates and sustains all levels of existence, including human existence. Indeed, God is that process within human communities that works to enrich human life, to save human beings from meaninglessness and despair, and to lead humankind to the greatest good possible.

The Conditions of Transformation

We've seen some of the reasons why Wieman believes that humankind is incapable of achieving its greatest good by its own resources. We can achieve our greatest good not by striving to satisfy the interests we believe ourselves to have, but only by giving ourselves over to that transforming process at work in our midst. The act of giving ourselves over to this creative process is, for Wieman, what religious faith is all about. Faith is an act of commitment, not a matter of belief. As such, Wieman argues, it involves two levels.

> I distinguish two levels in the self-giving of faith. At one level commitment is guided by the ideas which one happens to have at the time concerning what transforms man creatively. But there is a deeper level of commitment. At this second level, one is motivated to give himself, in the wholeness of his being so far as he is able, to what in truth does save and transform, no matter how different it may be from one's ideas of it.[18]

We have considered some of the basic points in Wieman's religious philosophy: (1) that human good is satisfaction of human interest, (2) that human ignorance of our deepest interests, the capacity for radical transformation, and the natural human resistance to such transformation combine to frustrate humankind's hope to achieve its greatest good by its own efforts, (3) that there is a process at work (creative good) such that if we give ourselves over to its transforming power we will be saved from evil and led to our greatest good, and (4) that the basic condition we must satisfy if we are to reach this greatness is the giving of ourselves in faith to the work of this divine process in our midst. The resulting problem for humankind is twofold. First, it must form some more or less correct idea of God, of that process to which it needs to give itself in faith. This is the *intellectual* problem. For unless an individual has some correct idea of what God is, he or she will end up giving himself or herself over to something other than God, ending in despair and destruction. Wieman's intellectual efforts were directed to discovering some correct ideas about God, about that process at work in our midst which, if we submit to it, will lead us to the best.

Second, after humankind has formed some correct idea of this divine process, it must overcome its own resistance to transformation, and give itself in faith and loyalty to this process, letting it work upon human life. This is the *religious* problem. It is the problem of living the life of faith, of committing ourselves totally and completely to that which might deliver us from evil. And this difficulty is made severe, Wieman believes, because the divine process cannot be controlled by human beings. They may know that if they give themselves completely over to the creative event, the result will be an increase of human good. But the nature of this good cannot be humanly predicted. The achievement of created good may necessitate a major transformation of our goals and desires. All human wishes and expectations may be broken by the goodness that is God. Every transformation toward greater good may mean the losing of one's life in order to gain it. Even our fondest ideas of God may be altered when we give ourselves over to the working of the divine process. Thus the life of faith is not a safe, comfortable life; it requires enormous courage and involves great risk. But it is the only life worth living, for it alone has the promise of saving us from evil and leading us to the best.

A RETURN TO THE FIRST QUESTION

In this final chapter we have had a look at two modern alternatives to traditional theism. The proponents of these alternatives reject the theistic idea of God—Tillich by identifying God with being-itself, a reality underlying all existing things, whether natural or supernatural; Wieman by identifying God with a process within nature creative of human good. Both thinkers have sought in different ways to avoid the troublesome issue of whether there are rational grounds for believing in the existence of God. Tillich sought to avoid the issue by placing God beyond the realm of existence altogether—only beings exist, and being-itself is not one being among others; it is that reality from which all beings derive their existence. Wieman endeavored to avoid the issue by defining the term *God* in such a way that the existence of God will be an indisputable fact. God is simply that natural process which works toward the realization of human good. Neither, however, has been fully successful in avoiding the fundamental problem of the existence of God. For the question remains whether the term *being-itself* refers to nothing whatsoever or whether there is a reality designated by the term. Similarly, the question can be raised as to whether there is a single, unified process in the universe which works for human good or whether, instead, there are a number of quite diverse things and processes, each of which is sometimes supportive of the satisfaction of human interests, and sometimes not. Thus, Tillich's theology and Wieman's theology face the problem of rational justification equally with the theology of traditional theism.

Religion is a near universal phenomenon in humankind's brief history in the universe. As such, it merits careful study from the various intellectual disciplines: philosophy, history, anthropology, and the rest. In this brief book we've examined some of the chief questions that have emerged in the philosophical study of religion. In particular, we have examined a number of major issues involved in the philosophical scrutiny of theistic religion. If the conclusions reached along the way are not as definitive as either theist or atheist would like, it must be remembered that in philosophy, as well as in life, what matters most is often the journey itself, and not its end point.

Notes

1. Mark 12:29 (Revised Standard Version).
2. Bertrand Russell, *Mysticism and Logic* (London: George Allen & Unwin Ltd., 1917), pp. 47–48.
3. Paul Tillich, "The Religious Symbol," *Religious Experience and Truth*, ed. Sidney Hook (New York: New York University Press, 1961), pp. 20–21.
4. Paul Tillich, *Dynamics of Faith* (New York: Harper & Row, Publishers, 1957), p. 81.
5. Tillich, *Dynamics*, p. 82.
6. Tillich, *Dynamics*, p. 82.
7. Tillich, *Dynamics*, p. 81.
8. Tillich, *Dynamics*, p. 84.

9. Tillich, *Dynamics*, p. 84.
10. Tillich, *Dynamics*, p. 85.
11. Tillich, *Dynamics*, p. 96.
12. Paul Tillich, *Systematic Theology*, Vol. I (Chicago: The University of Chicago Press, 1951), p. 216.
13. See, for example, the essays by Reinhold Niebuhr and A. T. Mollegen in *The Theology of Paul Tillich*, eds. C. W. Kegley and R. W. Bretall (New York: The Macmillan Company, 1959). Also see Alastair M. Macleod, *Tillich: An Essay on the Role of Ontology in His Philosophical Theology* (London: George Allen & Unwin Ltd., 1973), and William L. Rowe, *Religious Symbols and God: A Philosophical Study of Tillich's Theology* (Chicago: The University of Chicago Press, 1968).
14. Henry Nelson Wieman, *The Empirical Theology of Henry Nelson Wieman*, ed. R. W. Bretall (New York: The Macmillan Company, 1963), p. 3.
15. Wieman, "On Using the Word 'God': A Reply," *Journal of Philosophy*, XXX (1933), p. 401.
16. Wieman, *Man's Ultimate Commitment* (Carbondale, Illinois: Southern Illinois University Press, 1958), p. 20.
17. Wieman, *The Source of Human Good* (Chicago: The University of Chicago Press, 1946), pp. 38–39.
18. Wieman, *The Empirical Theology of Henry Nelson Wieman*, pp. 6–7.

Topics for Review

1. What are the two aspects of the central problem with which Tillich was concerned? Explain.
2. How does Tillich propose to explain the puzzling fact that finite objects become the focus of an unlimited concern? From what basic point does he begin his explanation?
3. Explain what Tillich means by the truth of faith.
4. How does Wieman's view about the limits of human knowledge influence his view of God?
5. What is Wieman's view of human good and why does he think that human beings by themselves cannot attain their greatest good?

Topics for Further Study

6. Do you think that Tillich's religious philosophy is a genuine alternative to theism for modern people? If so, why? If not, why not?
7. Do you think Wieman makes a proper use of the term *God* when he applies it to an impersonal process in the natural world? What place could such basic religious activities as prayer and worship have in Wieman's religious philosophy? Discuss.

FOR FURTHER READING

Note: Some references for further reading are contained in the footnotes to the various chapters of this book. The following suggestions for further reading fall into two groups. In the first group are listed a few anthologies containing readings from classical and contemporary authors who have made significant contributions to the philosophy of religion. Some of the major ideas of a number of these authors are discussed in this book. The second group contains books dealing in depth with various topics discussed in this book.

1. Anthologies

Hick, John, ed., *Classical and Contemporary Readings in the Philosophy of Religion.* 2d ed. Englewood Cliffs, N.J.: Prentice-Hall, Inc., 1970.

Pojman, Louis P., ed., *Philosophy of Religion: An Anthology.* Belmont, California: Wadsworth, 1987.

Rowe, William L. and William J. Wainwright, eds., *Philosophy of Religion: Selected Readings.* 2d ed. New York: Harcourt Brace Jovanovich, Inc., 1989.

2. Books dealing in depth with some of the topics included in this book.

Alston, William P., *Divine Nature and Human Language: Essays in Philosophical Theology.* Ithaca, New York: Cornell University Press, 1989.

Audi, Robert and William Wainwright, eds., *Rationality, Religious Belief, and Moral Commitment: New Essays in the Philosophy of Religion.* Ithaca, New York: Cornell University Press, 1986.

Broad, C. D., *Religion, Philosophy and Psychical Research.* New York: Humanities Press, 1969.

Davis, Stephen T., *Logic and The Nature of God.* Grand Rapids, Michigan: Eerdmans, 1983.

Delaney, C. F., ed., *Rationality and Religious Belief.* Notre Dame: University of Notre Dame Press, 1978.

Dore, Clement, *Theism.* Dordrecht, Netherlands: D. Reidel, 1984.

Ducasse, C. J., *A Philosophical Scrutiny of Religion.* New York: The Ronald Press, 1953.

Ducasse, Curt John, *A Critical Examination of the Belief in Life after Death.* Springfield, Illinois: Thomas, 1961.

Ferre, Frederick, *Language, Logic and God.* New York: Harper & Row Publishers, 1969.

Flew, Antony, *God and Philosophy.* New York: Harper and Row Publishers, 1961.

Geach, Peter, *Providence and Evil.* Cambridge: Cambridge University Press, 1977.

Gutting, Gary, *Religious Belief and Religious Skepticism.* Notre Dame: University of Notre Dame Press, 1982.

Hasker, William, *God, Time, and Knowledge.* Ithaca, New York: Cornell University Press, 1989.

Hepburn, Ronald W., *Christianity and Paradox.* London: C. A. Watts & Company Ltd., 1958.

Hick, John, *Arguments for the Existence of God.* New York: Herder and Herder, 1971.

————, *Evil and the God of Love.* New York: Harper & Row Publishers, 1966.

James, William, *Varieties of Religious Experience.* New York: Longmans, Green and Company, 1902.

Katz, Steven T., ed., *Mysticism and Philosophical Analysis.* Oxford: Oxford University Press, 1978.

Kellenberger, J., *Religious Discovery, Faith and Knowledge.* Englewood Cliffs, New Jersey: Prentice-Hall, 1972.

Kenny, Anthony, *The God of the Philosophers.* Oxford: Oxford University Press, 1979.

Lewis, C. S., *Miracles.* New York: The Macmillan Co., 1963.

Lewis, H. D., *Our Experience of God.* London: George Allen & Unwin Ltd., 1959.

Mackie, J. L., *The Miracle of Theism.* Oxford: Oxford University Press, 1982.

Martin, Michael, *Atheism: A Philosophical Justification.* Philadelphia: Temple University Press, 1990.

Mascall, E. L., *Existence and Analogy.* New York: Longman Group Limited, 1949.

Matson, Wallace I., *The Existence of God.* Ithaca, New York: Cornell University Press, 1965.

Mavrodes, George I., *Belief in God.* New York: Random House, Inc., 1970.

Otto, Rudolf, *The Idea of the Holy.* Oxford: Oxford University Press, 1958.

Penelhum, Terence, *Immortality.* Belmont, California: Wadsworth, 1973.

Penelhum, Terence, *Religion and Rationality.* New York: Random House, Inc., 1971.

Pike, Nelson, *God and Timelessness.* New York: Schocken Books, Inc., 1970.

Plantinga, Alvin, *God, Freedom, and Evil*. New York: Harper & Row Publishers, 1974.

Plantinga, Alvin, and Nicholas Wolterstorff, eds., *Faith and Rationality: Reason and Belief in God*. Notre Dame: University of Notre Dame Press, 1983.

Reichenbach, Bruce, *Evil and A Good God*. New York: Fordham University Press, 1982.

Ross, James F., *Philosophical Theology*. New York: The Bobbs-Merrill Company, Inc., 1969.

Rowe, William L., *The Cosmological Argument*. Princeton: Princeton University Press, 1975.

Schlesinger, George, *Religion and Scientific Method*. Dordrecht, Netherlands: D. Reidel, 1977.

Smart, Ninian, *Reasons and Faiths*. London: Routledge and Kegan Paul Ltd., 1958.

Stace, W. T., *Mysticism and Philosophy*. New York: J. B. Lippincott Co., 1960.

Swinburne, Richard, *The Coherence of Theism*. Oxford: Oxford University Press, 1977.

Taylor, A. E., *Does God Exist?* London: The Macmillan Co., 1945.

Thomas, George F., *Philosophy and Religious Belief*. New York: Charles Scribner's Sons, 1970.

Tillich, Paul, *Biblical Religion and the Search for Ultimate Reality*. Chicago: University of Chicago Press, 1955.

———, *Dynamics of Faith*. New York: Harper & Row Publishers, 1957.

Wainwright, William, *Mysticism: A Study of Its Nature, Cognitive Value, and Moral Implications*. Madison, Wisconsin: University of Wisconsin Press, 1981.

Wieman, Henry Nelson, *Man's Ultimate Commitment*. Carbondale, Illinois: Southern Illinois University Press, 1958.

———, *The Source of Human Good*. Chicago: University of Chicago Press, 1946.

Wierenga, Edward R., *The Nature of God: An Inquiry into Divine Attributes*. Ithaca, New York: Cornell University Press, 1989.

Yandell, Keith, *Christianity and Philosophy*. Grand Rapids, Michigan: Eerdmans, 1984.

INDEX